Volume 2

by
NICK SELUK

Layout assists by **Jimmy Deoquino**

Rocketship Entertainment, LLC

Tom Akel, CEO & Publisher
Rob Feldman, CTO
Jeanmarie McNeely, CFO
Brandon Freeberg, Dir. of Campaign Mgmt.
Phil Smith, Art Director
Aram Alekyan, Designer
Jimmy Deoquino, Designer
Jed Keith, Social Media
Jerrod Clark, Publicity

rocketshipent.com

LARS THE AWKWARD YETI VOLUME 2
ISBN SOFTCOVER: 978-1-962298-03-2
ISBN HARDCOVER: 978-1-962298-04-9
First printing. June 2024. Copyright © The Awkward Yeti, LLC. All rights
reserved. Published by Rocketship Entertainment, LLC. 136 Westbury
Ct., Doylestown, PA 18901. "Lars the Awkward Yeti", the Awkward Yeti
logo, and the likenesses of all characters herein are trademarks of
The Awkward Yeti, LLC. "Rocketship" and the Rocketship logo are
trademarks of Rocketship Entertainment, LLC. No part of this publication
may be reproduced or transmitted, in any form or by any means, without
the express written consent of The Awkward Yeti, LLC or Rocketship
Entertainment, LLC. All names, characters, events, and locales in this
publication are entirely fictional. Any resemblance to actual persons
(living or dead), events, or places, without satiric intent, is coincidental.
Printed in China.

He Thinks He's People

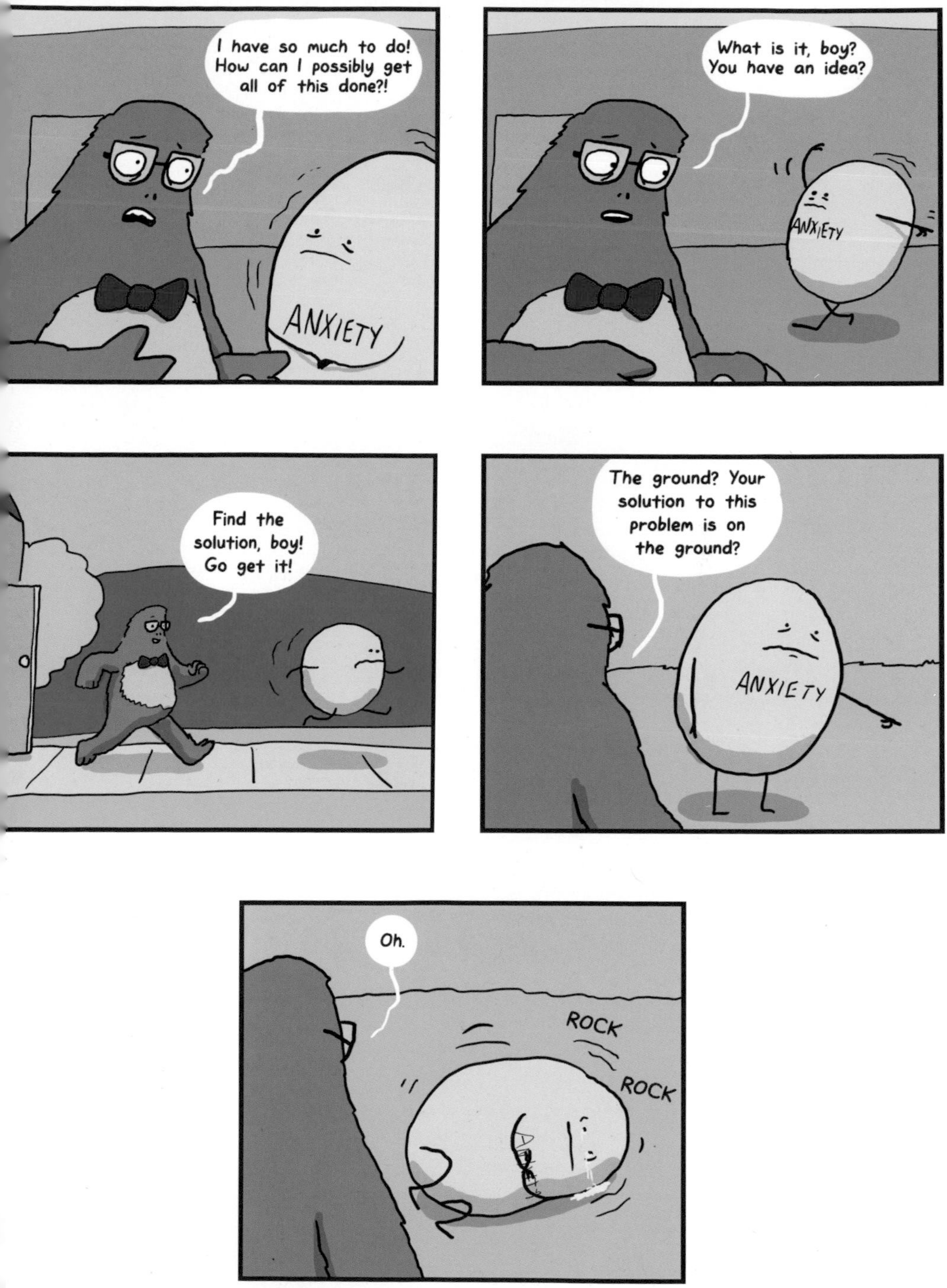

I have so much to do! How can I possibly get all of this done?!
ANXIETY
What is it, boy? You have an idea?
ANXIETY
Find the solution, boy! Go get it!
The ground? Your solution to this problem is on the ground?
ANXIETY
Oh.
ROCK
ROCK

Stress of the World

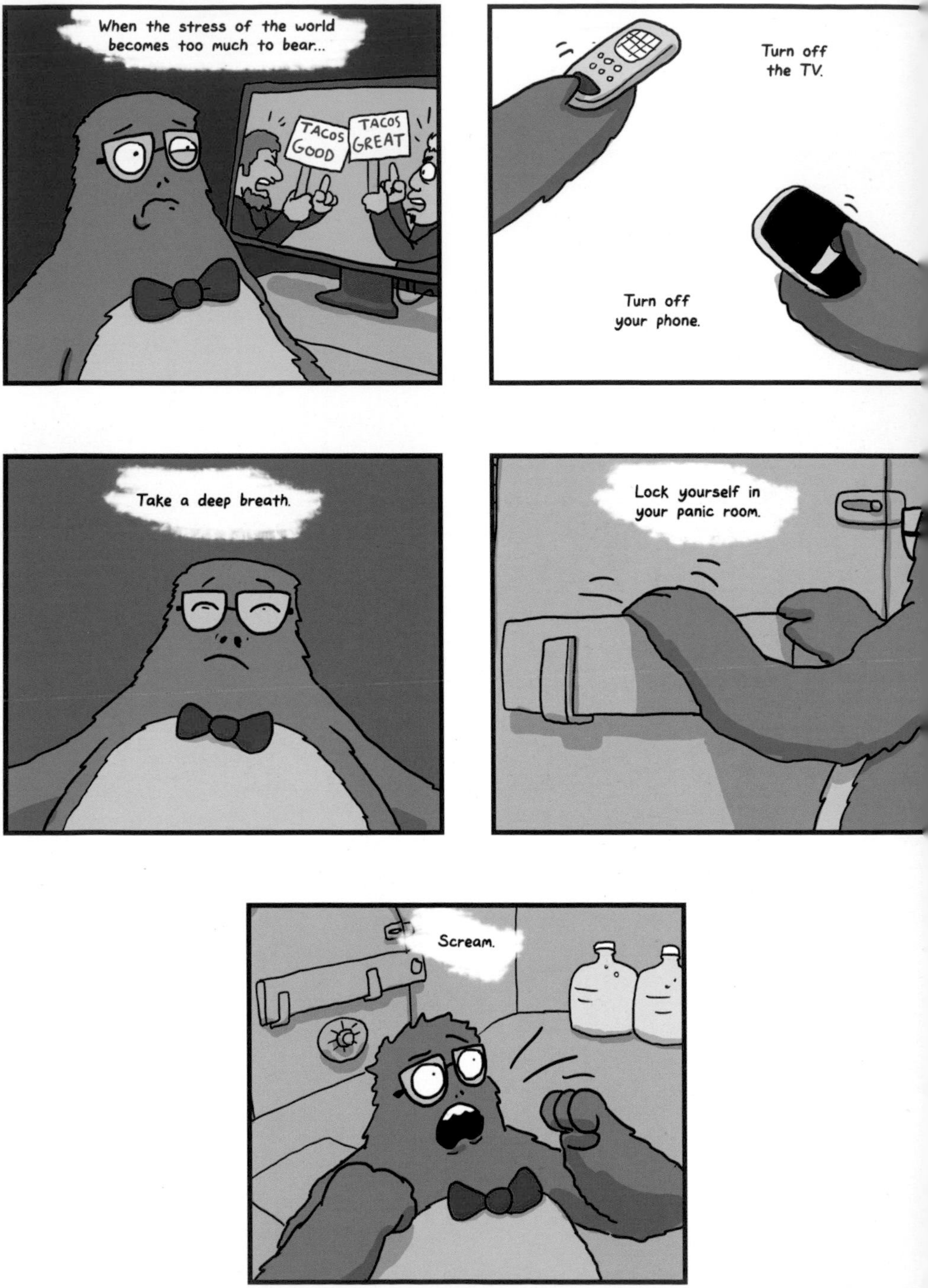
When the stress of the world becomes too much to bear...
TACOS GOOD
TACOS GREAT
Turn off the TV.
Turn off your phone.
Take a deep breath.
Lock yourself in your panic room.
Scream.

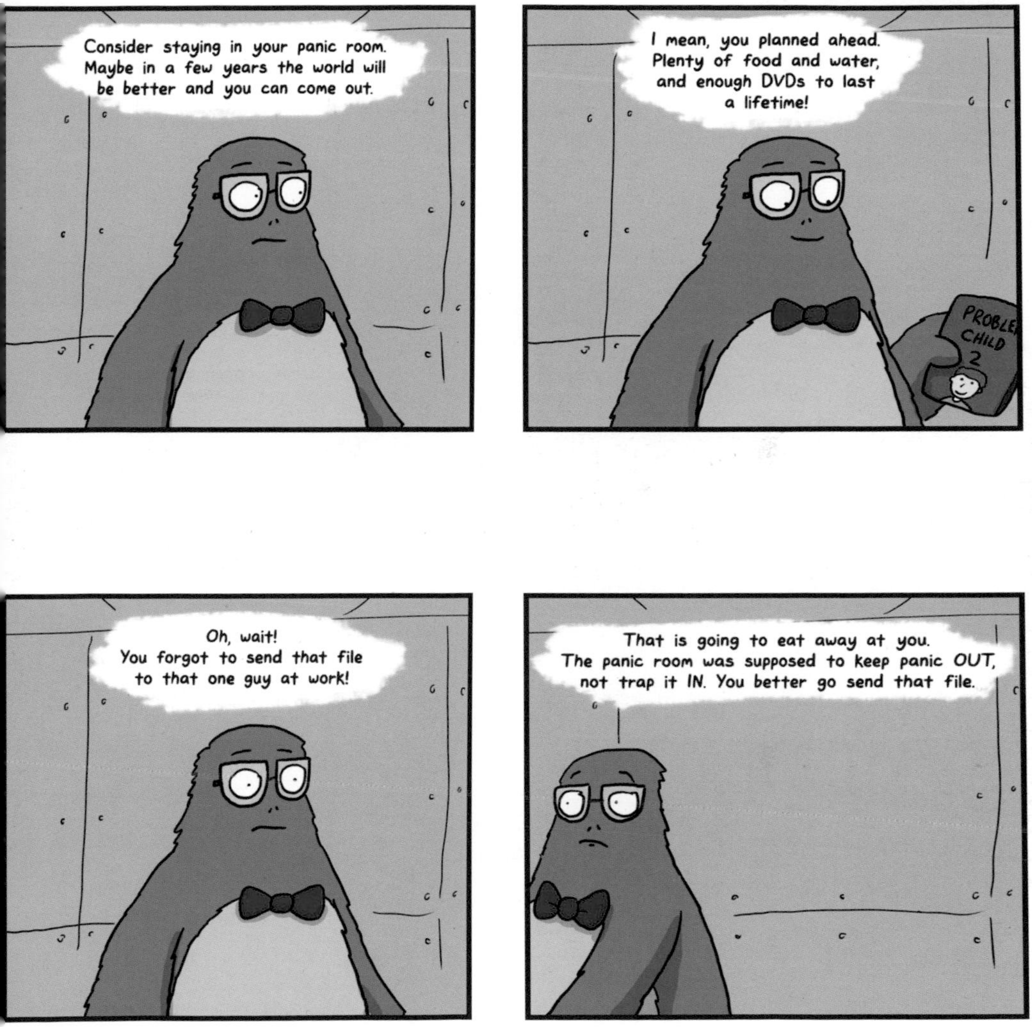
Consider staying in your panic room. Maybe in a few years the world will be better and you can come out.
I mean, you planned ahead. Plenty of food and water, and enough DVDs to last a lifetime!
PROBLE
CHILD
2
Oh, wait! You forgot to send that file to that one guy at work!
That is going to eat away at you. The panic room was supposed to keep panic OUT, not trap it IN. You better go send that file.

Lars Stands Up to Anxiety

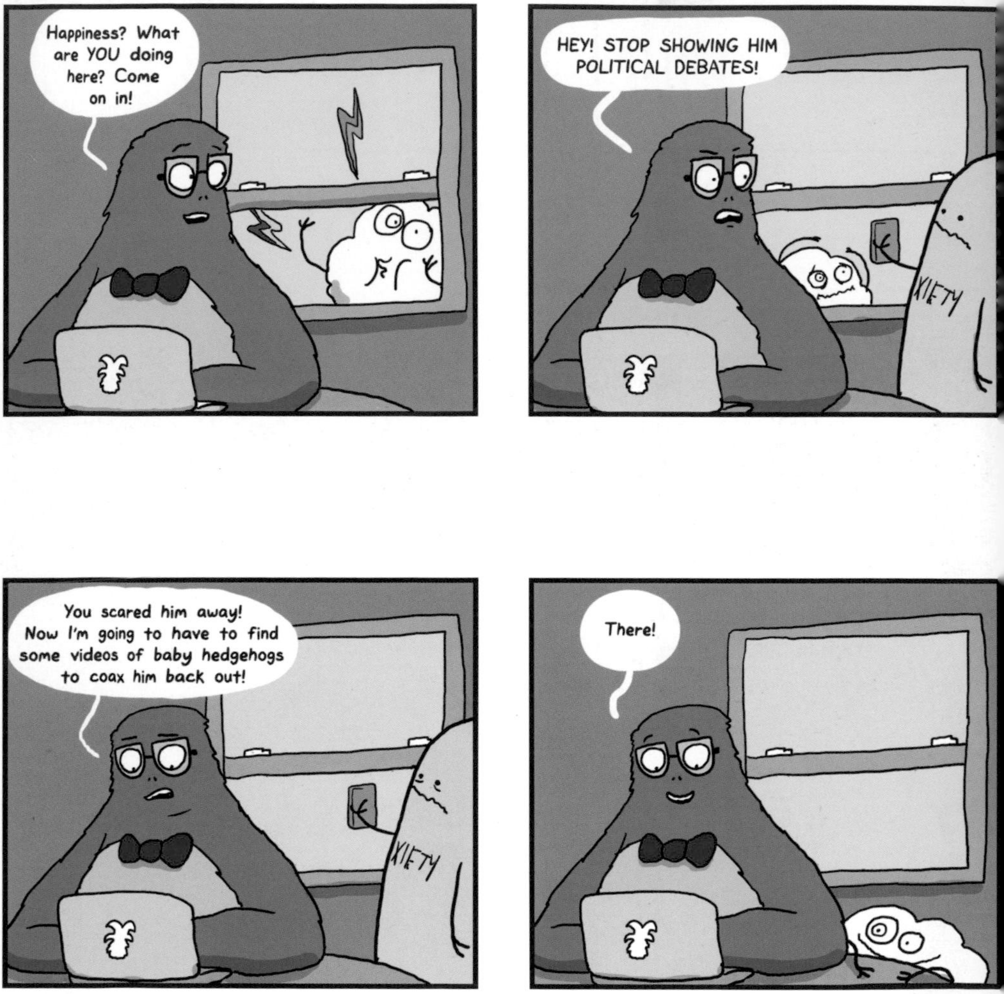
Happiness? What are YOU doing here? Come on in!
HEY! STOP SHOWING HIM POLITICAL DEBATES!
XIETY
You scared him away! Now I'm going to have to find some videos of baby hedgehogs to coax him back out!
XIETY
There!

ArachNOPEphobia

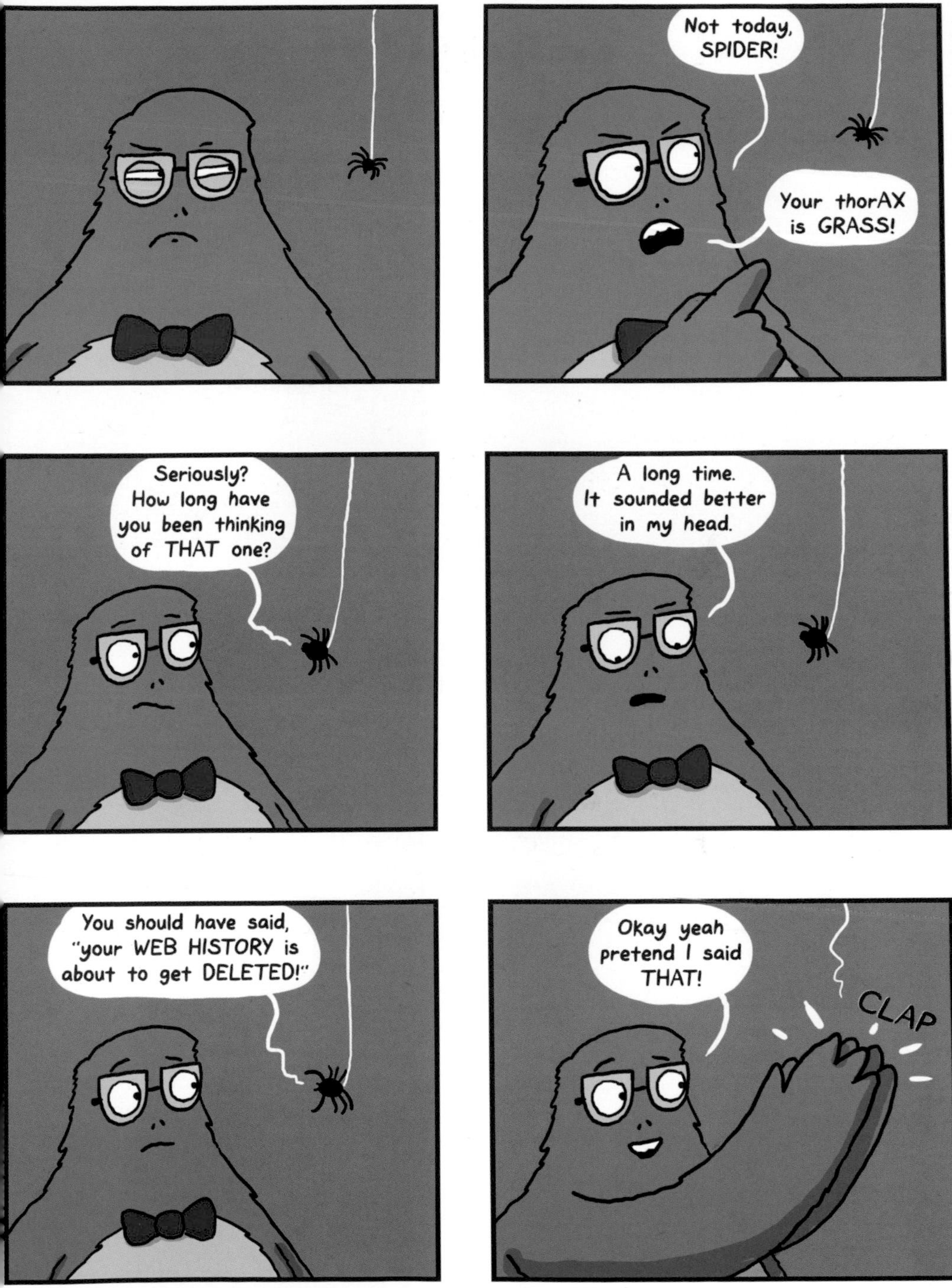
Not today, SPIDER!
Your thorAX is GRASS!
Seriously? How long have you been thinking of THAT one?
A long time. It sounded better in my head.
You should have said, "your WEB HISTORY is about to get DELETED!"
Okay yeah pretend I said THAT!
CLAP

Brotherly Advice

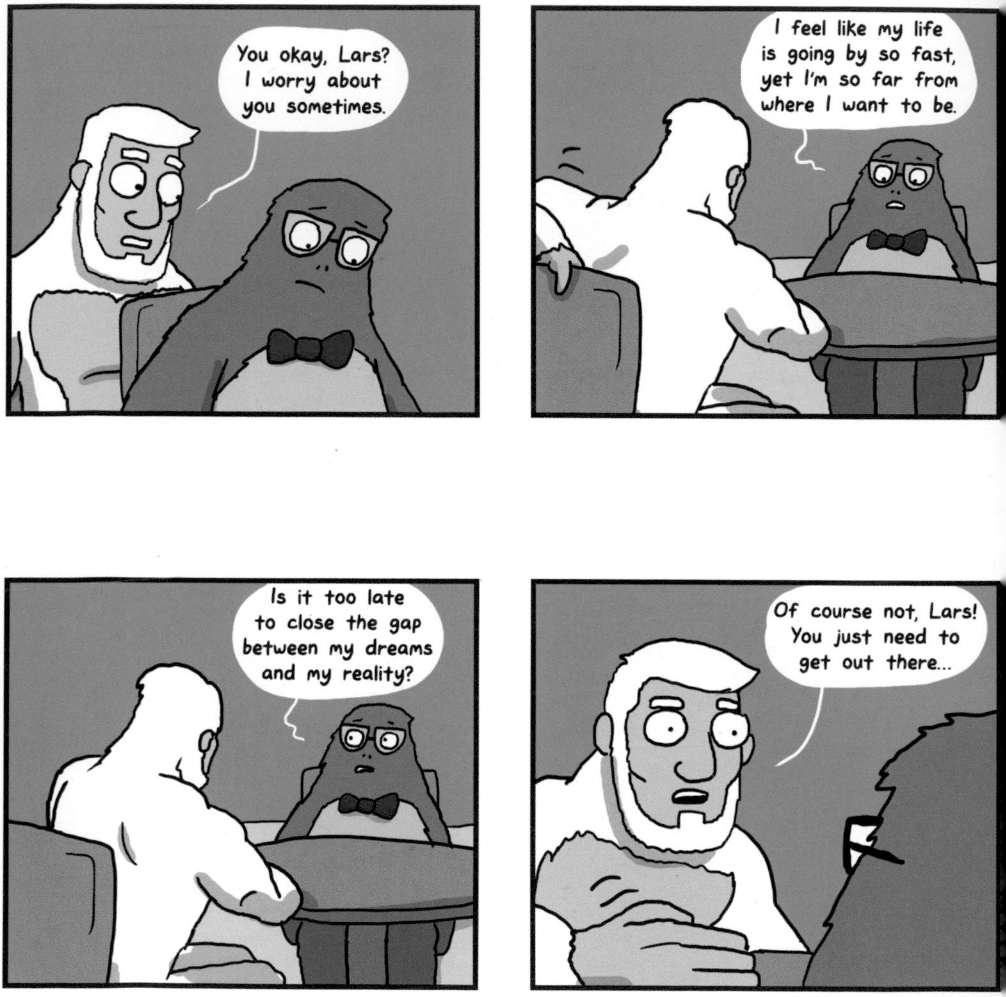
You okay, Lars? I worry about you sometimes.
I feel like my life is going by so fast, yet I'm so far from where I want to be.
Is it too late to close the gap between my dreams and my reality?
Of course not, Lars! You just need to get out there...

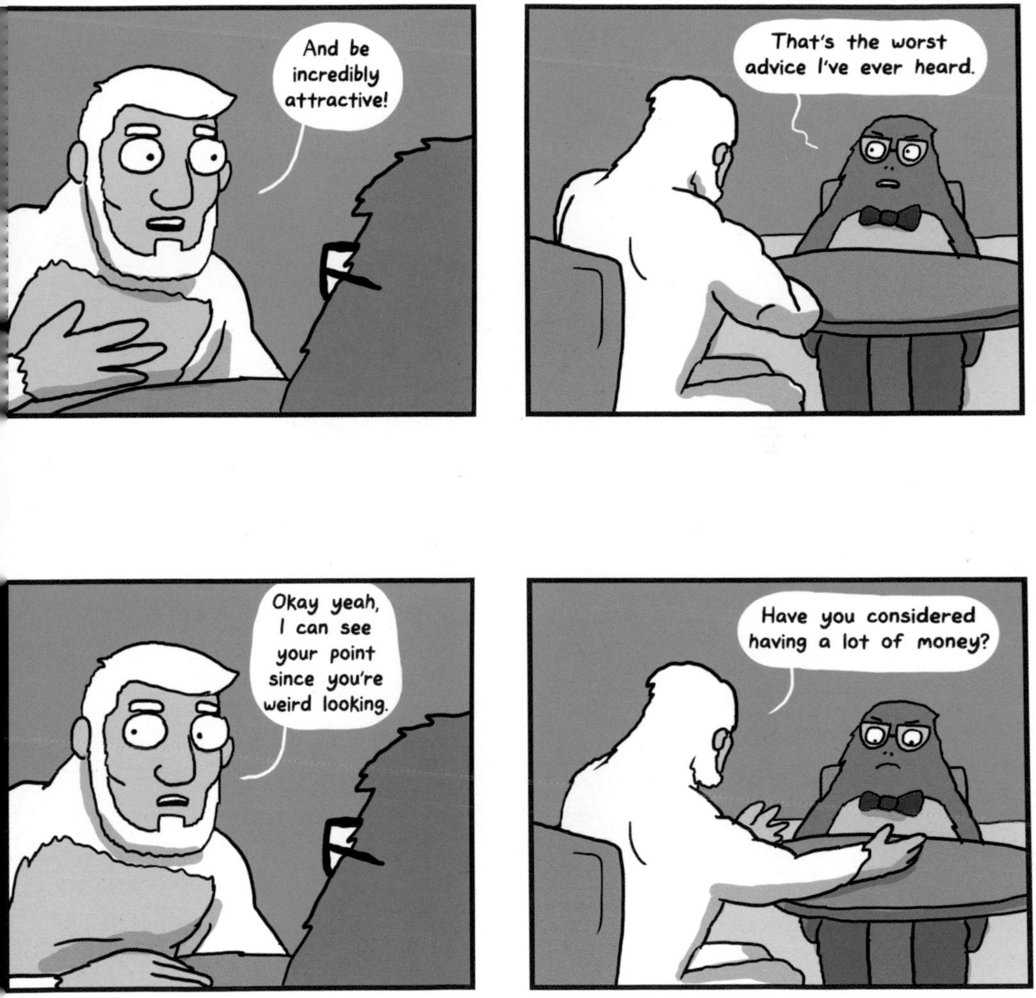
And be incredibly attractive!
That's the worst advice I've ever heard.
Okay yeah, I can see your point since you're weird looking.
Have you considered having a lot of money?

Tech Support

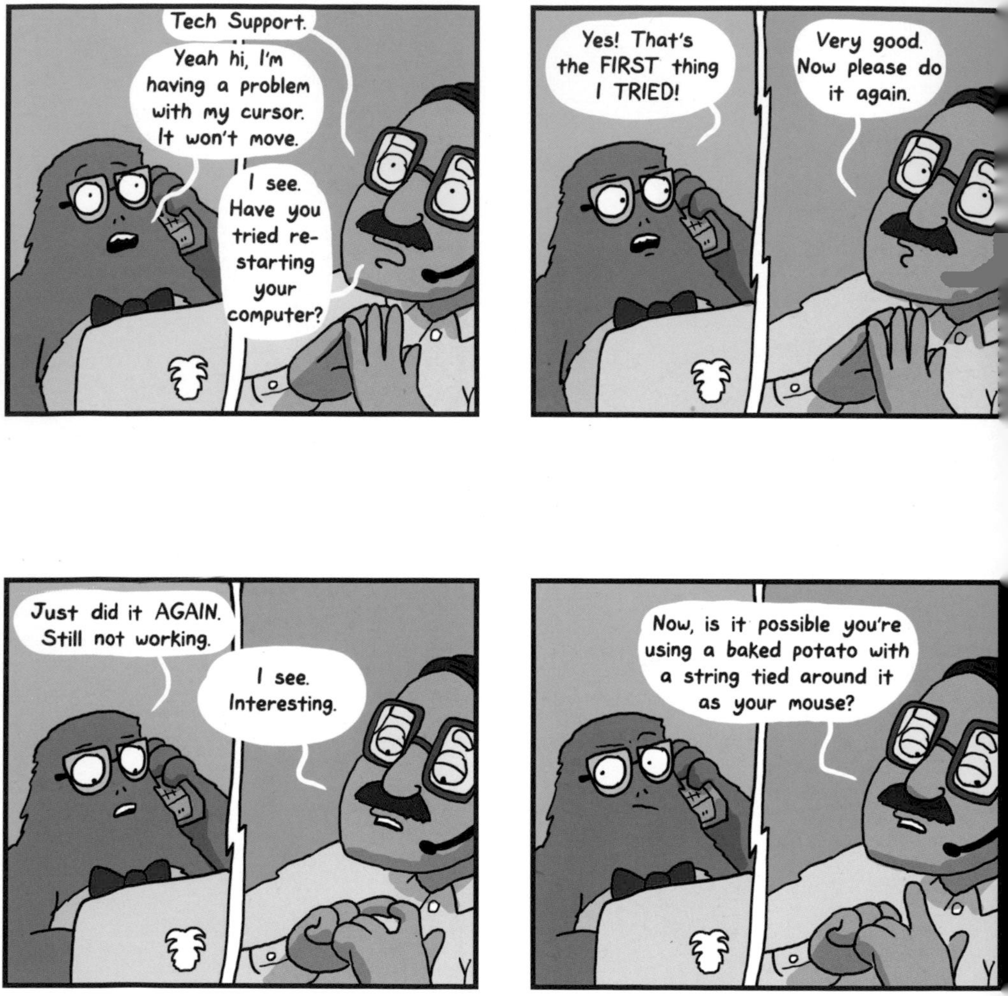

Tech Support.
Yeah hi, I'm having a problem with my cursor. It won't move.
I see. Have you tried re-starting your computer?
Yes! That's the FIRST thing I TRIED!
Very good. Now please do it again.
Just did it AGAIN. Still not working.
I see. Interesting.
Now, is it possible you're using a baked potato with a string tied around it as your mouse?

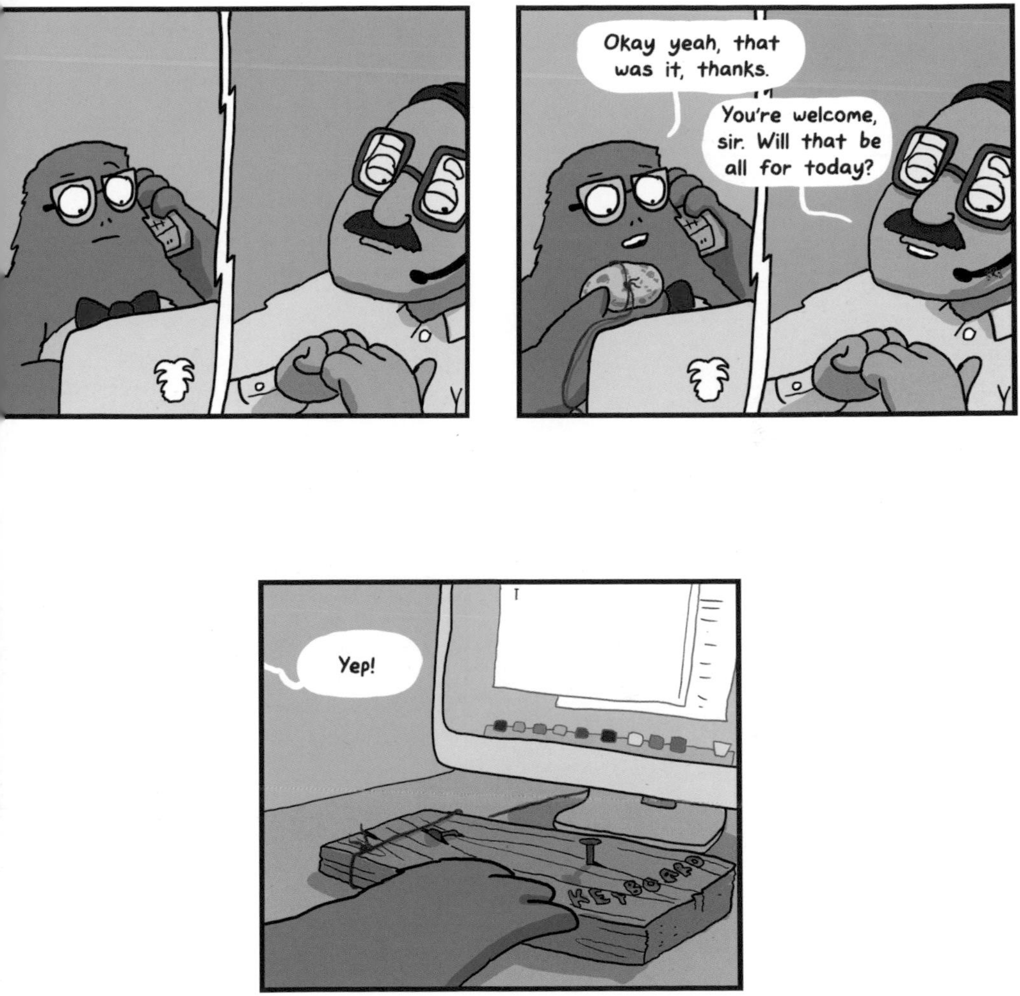
Okay yeah, that was it, thanks.
You're welcome, sir. Will that be all for today?
Yep!
KEYBOARD

Thoughts

What's on your mind, big guy?
What if we've become so distracted by our newfound ability to be heard via the Internet that we aren't even being proactive about change anymore - rather, we fight amongst ourselves with no real objectives, and allow the 'powers that be' free reign to continue their corruption uninterrupted?!
I mean... I was thinking about last night's sports game...
WHAT A GAME!

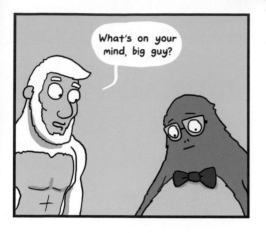

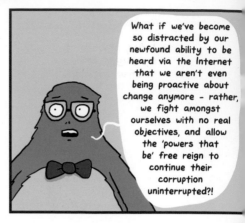

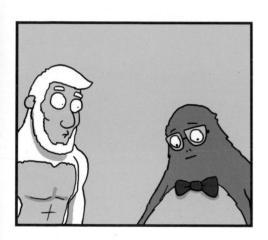

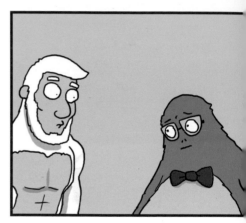

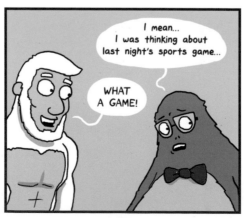

The Musician

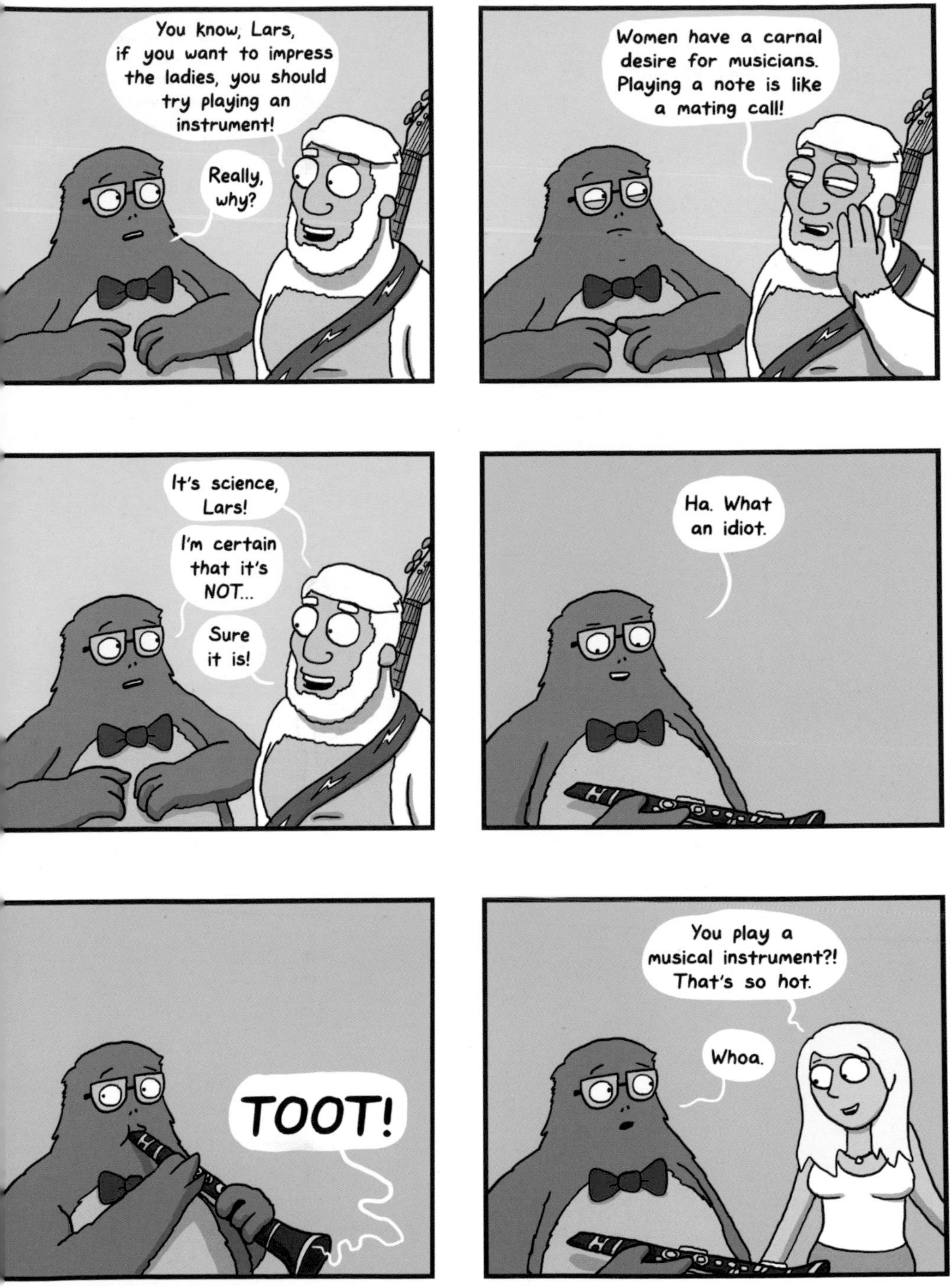
You know, Lars, if you want to impress the ladies, you should try playing an instrument!
Really, why?
Women have a carnal desire for musicians. Playing a note is like a mating call!
It's science, Lars!
I'm certain that it's NOT...
Sure it is!
Ha. What an idiot.
TOOT!
You play a musical instrument?! That's so hot.
Whoa.

Moving On

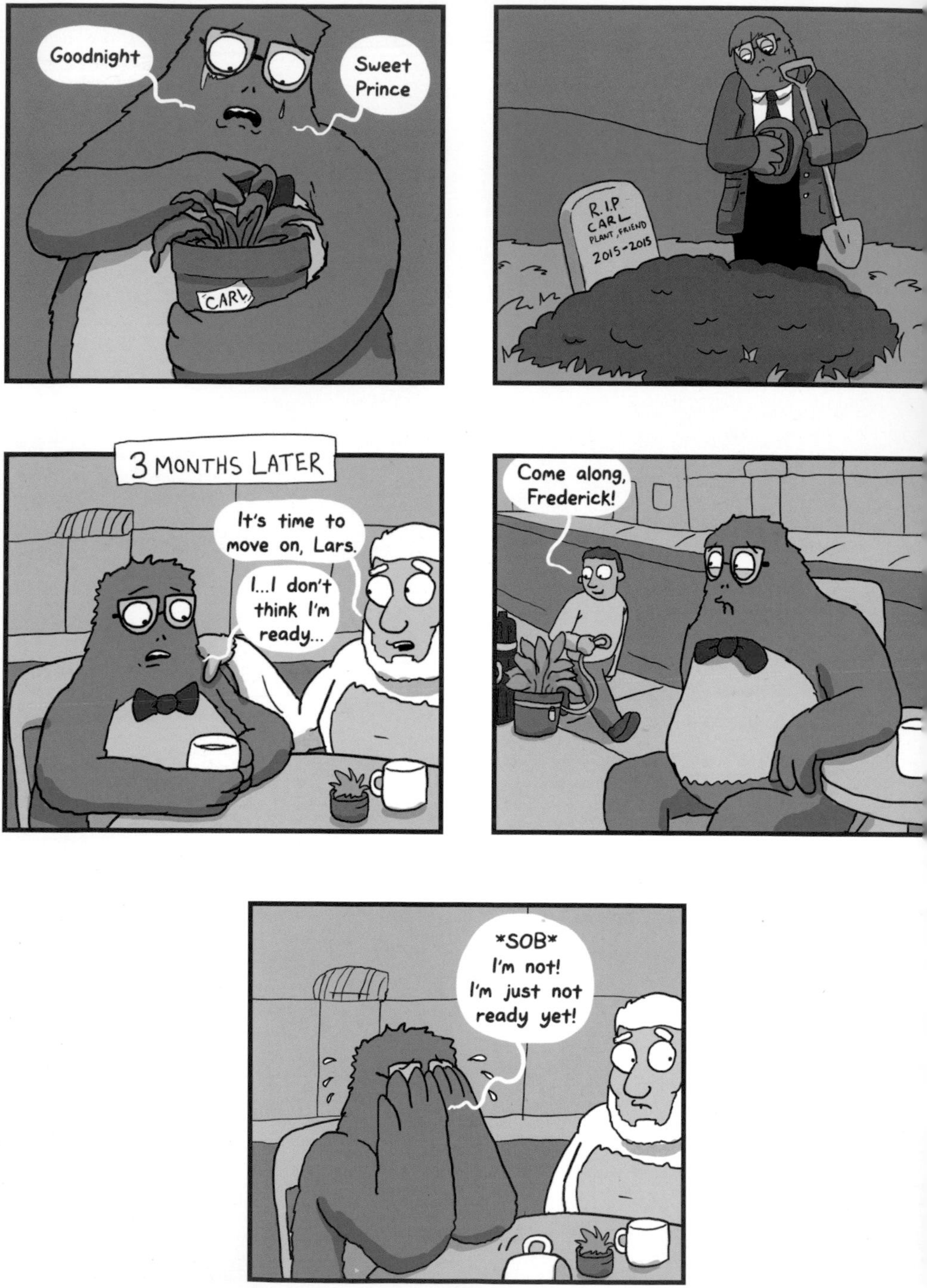
Goodnight
Sweet Prince
CARL
R.I.P
CARL
PLANT, FRIEND
2015-2015
3 MONTHS LATER
It's time to move on, Lars.
I...I don't think I'm ready...
Come along, Frederick!
SOB
I'm not!
I'm just not ready yet!

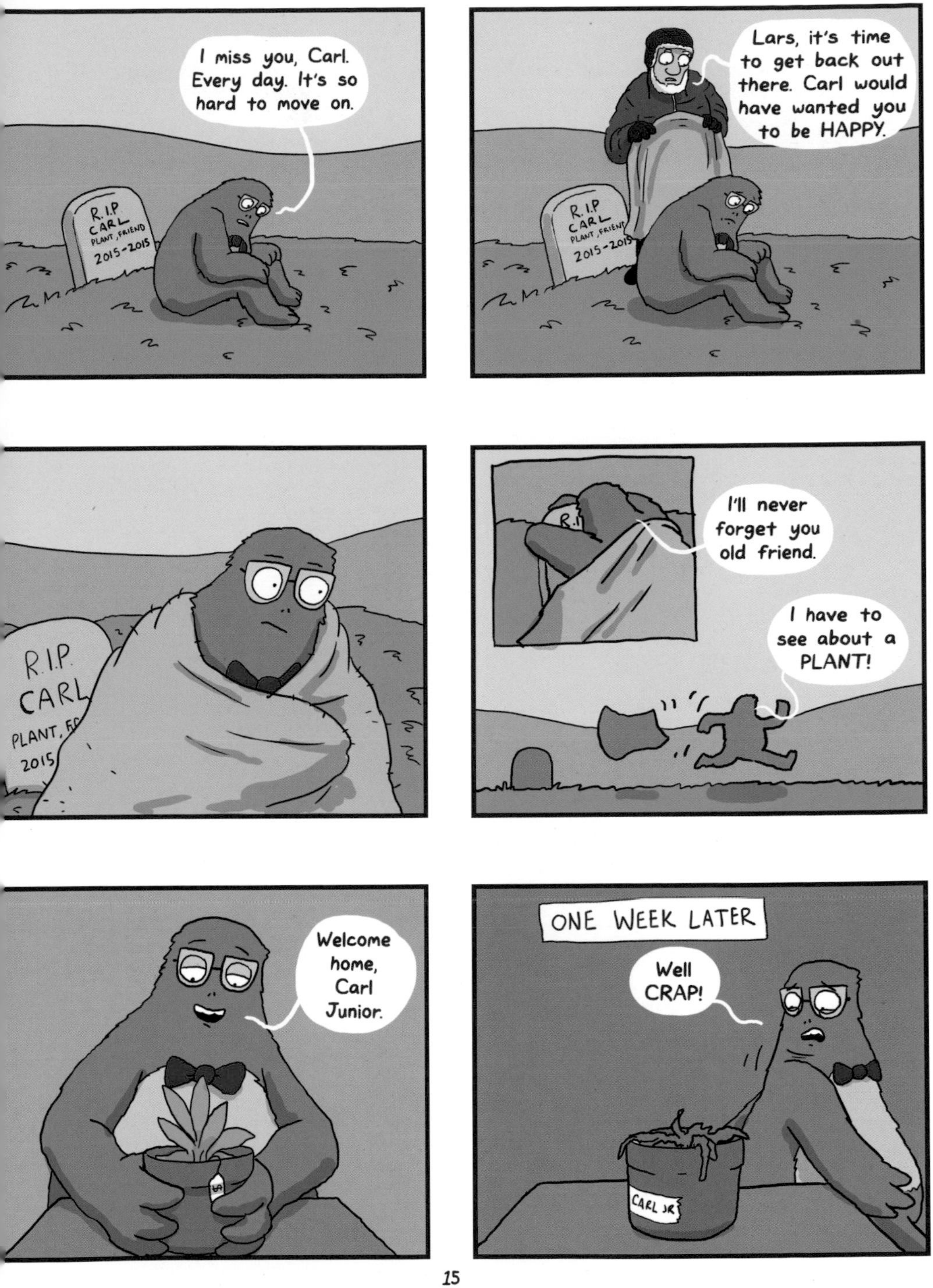
I miss you, Carl. Every day. It's so hard to move on.
R.I.P CARL PLANT, FRIEND 2015-2015
Lars, it's time to get back out there. Carl would have wanted you to be HAPPY.
R.I.P CARL PLANT, FRIEND 2015-2015
R.I.P. CARL PLANT, F 2015
I'll never forget you old friend.
I have to see about a PLANT!
Welcome home, Carl Junior.
ONE WEEK LATER
Well CRAP!
CARL JR

Adulthood

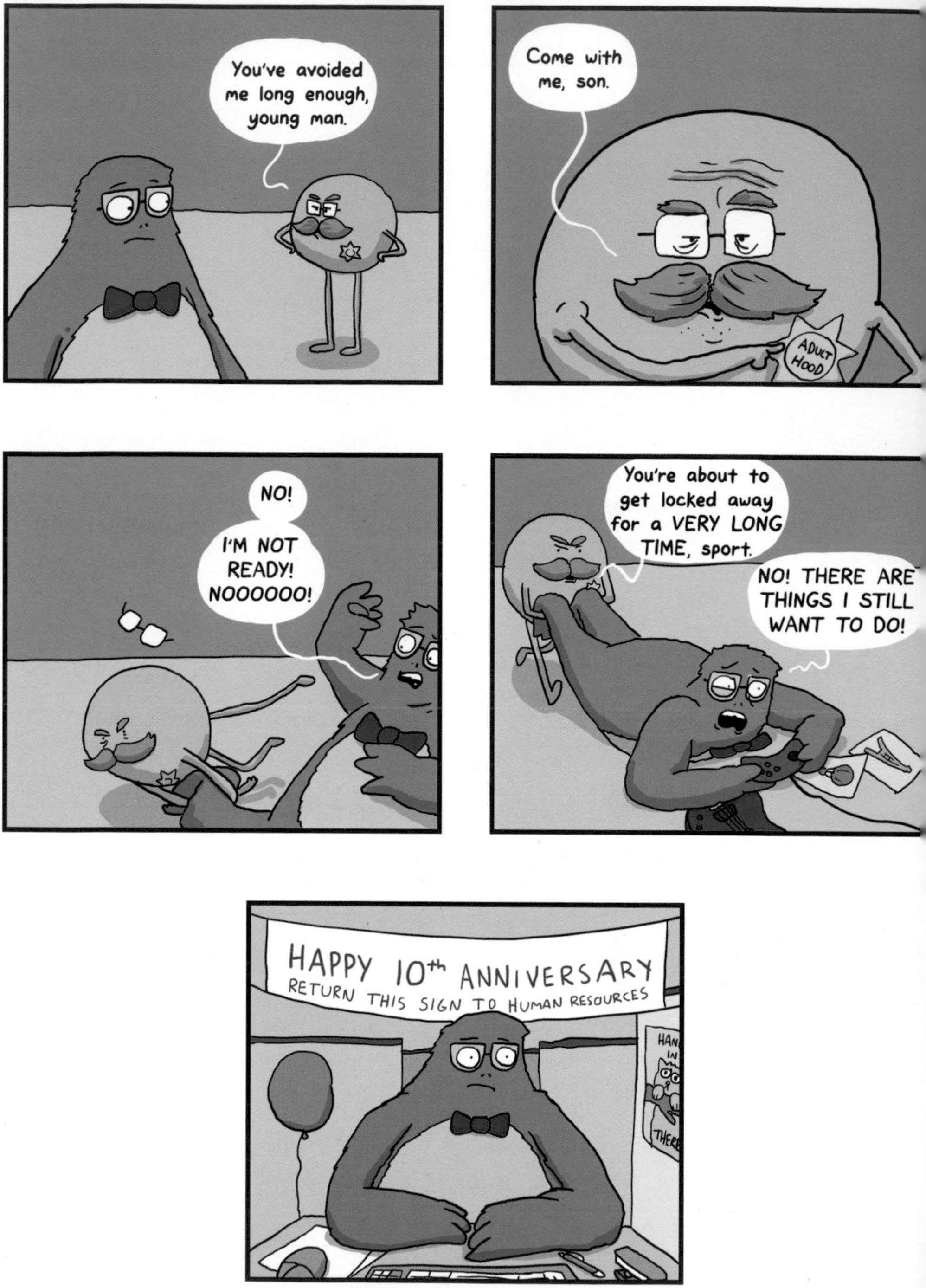

You've avoided me long enough, young man.
Come with me, son.
ADULT HOOD
NO!
I'M NOT READY! NOOOOOO!
You're about to get locked away for a VERY LONG TIME, sport.
NO! THERE ARE THINGS I STILL WANT TO DO!
HAPPY 10th ANNIVERSARY
RETURN THIS SIGN TO HUMAN RESOURCES

Adulthood Part 2: The Myth

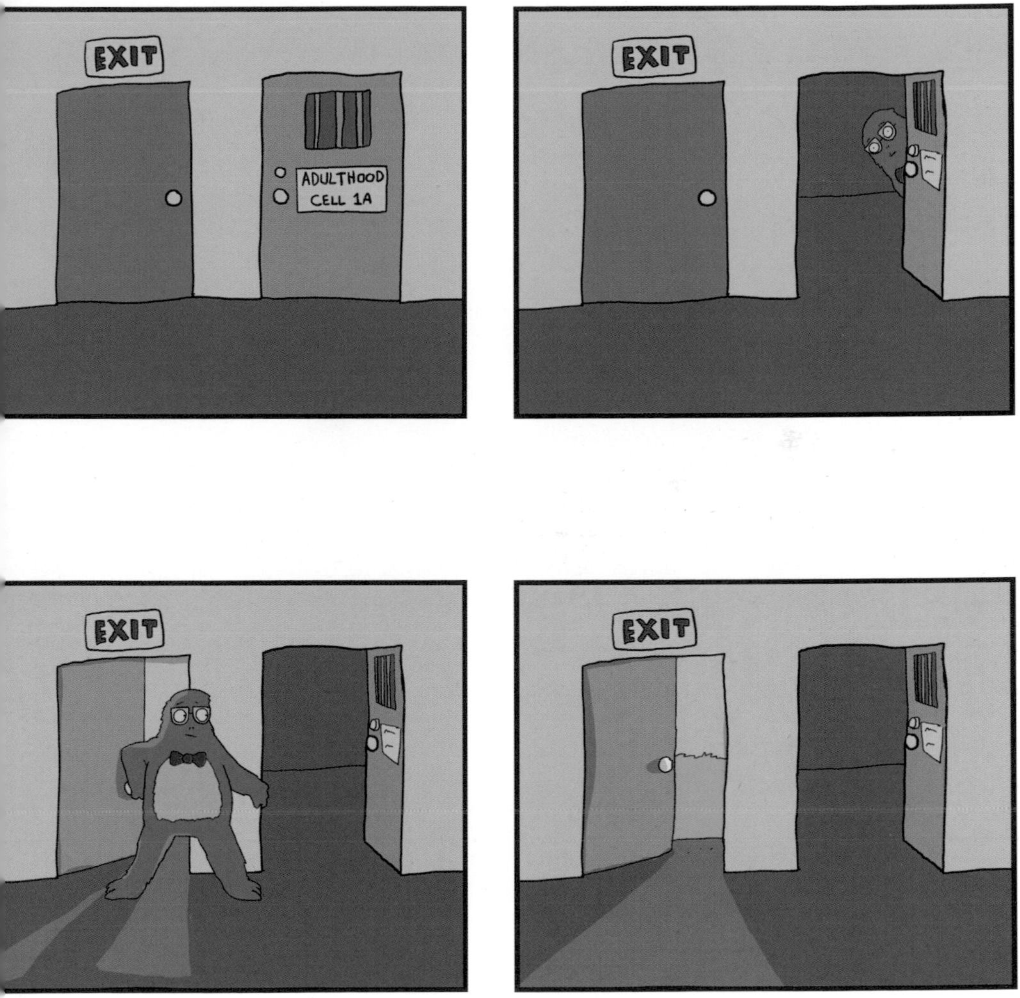
EXIT
ADULTHOOD
CELL 1A
EXIT
EXIT
EXIT

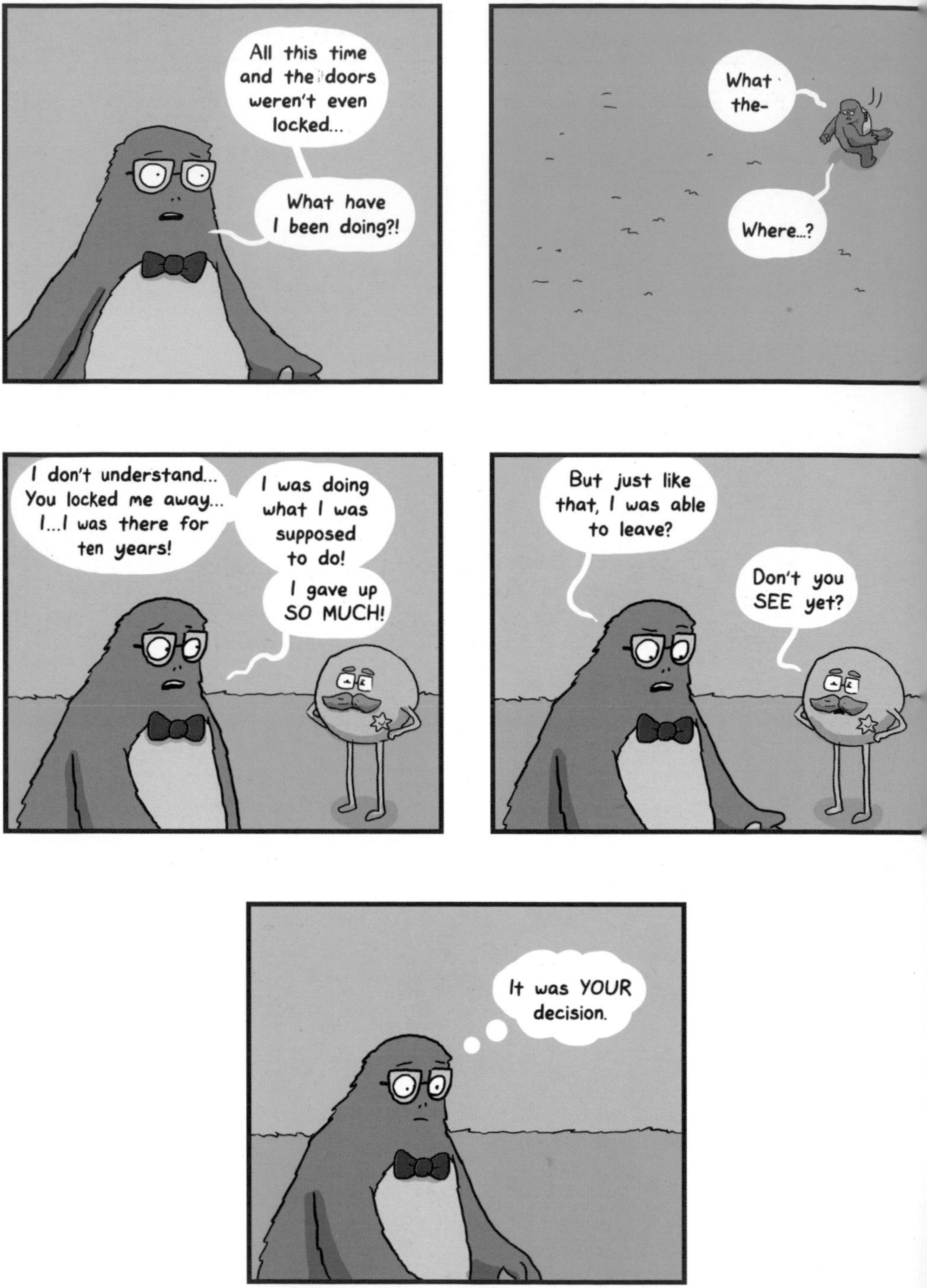
All this time and the doors weren't even locked...
What have I been doing?!
What the-
Where...?
I don't understand... You locked me away... I...I was there for ten years!
I was doing what I was supposed to do!
I gave up SO MUCH!
But just like that, I was able to leave?
Don't you SEE yet?
It was YOUR decision.

Stopping the Cycle

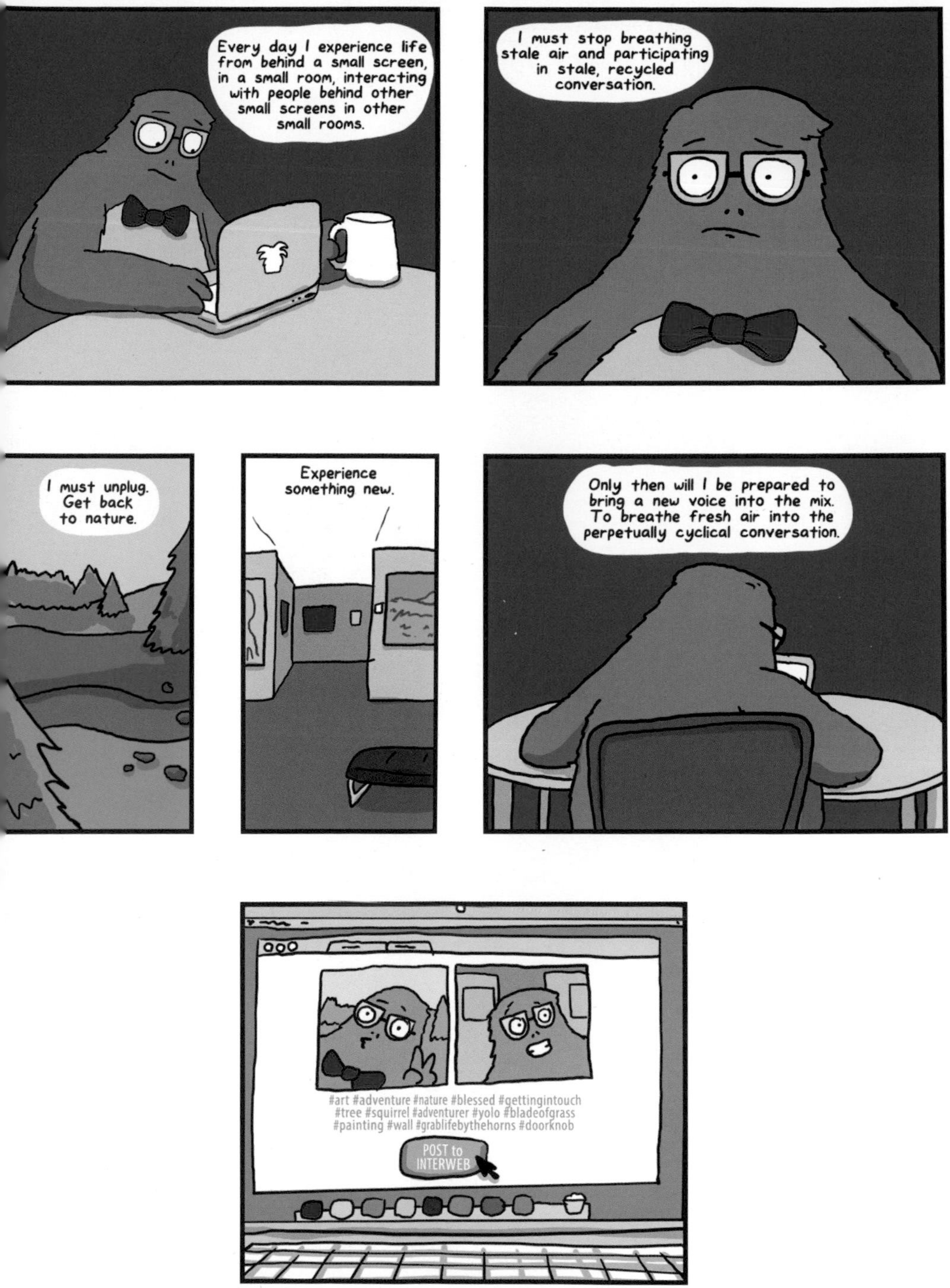

Every day I experience life from behind a small screen, in a small room, interacting with people behind other small screens in other small rooms.
I must stop breathing stale air and participating in stale, recycled conversation.
I must unplug. Get back to nature.
Experience something new.
Only then will I be prepared to bring a new voice into the mix. To breathe fresh air into the perpetually cyclical conversation.
#art #adventure #nature #blessed #gettingintouch #tree #squirrel #adventurer #yolo #bladeofgrass #painting #wall #grablifebythehorns #doorknob
POST to INTERWEB

You Think Coffee Is Your Ally? You Merely Adopted Coffee.

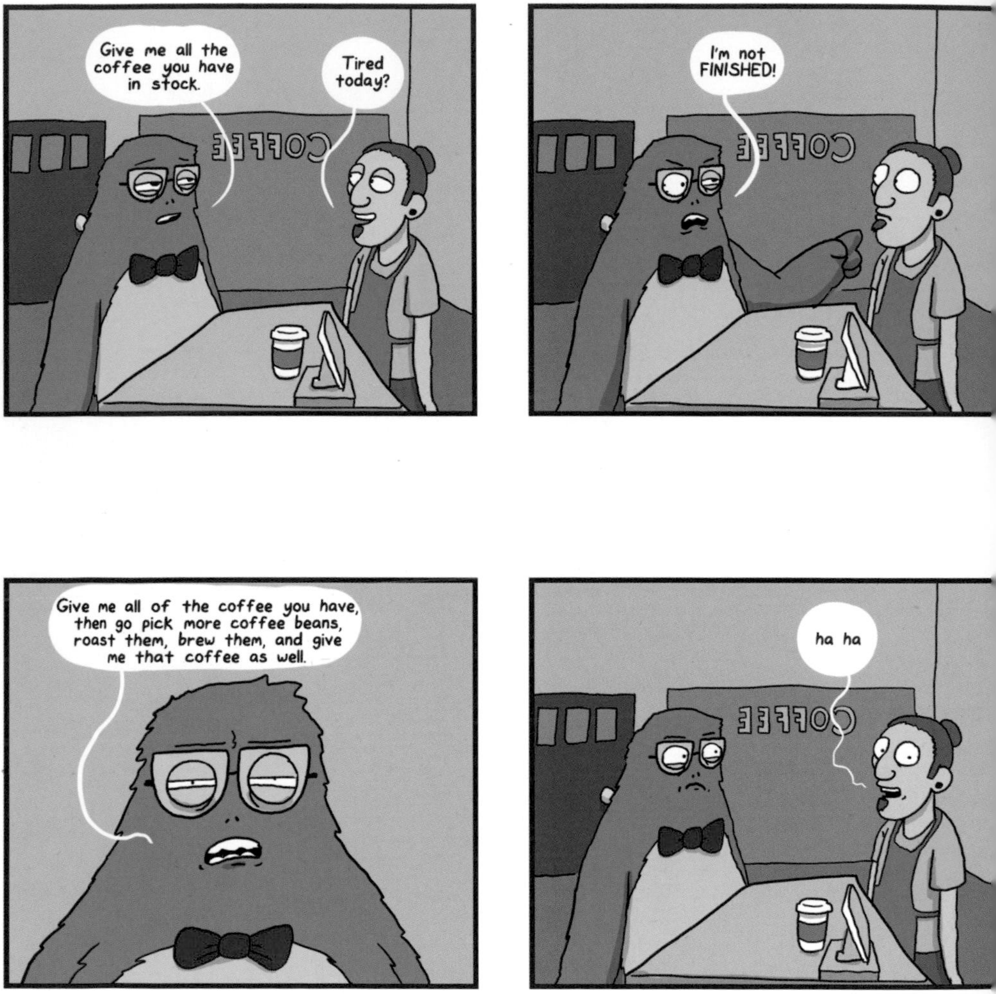
Give me all the coffee you have in stock.
Tired today?
I'm not FINISHED!
Give me all of the coffee you have, then go pick more coffee beans, roast them, brew them, and give me that coffee as well.
ha ha

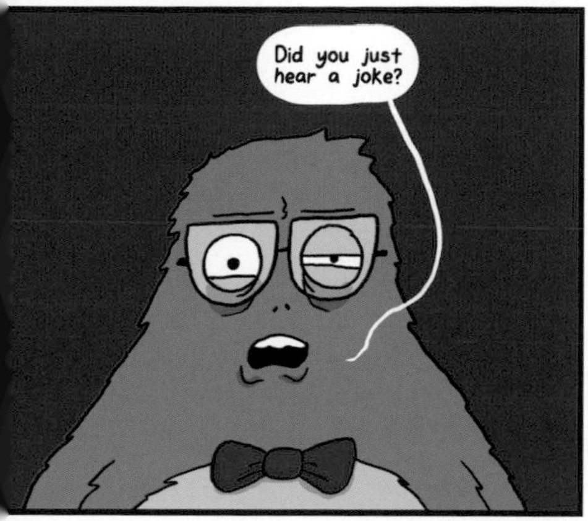
Did you just hear a joke?

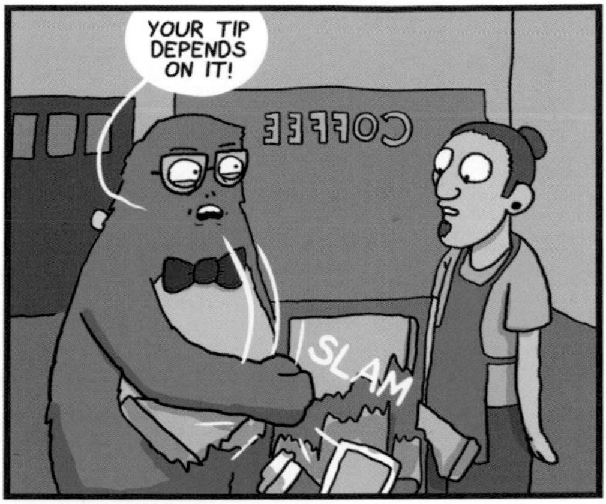
YOUR TIP DEPENDS ON IT!
SLAM

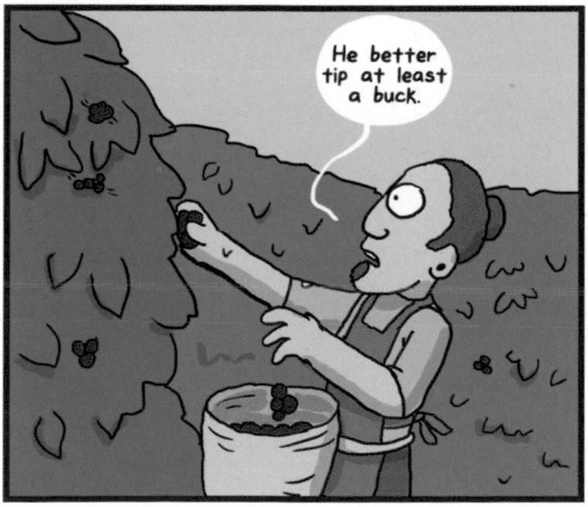
He better tip at least a buck.

Resolutions

Hey little bro, how are your New Year's resolutions going?
So far, not so good.
I wanted to eat better, but I also wanted to be less wasteful.
Problem is, I had a LOT of junk food still in my house!
Ah, so did you donate all that food to the needy or something?
Yep!
Well don't get down on yourself, you're off to a great start!
CHIPS

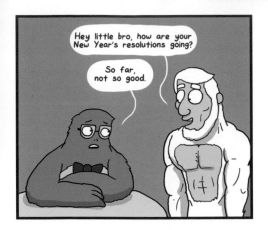

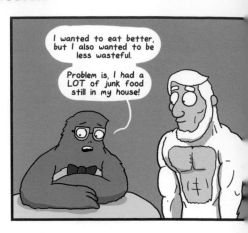

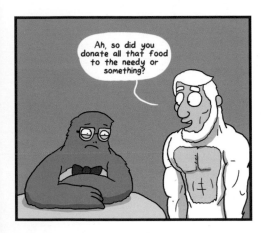

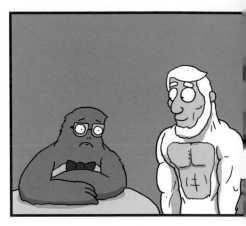

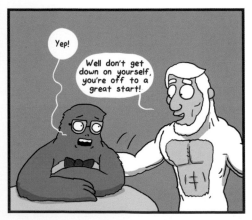

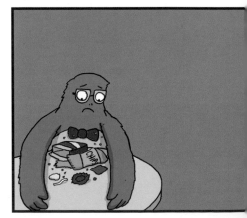

Escape

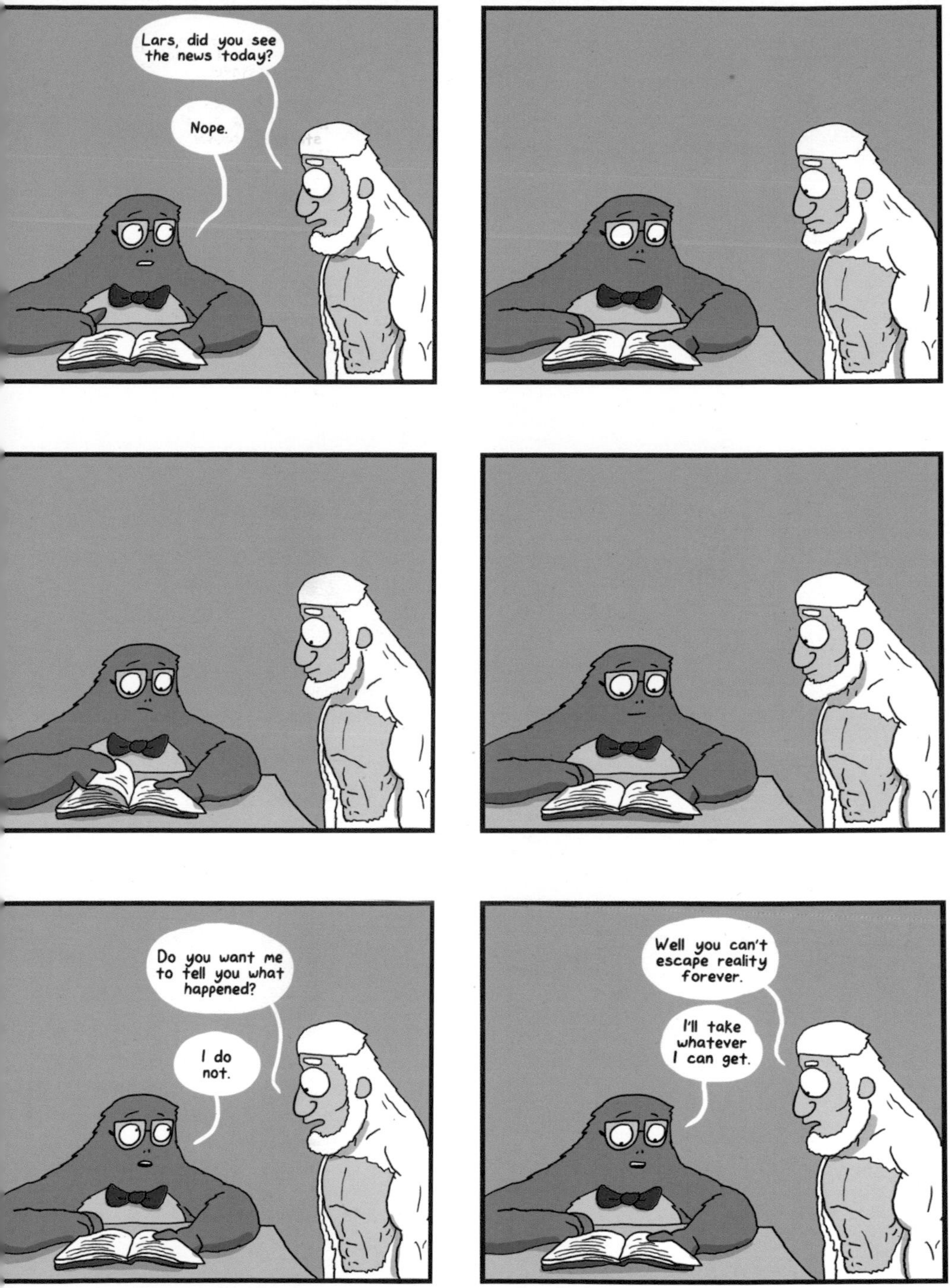
Lars, did you see the news today?
Nope.
Do you want me to tell you what happened?
I do not.
Well you can't escape reality forever.
I'll take whatever I can get.

Anxiety Parties

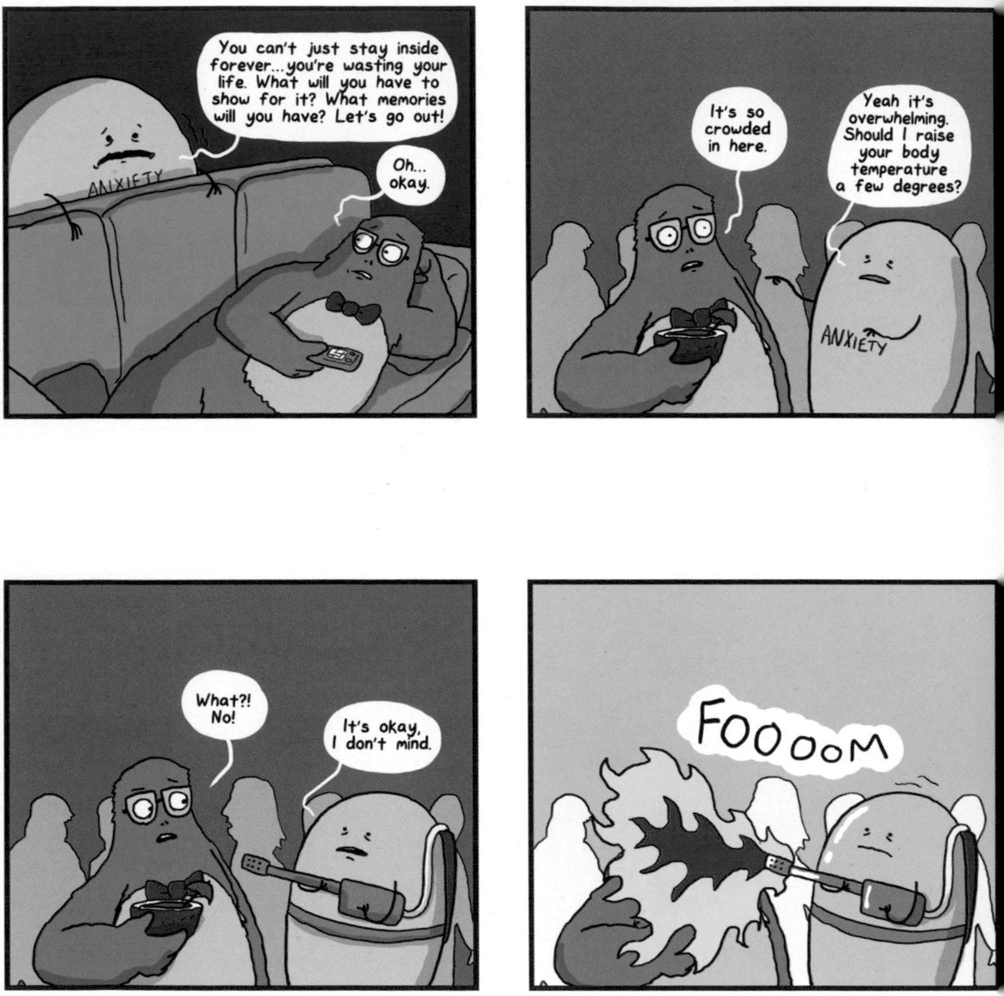

You can't just stay inside forever...you're wasting your life. What will you have to show for it? What memories will you have? Let's go out!
ANXIETY
Oh... okay.
It's so crowded in here.
Yeah it's overwhelming. Should I raise your body temperature a few degrees?
ANXIETY
What?! No!
It's okay, I don't mind.
FOOOOOM

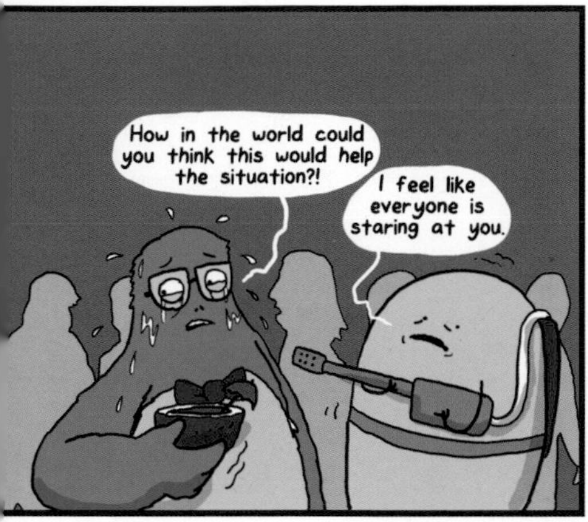
How in the world could you think this would help the situation?!
I feel like everyone is staring at you.

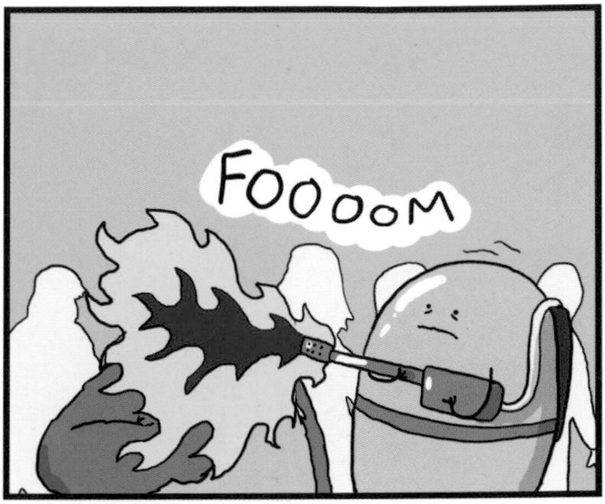
FOOOOOM

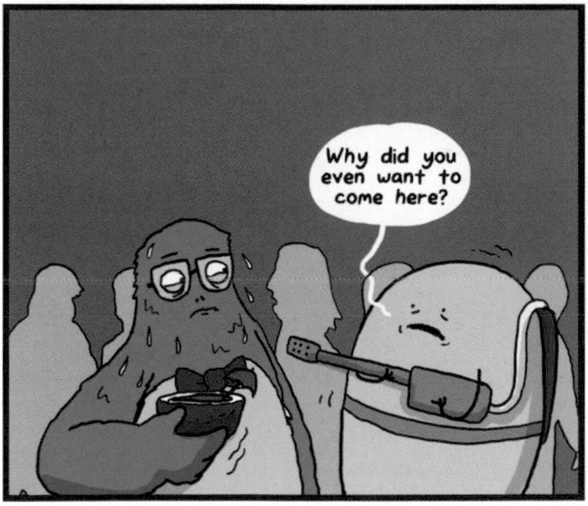
Why did you even want to come here?

The Adventures of Overly Dramatic Doctor

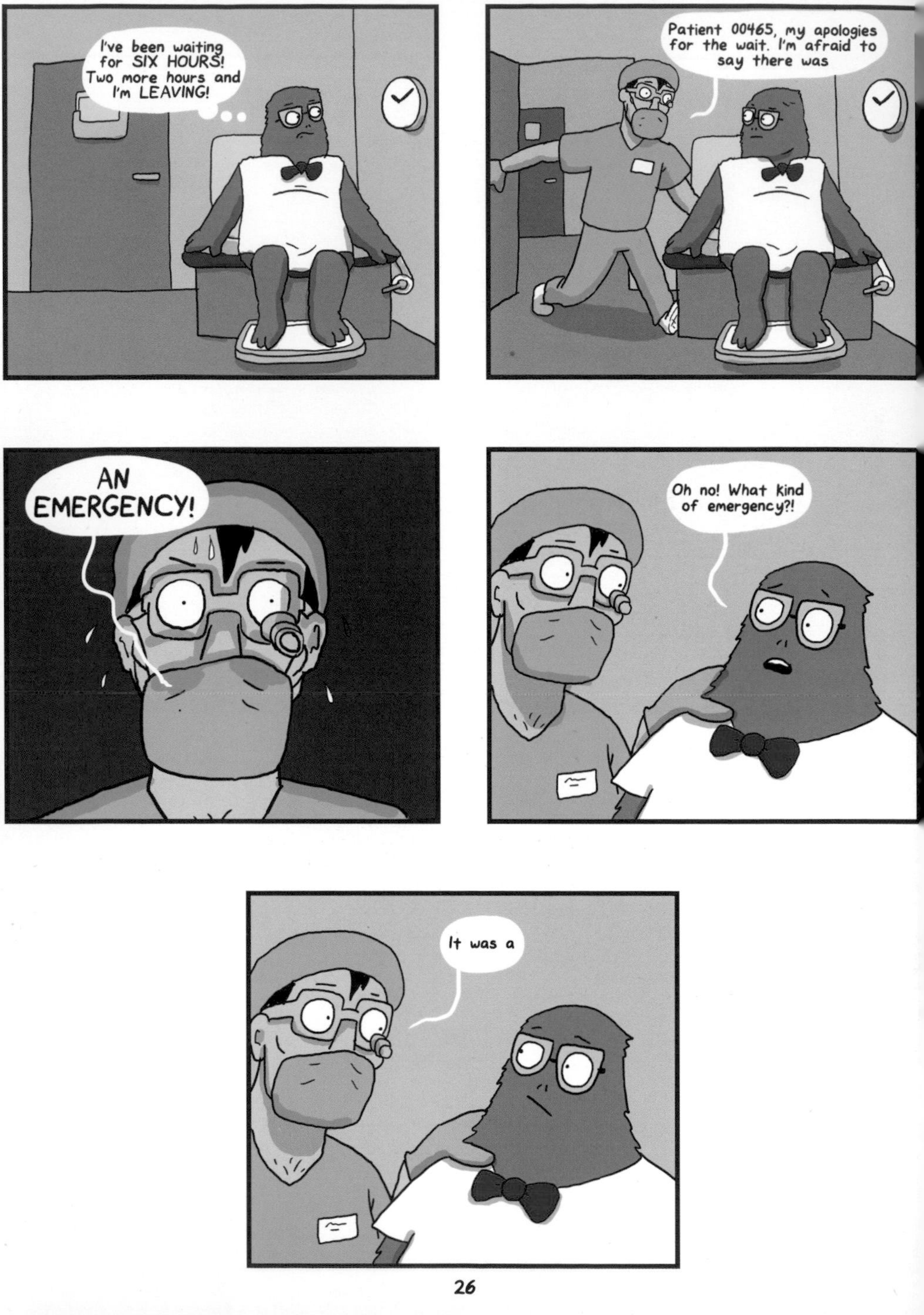

I've been waiting for SIX HOURS! Two more hours and I'm LEAVING!
Patient 00465, my apologies for the wait. I'm afraid to say there was
AN EMERGENCY!
Oh no! What kind of emergency?!
It was a

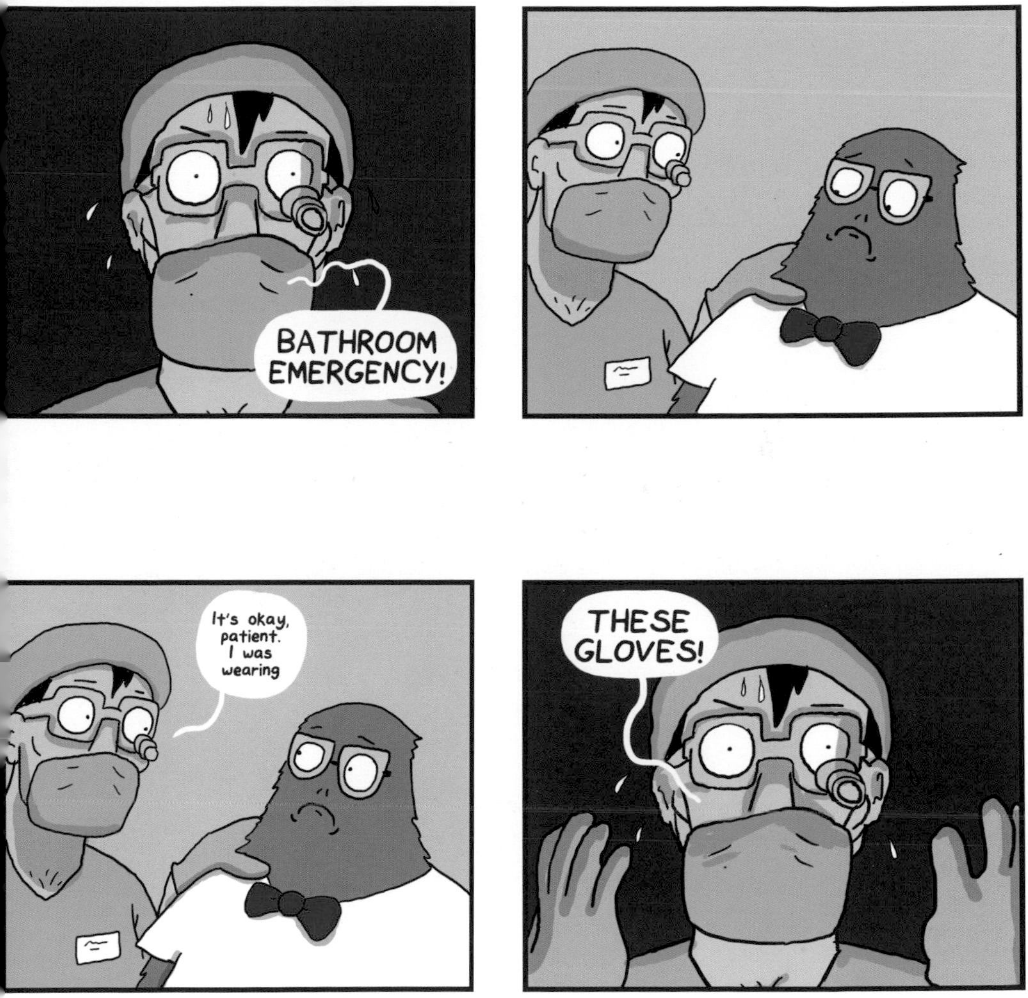
BATHROOM EMERGENCY!
It's okay, patient. I was wearing
THESE GLOVES!

Silky Smooth

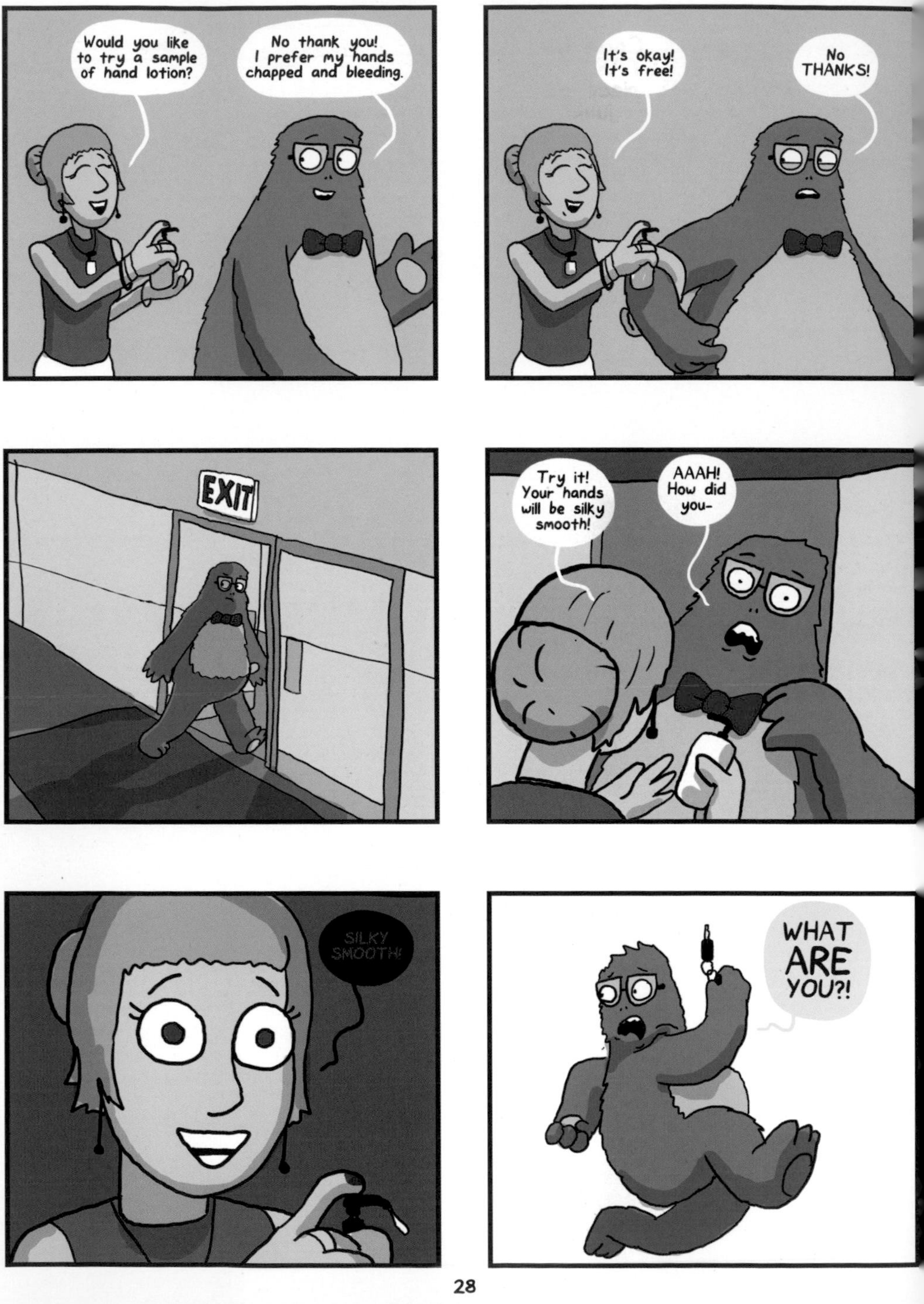

Would you like to try a sample of hand lotion?
No thank you! I prefer my hands chapped and bleeding.
It's okay! It's free!
No THANKS!
EXIT
Try it! Your hands will be silky smooth!
AAAH! How did you-
SILKY SMOOTH!
WHAT ARE YOU?!

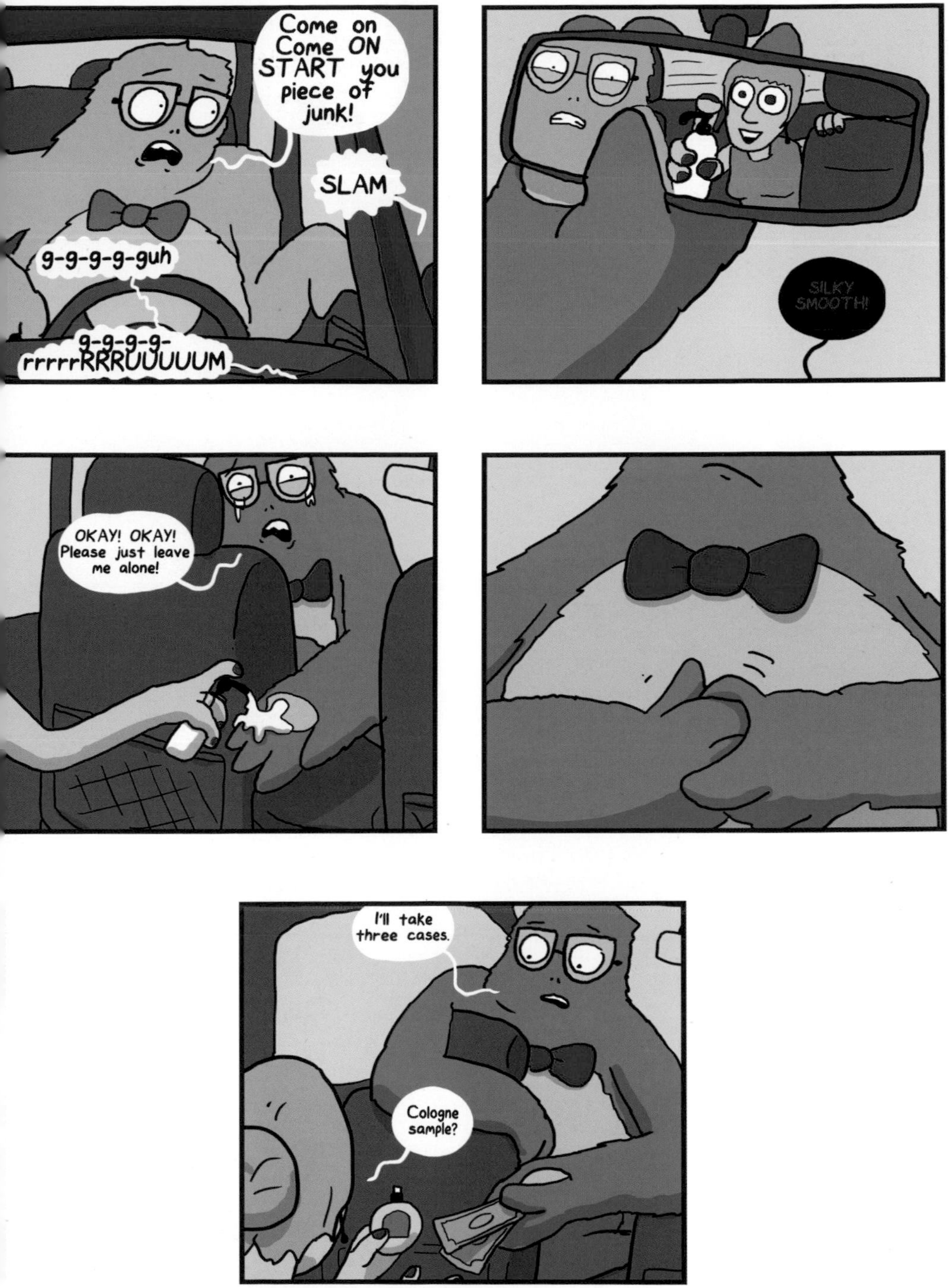
Come on Come ON START you piece of junk!
SLAM
g-g-g-g-guh
g-g-g-g-rrrrrRRRUUUUUM
SILKY SMOOTH!
OKAY! OKAY! Please just leave me alone!
I'll take three cases.
Cologne sample?

MD Banter

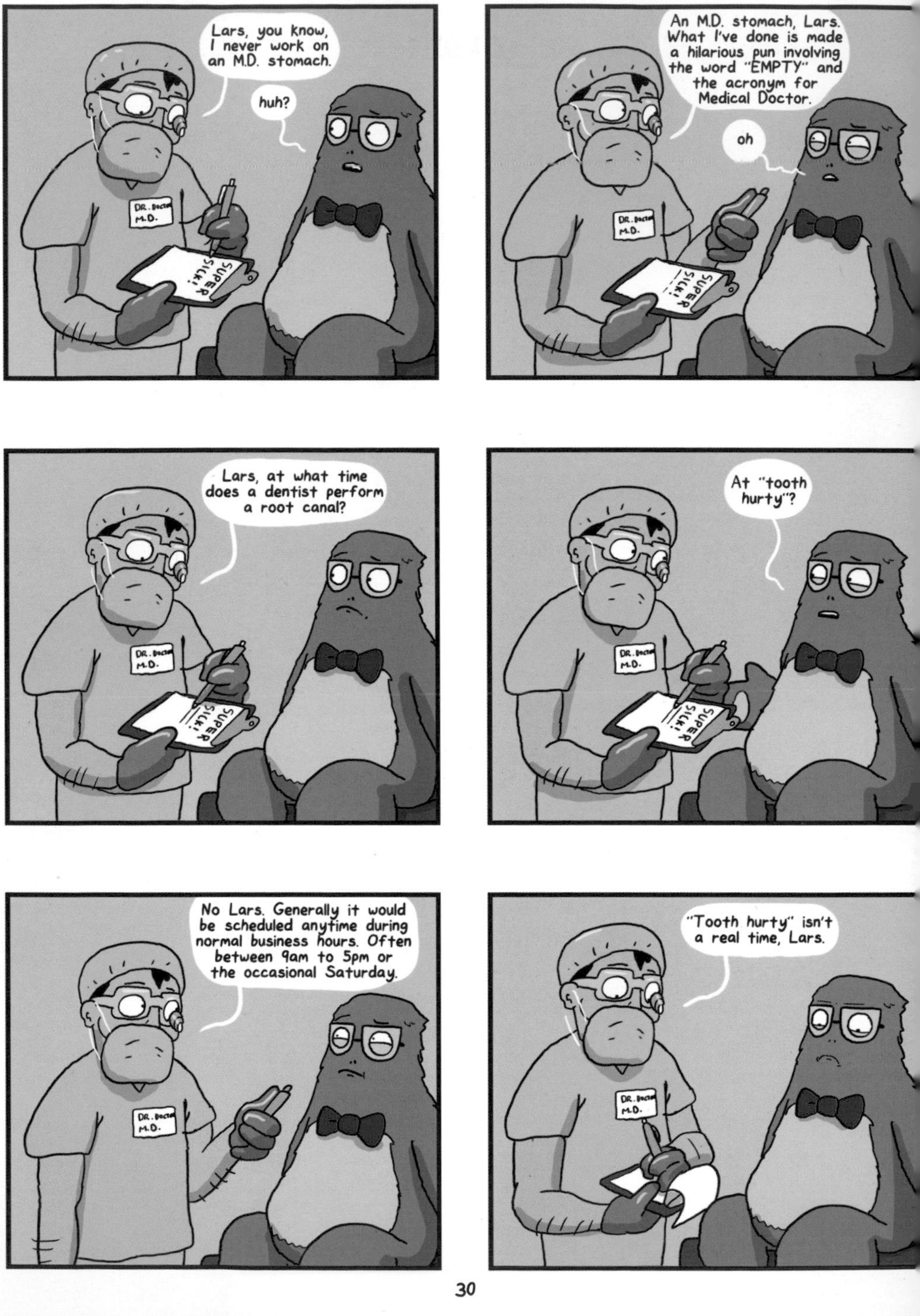
Lars, you know, I never work on an M.D. stomach.
huh?
DR. Doctor M.D.
SUPER SICK!
An M.D. stomach, Lars. What I've done is made a hilarious pun involving the word "EMPTY" and the acronym for Medical Doctor.
oh
Lars, at what time does a dentist perform a root canal?
At "tooth hurty"?
No Lars. Generally it would be scheduled anytime during normal business hours. Often between 9am to 5pm or the occasional Saturday.
"Tooth hurty" isn't a real time, Lars.

First Contact

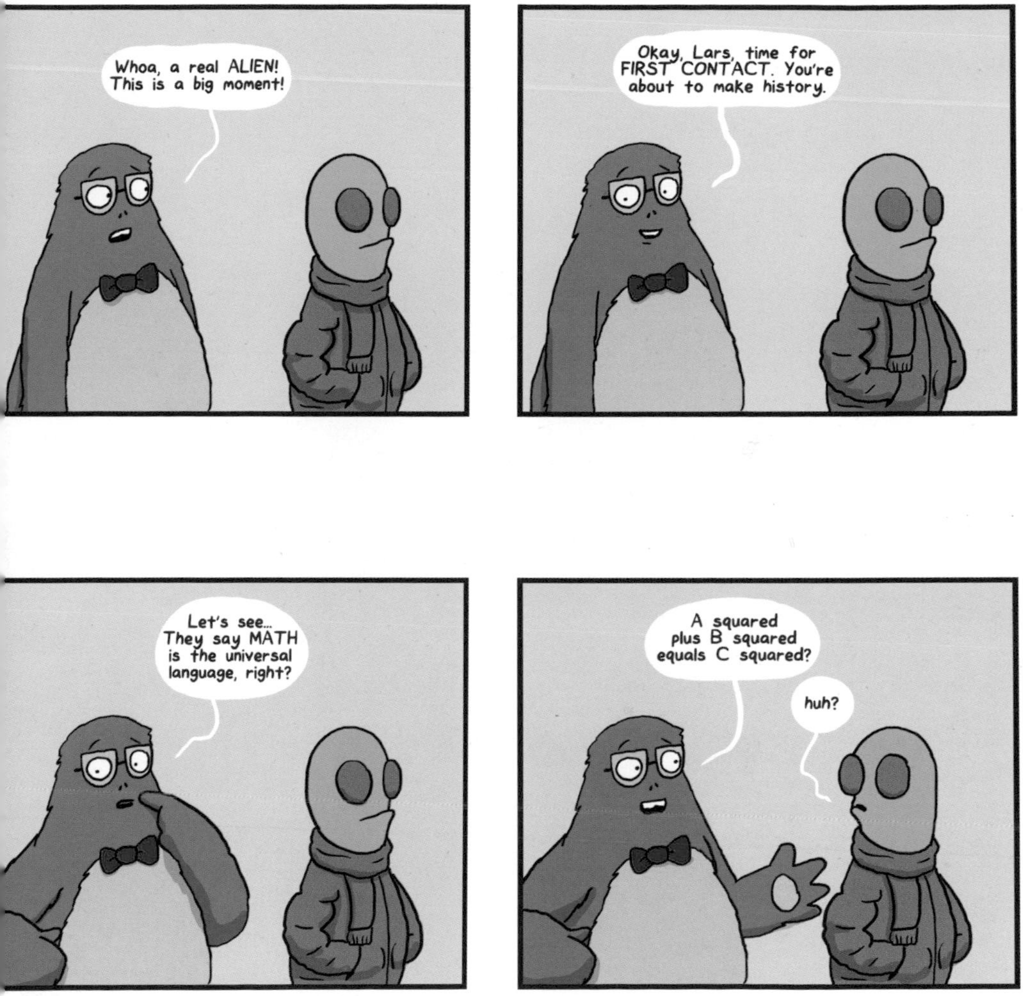
Whoa, a real ALIEN! This is a big moment!
Okay, Lars, time for FIRST CONTACT. You're about to make history.
Let's see... They say MATH is the universal language, right?
A squared plus B squared equals C squared?
huh?

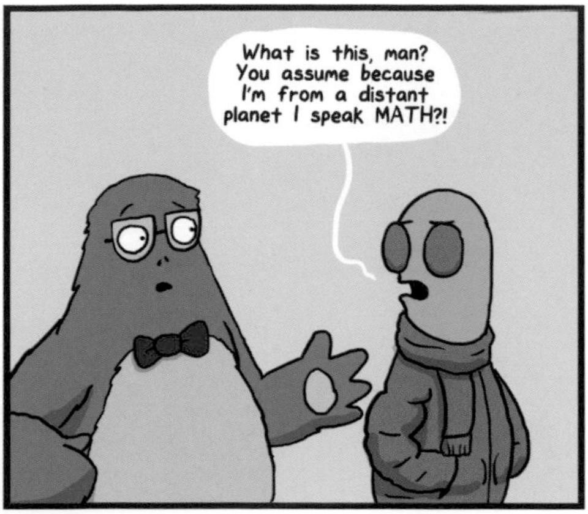
What is this, man? You assume because I'm from a distant planet I speak MATH?!

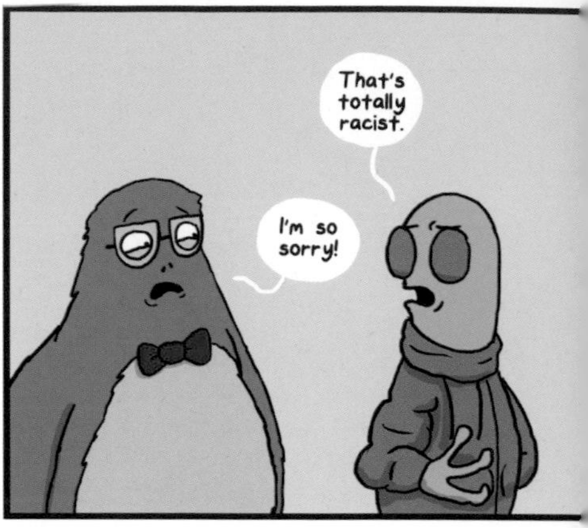
That's totally racist.
I'm so sorry!

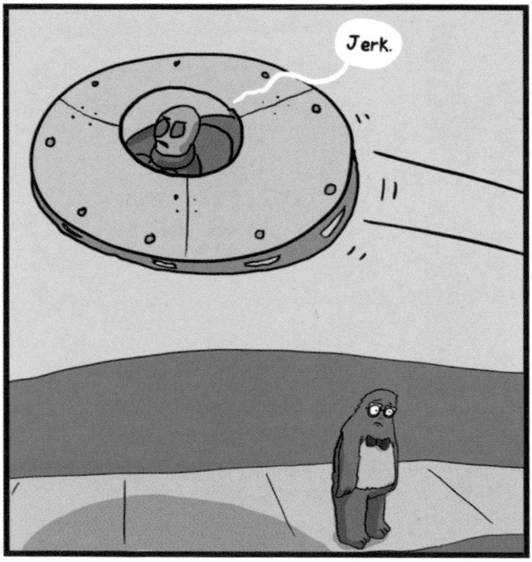
Jerk.

The Walk-In

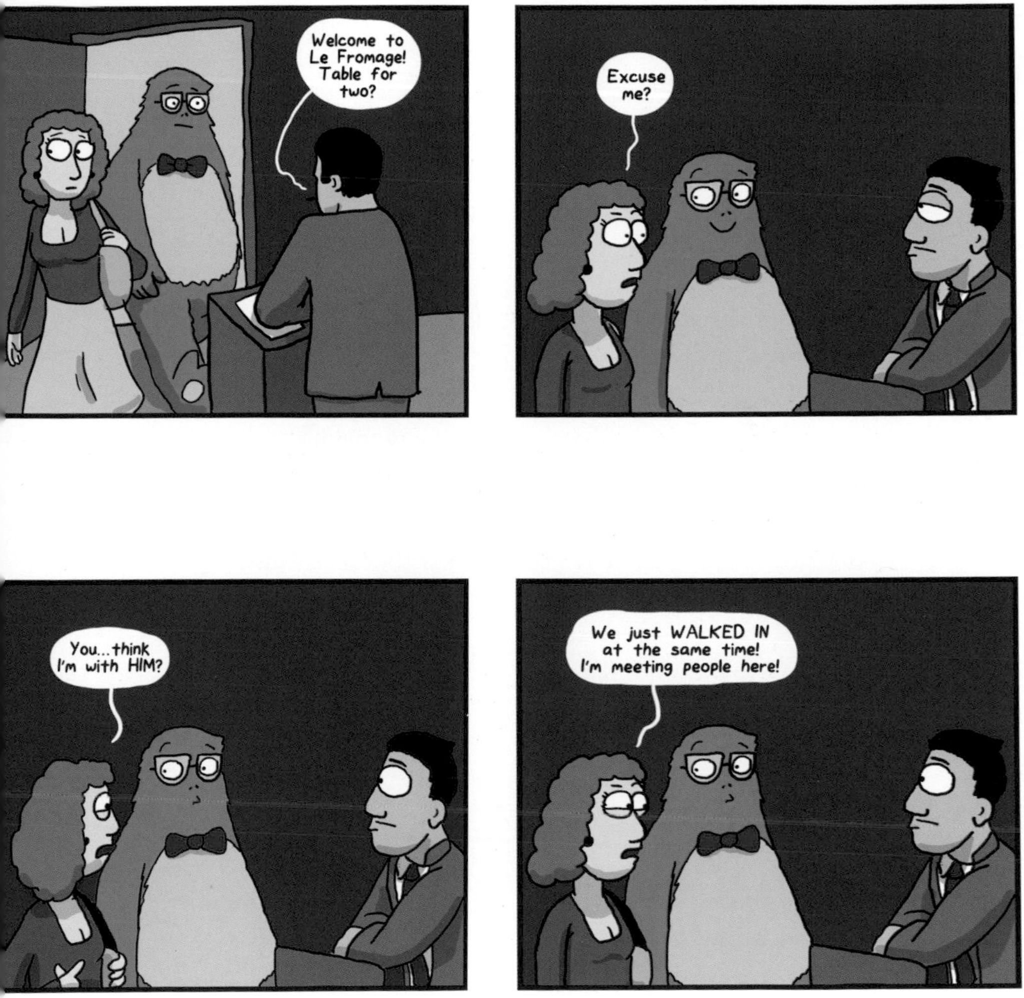
Welcome to Le Fromage! Table for two?
Excuse me?
You...think I'm with HIM?
We just WALKED IN at the same time! I'm meeting people here!

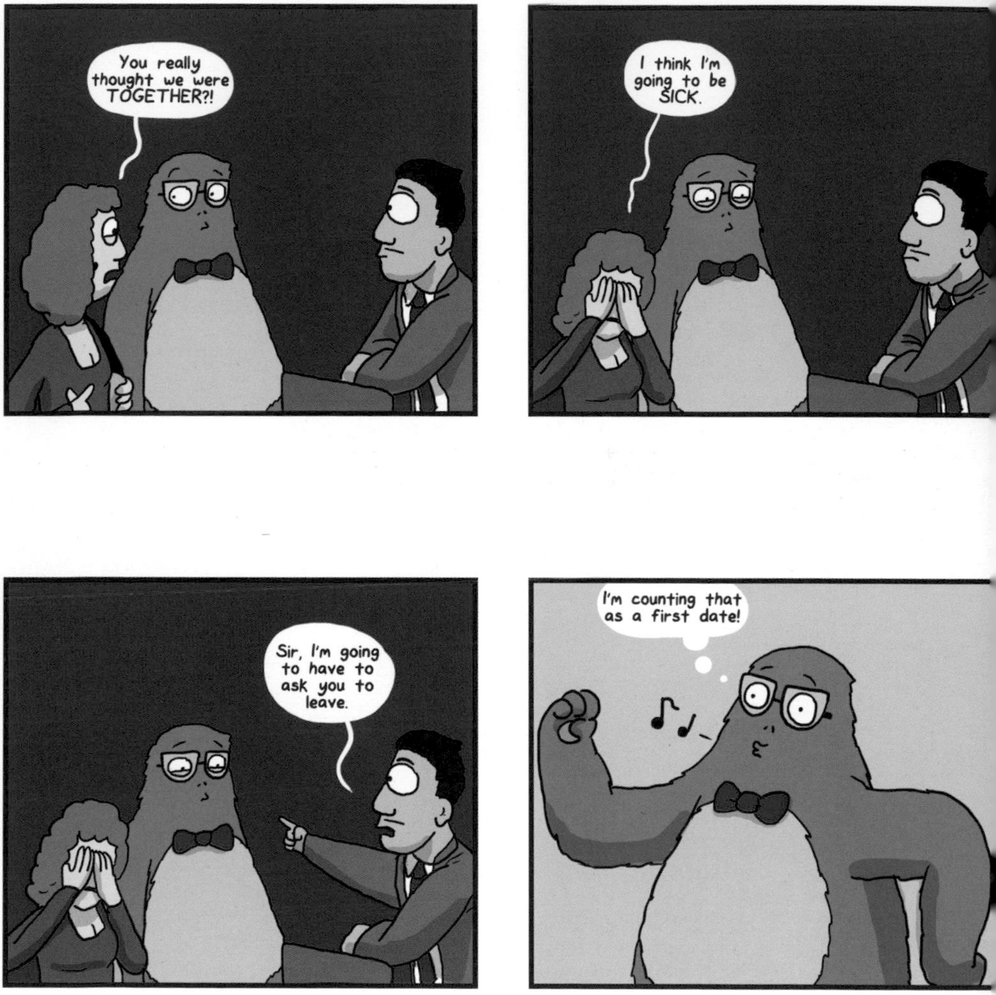
You really thought we were TOGETHER?!
I think I'm going to be SICK.
Sir, I'm going to have to ask you to leave.
I'm counting that as a first date!

Connection

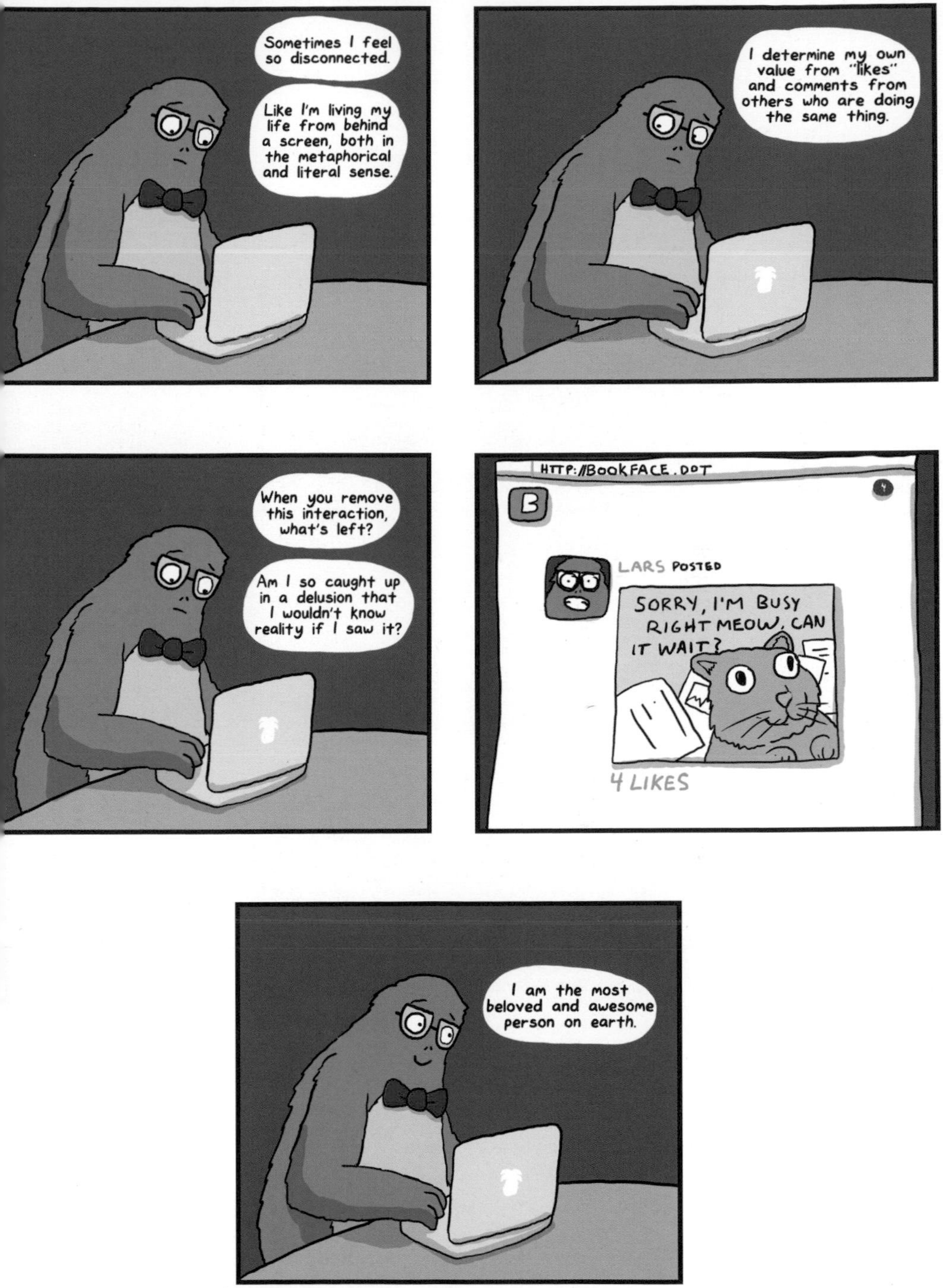
Sometimes I feel so disconnected.
Like I'm living my life from behind a screen, both in the metaphorical and literal sense.
I determine my own value from "likes" and comments from others who are doing the same thing.
When you remove this interaction, what's left?
Am I so caught up in a delusion that I wouldn't know reality if I saw it?
HTTP://BOOKFACE.DOT
LARS POSTED
SORRY, I'M BUSY RIGHT MEOW, CAN IT WAIT?
4 LIKES
I am the most beloved and awesome person on earth.

Action Guy 4

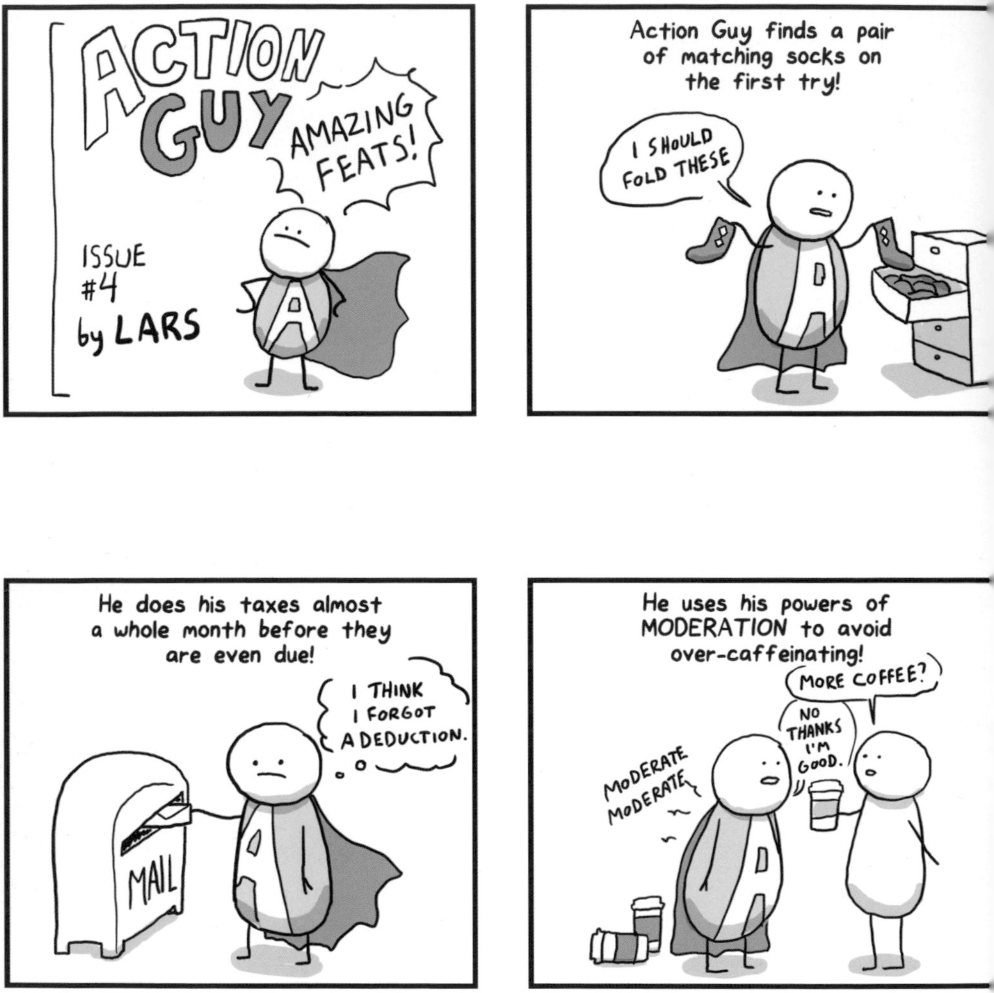
ACTION GUY
AMAZING FEATS!
ISSUE #4
by LARS
Action Guy finds a pair of matching socks on the first try!
I SHOULD FOLD THESE
He does his taxes almost a whole month before they are even due!
I THINK I FORGOT A DEDUCTION.
MAIL
He uses his powers of MODERATION to avoid over-caffeinating!
MORE COFFEE?
NO THANKS I'M GOOD.
MODERATE MODERATE

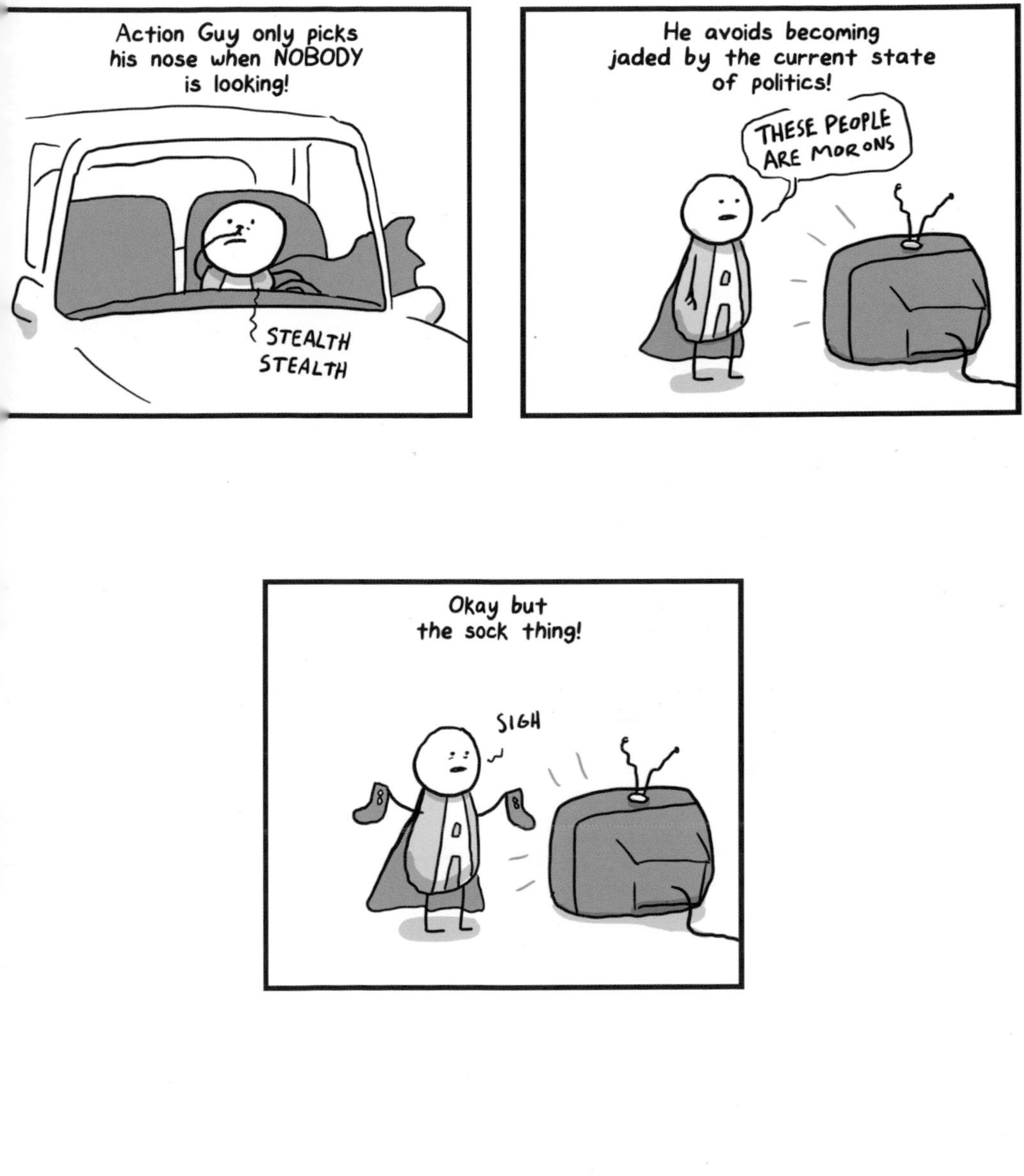
Action Guy only picks his nose when NOBODY is looking!
STEALTH STEALTH
He avoids becoming jaded by the current state of politics!
THESE PEOPLE ARE MORONS
Okay but the sock thing!
SIGH

Sports Chat

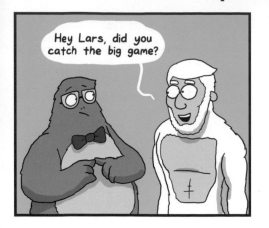

Hey Lars, did you catch the big game?

Talk about some EXPERT SPORTSING! They sure did some athletics!

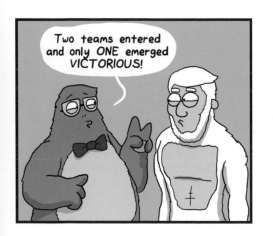

Two teams entered and only ONE emerged VICTORIOUS!

Point made, Lars. Just because you don't like sports doesn't mean you have to be sarcastic about it. Let people enjoy things!

I was being serious...

Fair

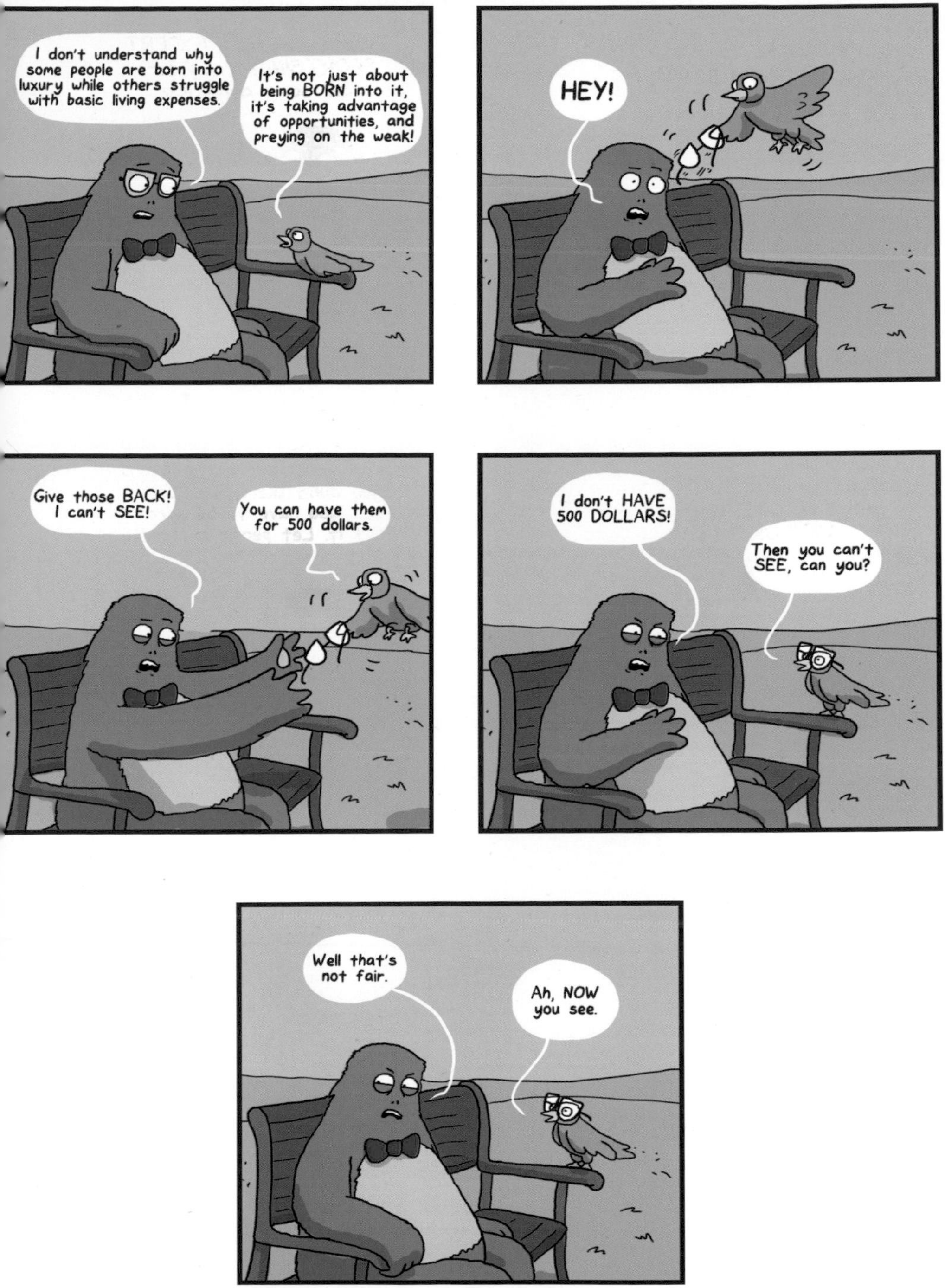

I don't understand why some people are born into luxury while others struggle with basic living expenses.
It's not just about being BORN into it, it's taking advantage of opportunities, and preying on the weak!
HEY!
Give those BACK! I can't SEE!
You can have them for 500 dollars.
I don't HAVE 500 DOLLARS!
Then you can't SEE, can you?
Well that's not fair.
Ah, NOW you see.

Last Slice

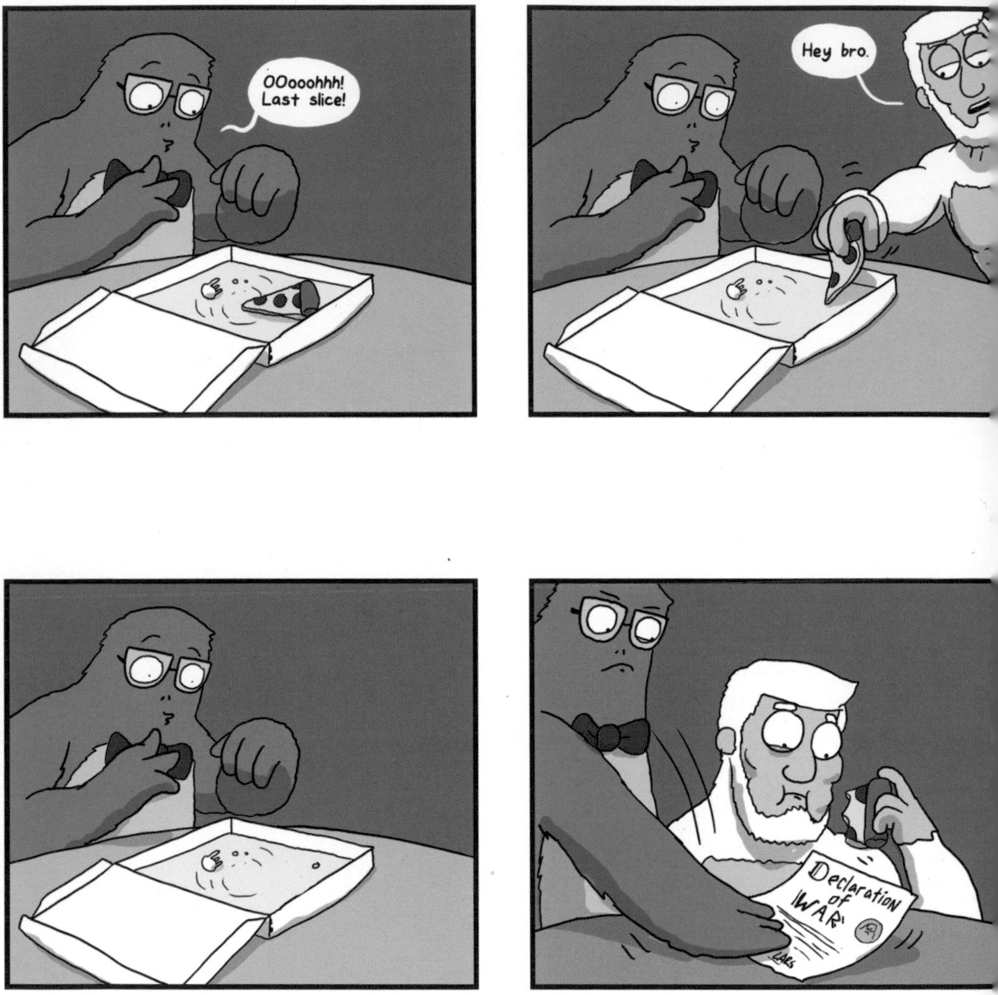
OOooohhh! Last slice!
Hey bro.
Declaration of WAR!

The Day Dream

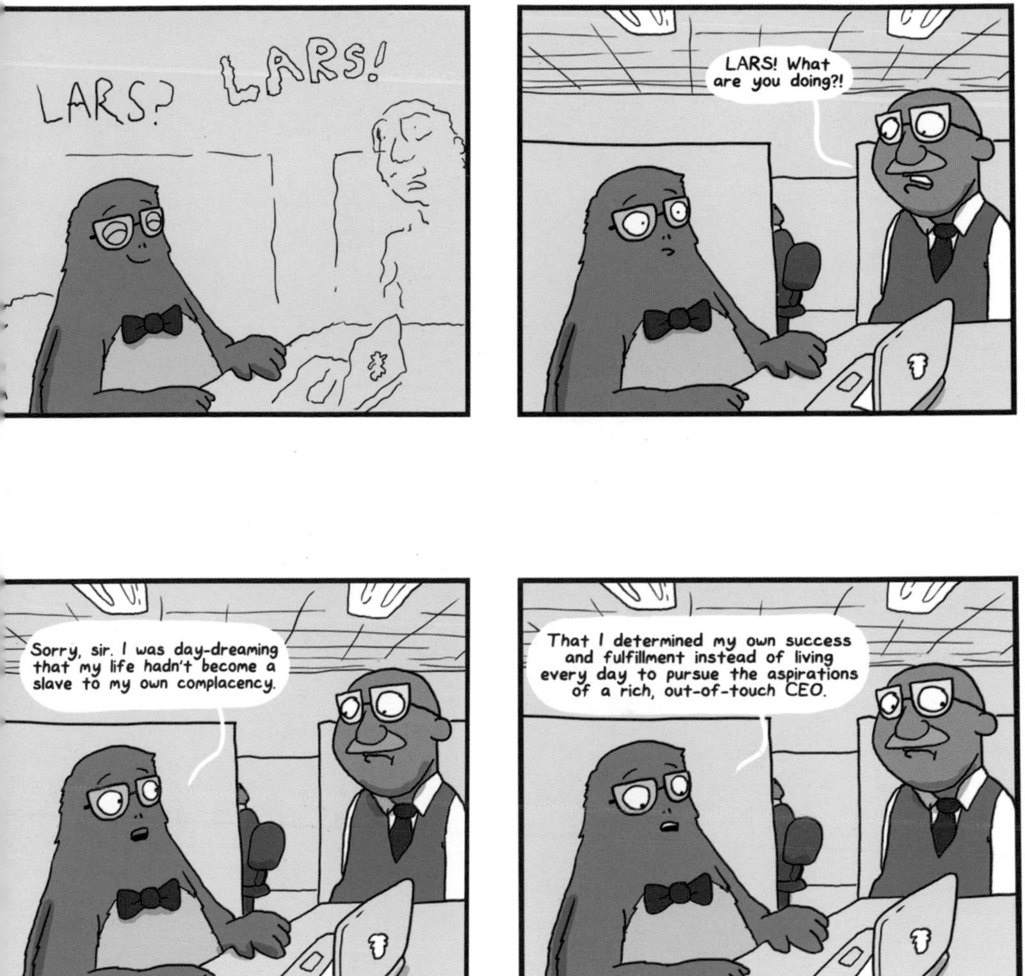
LARS?
LARS!
LARS! What are you doing?!
Sorry, sir. I was day-dreaming that my life hadn't become a slave to my own complacency.
That I determined my own success and fulfillment instead of living every day to pursue the aspirations of a rich, out-of-touch CEO.

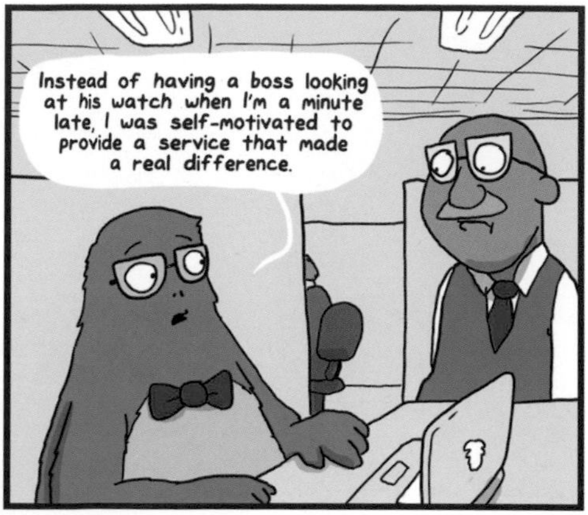
Instead of having a boss looking at his watch when I'm a minute late, I was self-motivated to provide a service that made a real difference.

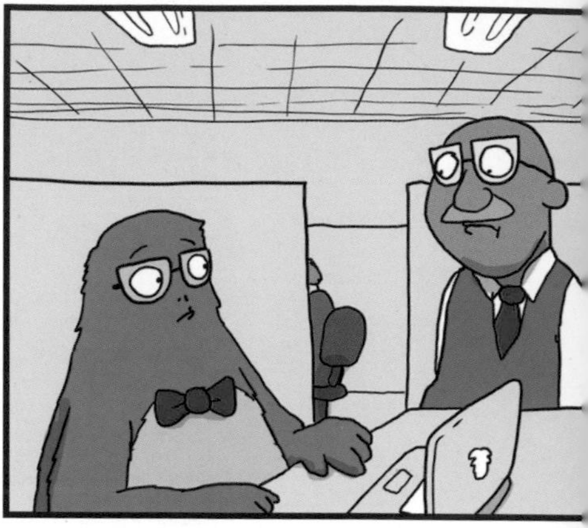

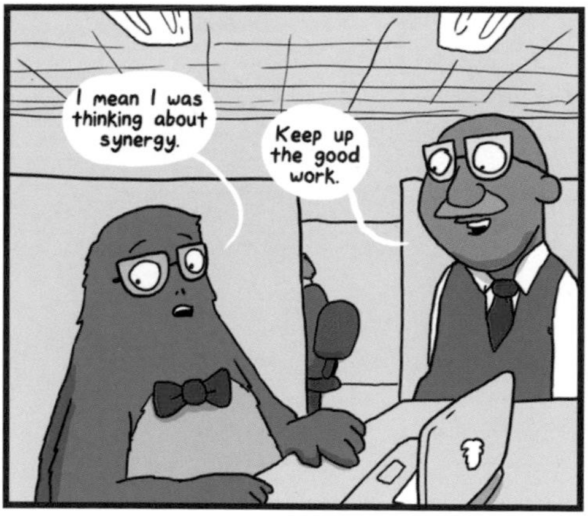
I mean I was thinking about synergy.
Keep up the good work.

World Traveler

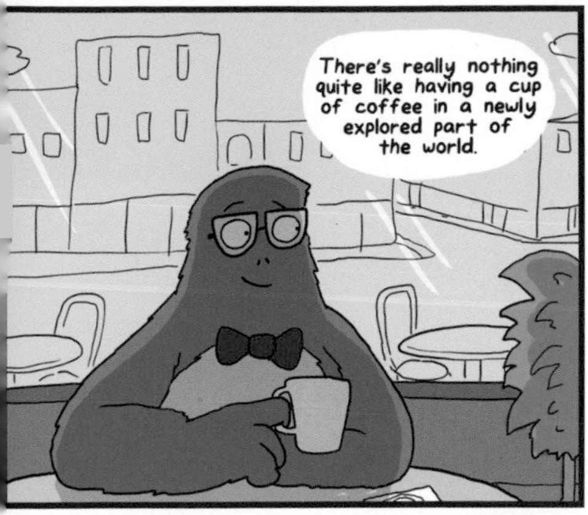
There's really nothing quite like having a cup of coffee in a newly explored part of the world.

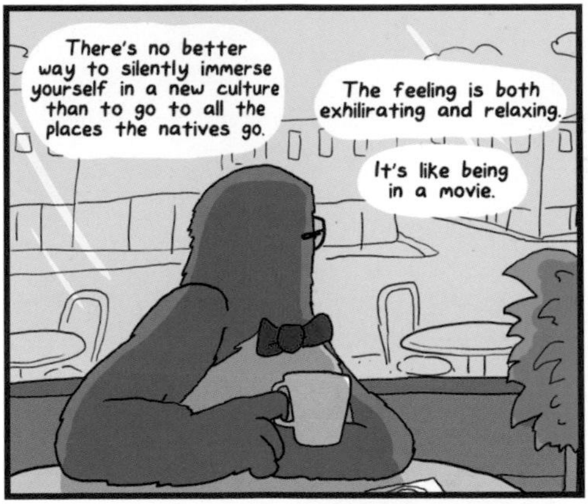
There's no better way to silently immerse yourself in a new culture than to go to all the places the natives go.
The feeling is both exhilirating and relaxing.
It's like being in a movie.

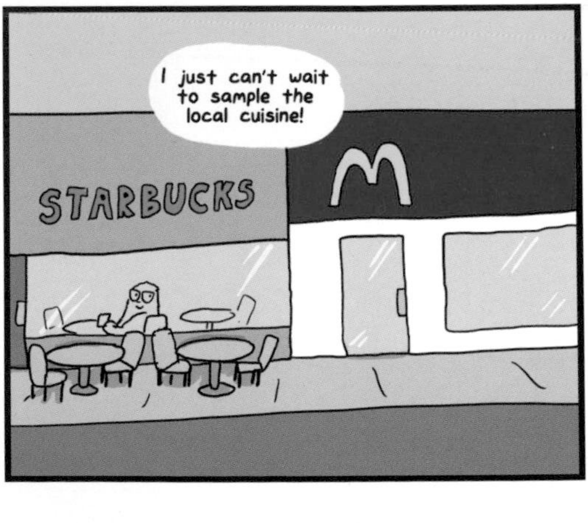
I just can't wait to sample the local cuisine!
STARBUCKS

Anxiety vs Friendship

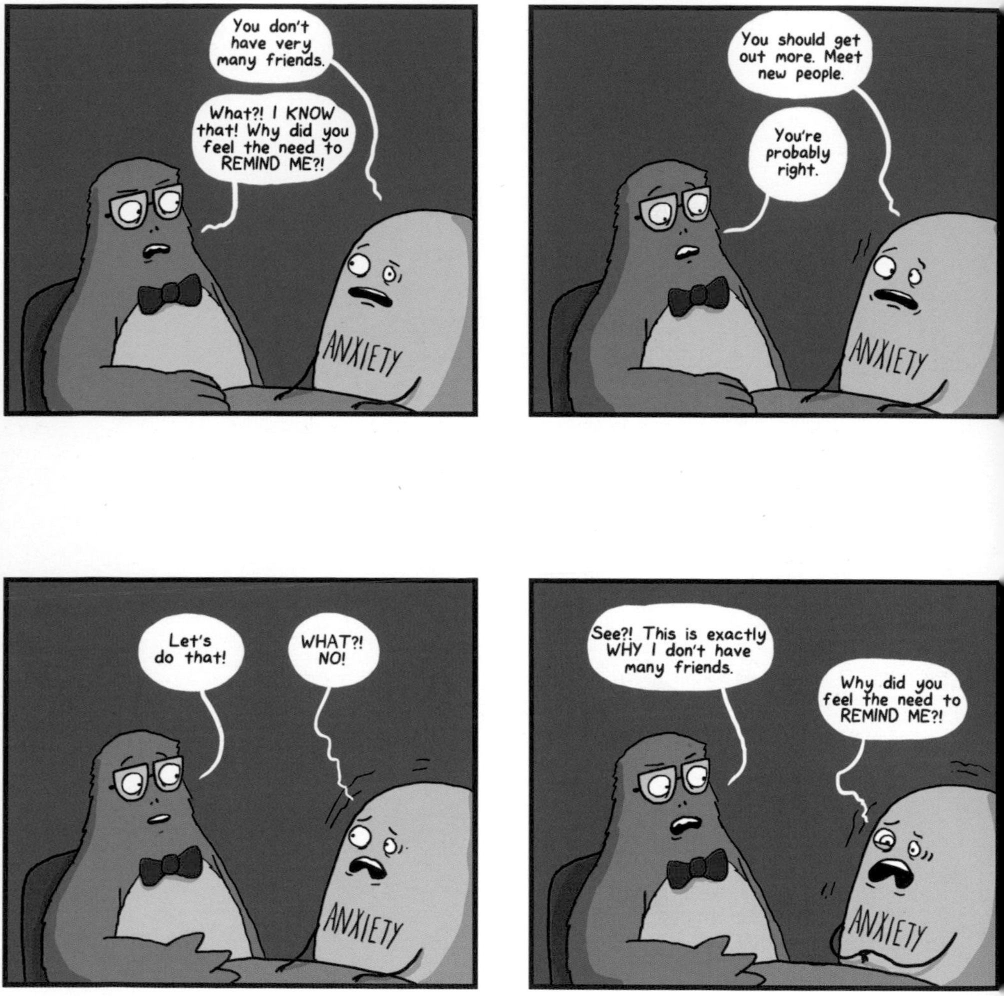

You don't have very many friends.
What?! I KNOW that! Why did you feel the need to REMIND ME?!
ANXIETY
You should get out more. Meet new people.
You're probably right.
ANXIETY
Let's do that!
WHAT?! NO!
ANXIETY
See?! This is exactly WHY I don't have many friends.
Why did you feel the need to REMIND ME?!
ANXIETY

Party Animal

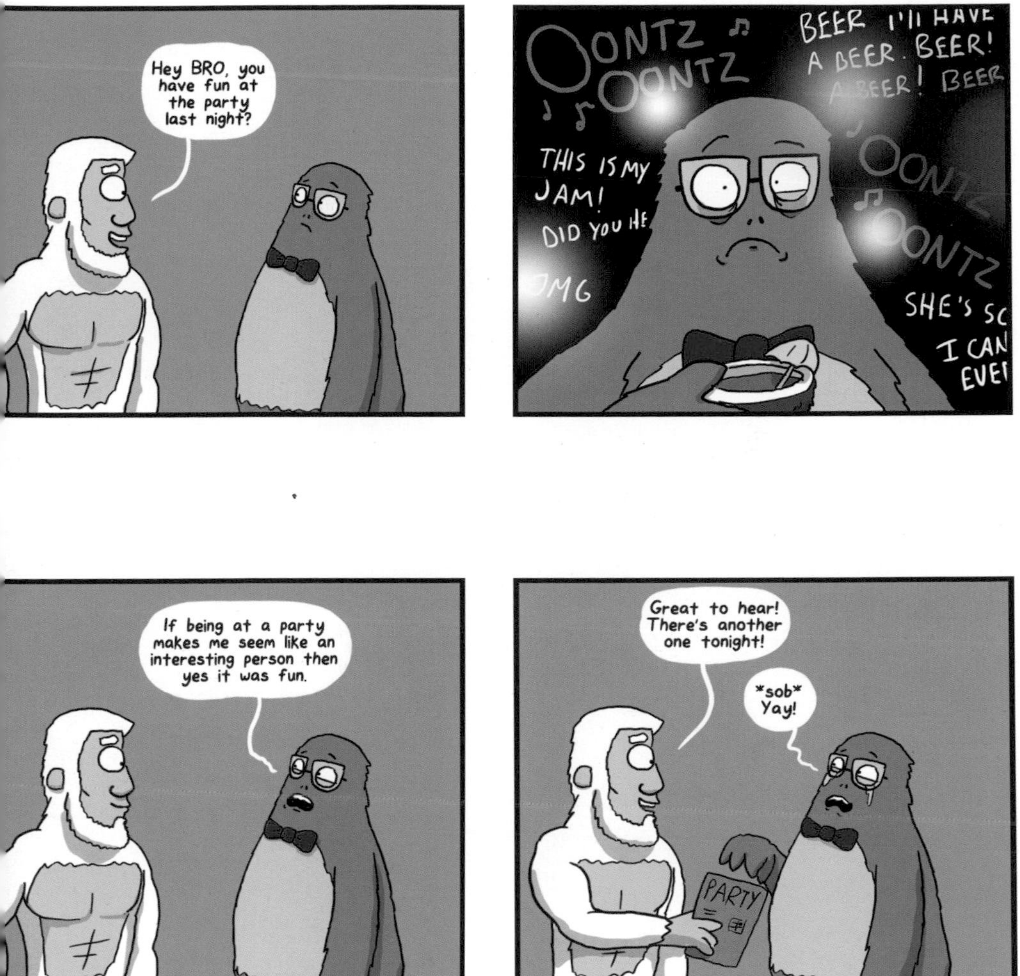
Hey BRO, you have fun at the party last night?
OONTZ OONTZ
BEER I'll HAVE A BEER. BEER! A BEER! BEER
THIS IS MY JAM!
DID YOU HE
OMG
OONTZ OONTZ
SHE'S SC
I CAN
EVE
If being at a party makes me seem like an interesting person then yes it was fun.
Great to hear! There's another one tonight!
sob Yay!
PARTY

When Your Jam Comes On

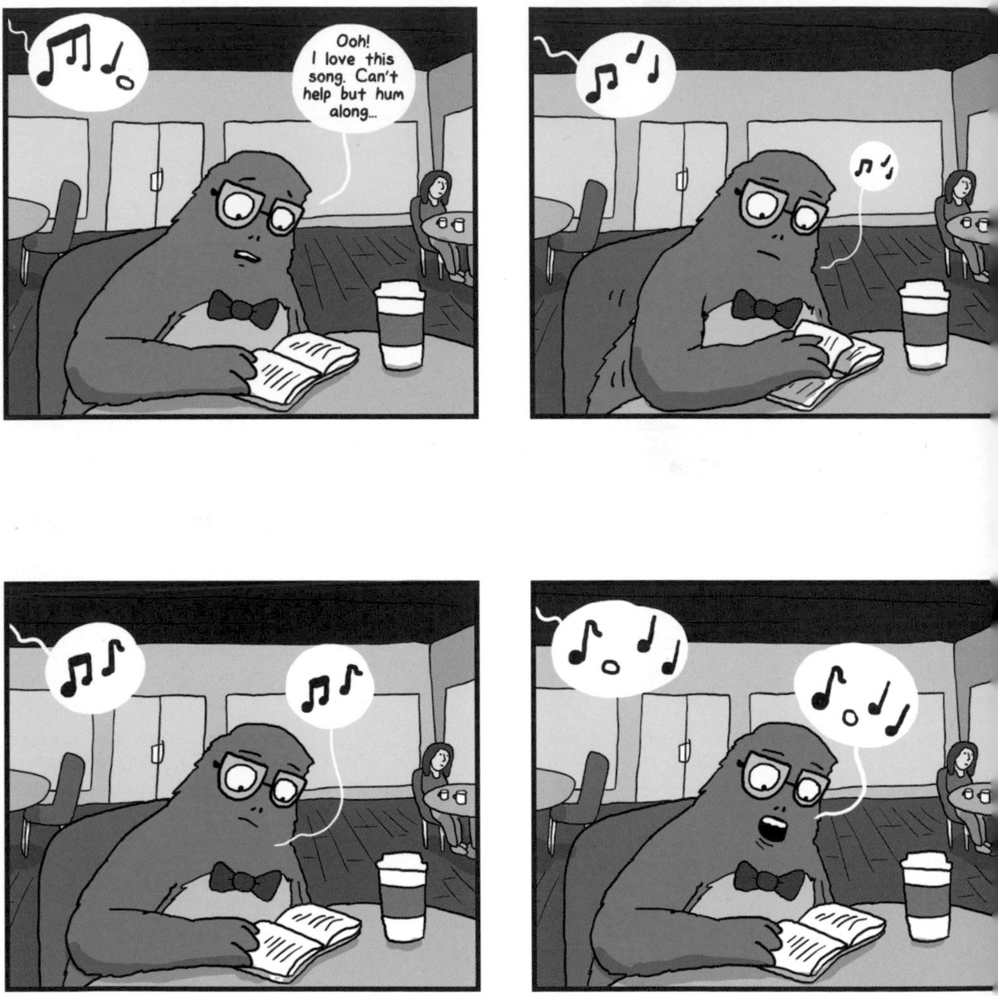
Ooh!
I love this song. Can't help but hum along...

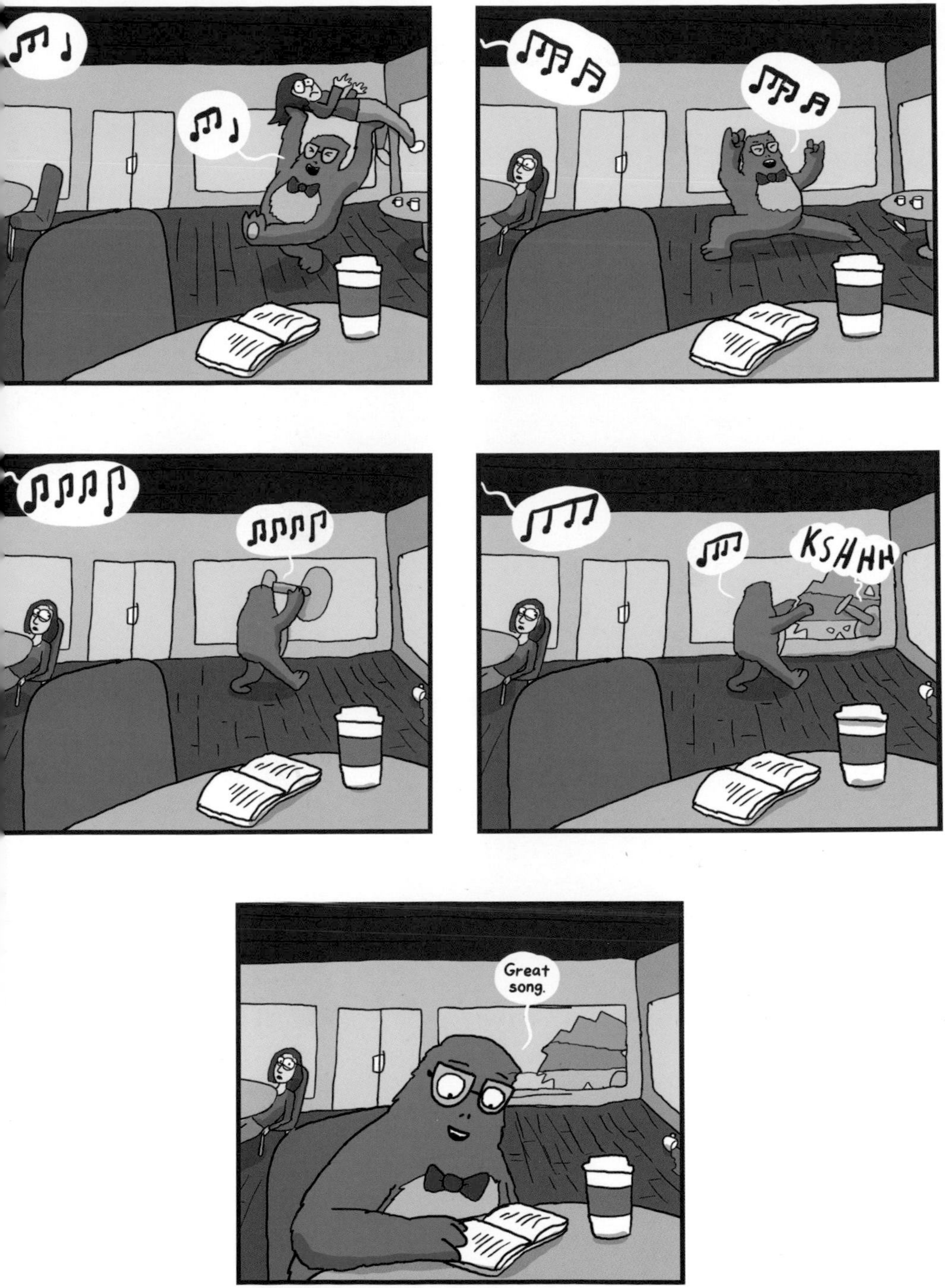
KSHHH
Great song.

Dessert

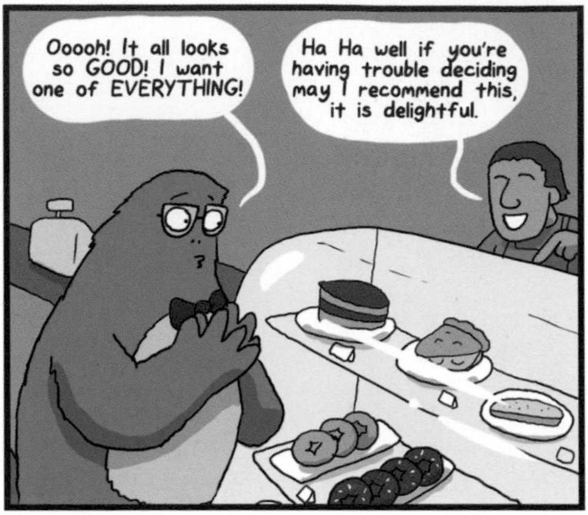

Ooooh! It all looks so GOOD! I want one of EVERYTHING!
Ha Ha well if you're having trouble deciding may I recommend this, it is delightful.

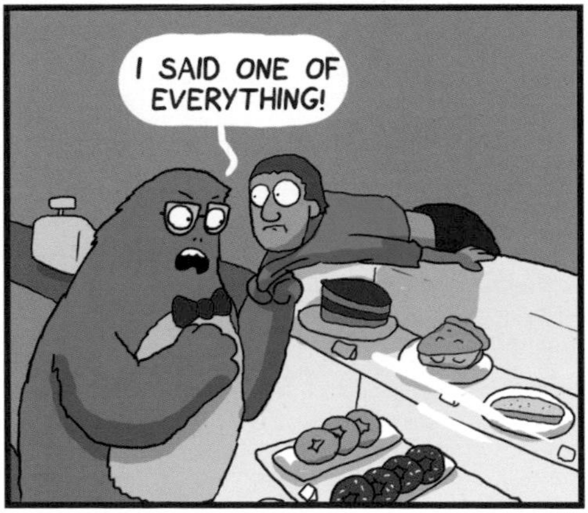

I SAID ONE OF EVERYTHING!

Opportunity for Excuses

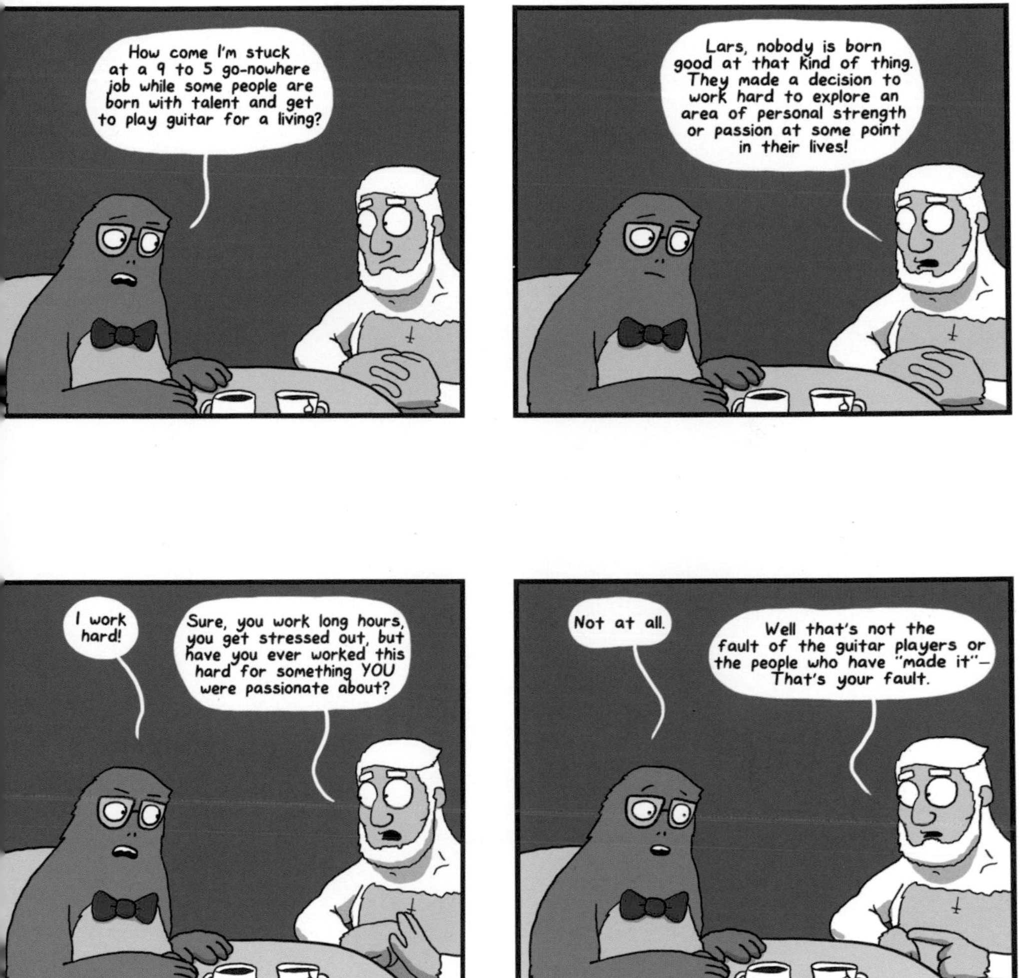
How come I'm stuck at a 9 to 5 go-nowhere job while some people are born with talent and get to play guitar for a living?
Lars, nobody is born good at that kind of thing. They made a decision to work hard to explore an area of personal strength or passion at some point in their lives!
I work hard!
Sure, you work long hours, you get stressed out, but have you ever worked this hard for something YOU were passionate about?
Not at all.
Well that's not the fault of the guitar players or the people who have "made it"— That's your fault.

Okay, but I never had the opportunities or connections to make it happen!
You have more connections than any generation before you! You have the internet!

People used to learn guitar by listening to records in their basements and trying to guess the notes. Now you can be trained by EXPERTS for FREE, and instantly share your progress with people!

Lars, you aren't stuck anywhere. You're lazy.
WHY OH WHY WAS I BORN LAZY?!
Stop, Lars. Just stop.

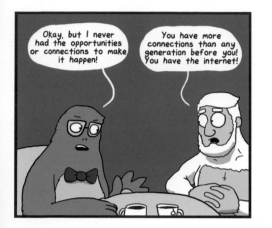

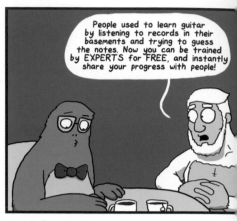

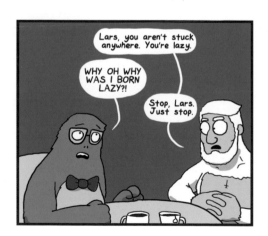

Are We Seeing the Same Thing?

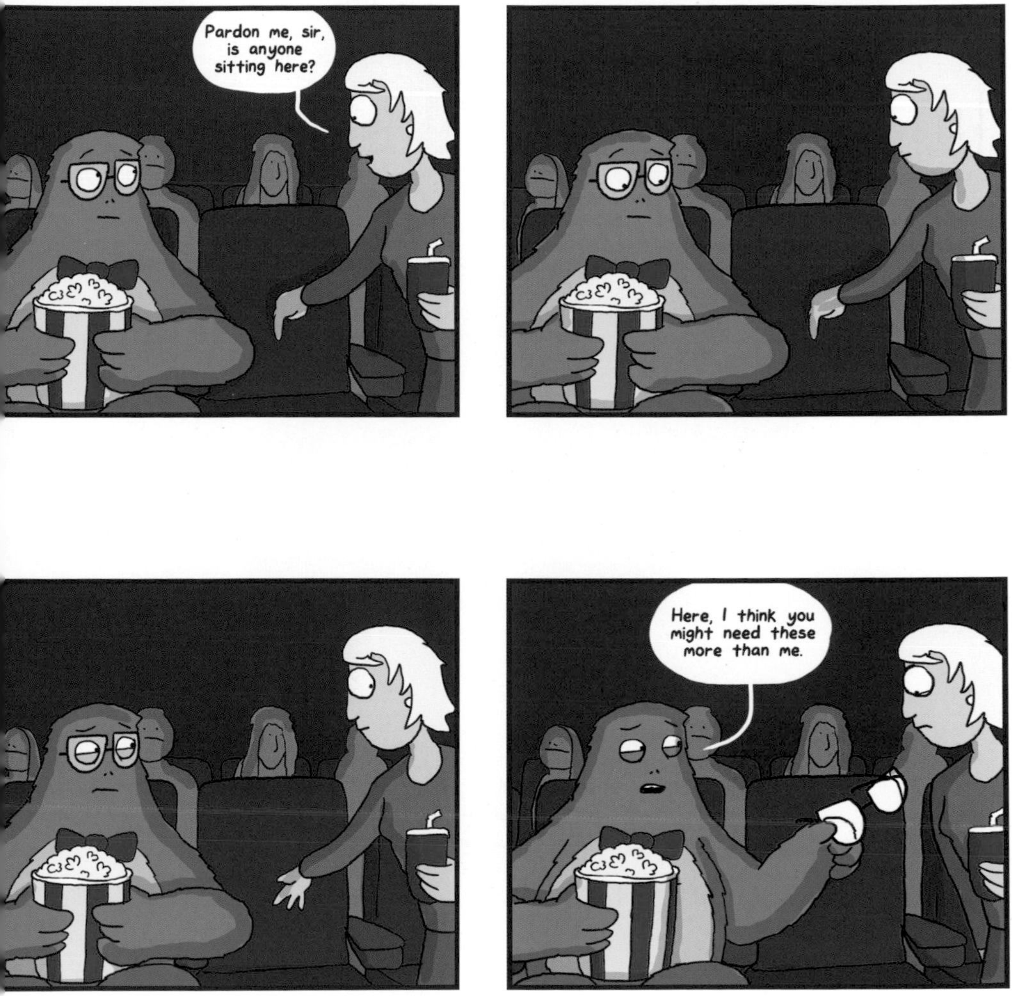
Pardon me, sir, is anyone sitting here?
Here, I think you might need these more than me.

Nuturing Talent

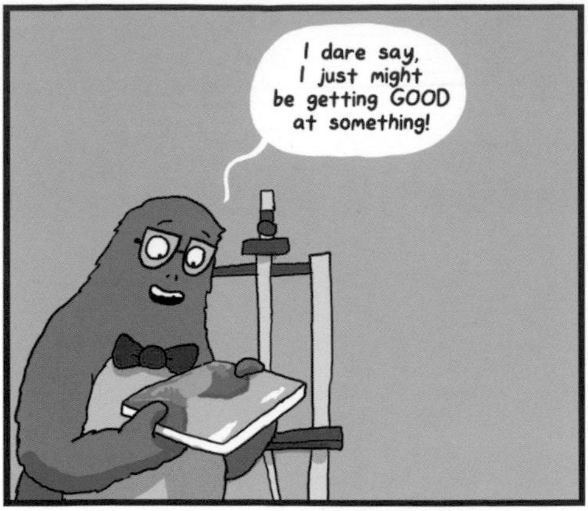
I dare say, I just might be getting GOOD at something!

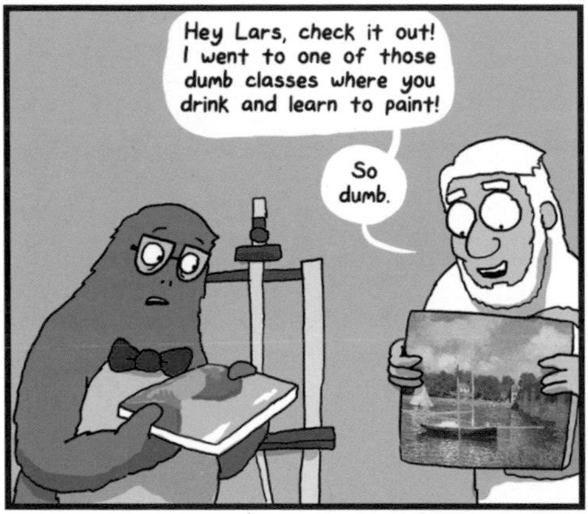
Hey Lars, check it out! I went to one of those dumb classes where you drink and learn to paint!
So dumb.

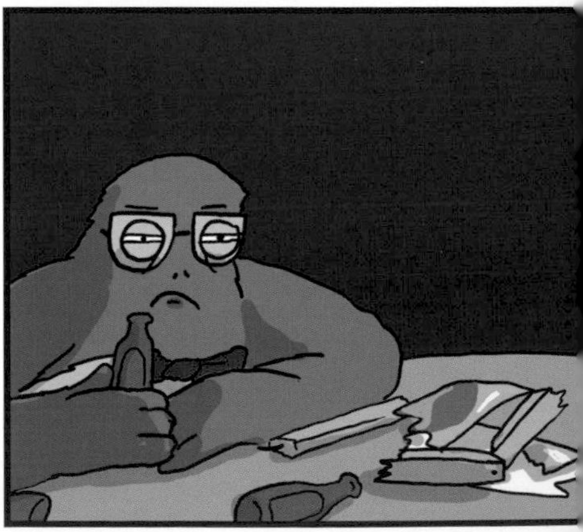

What's in a Name?

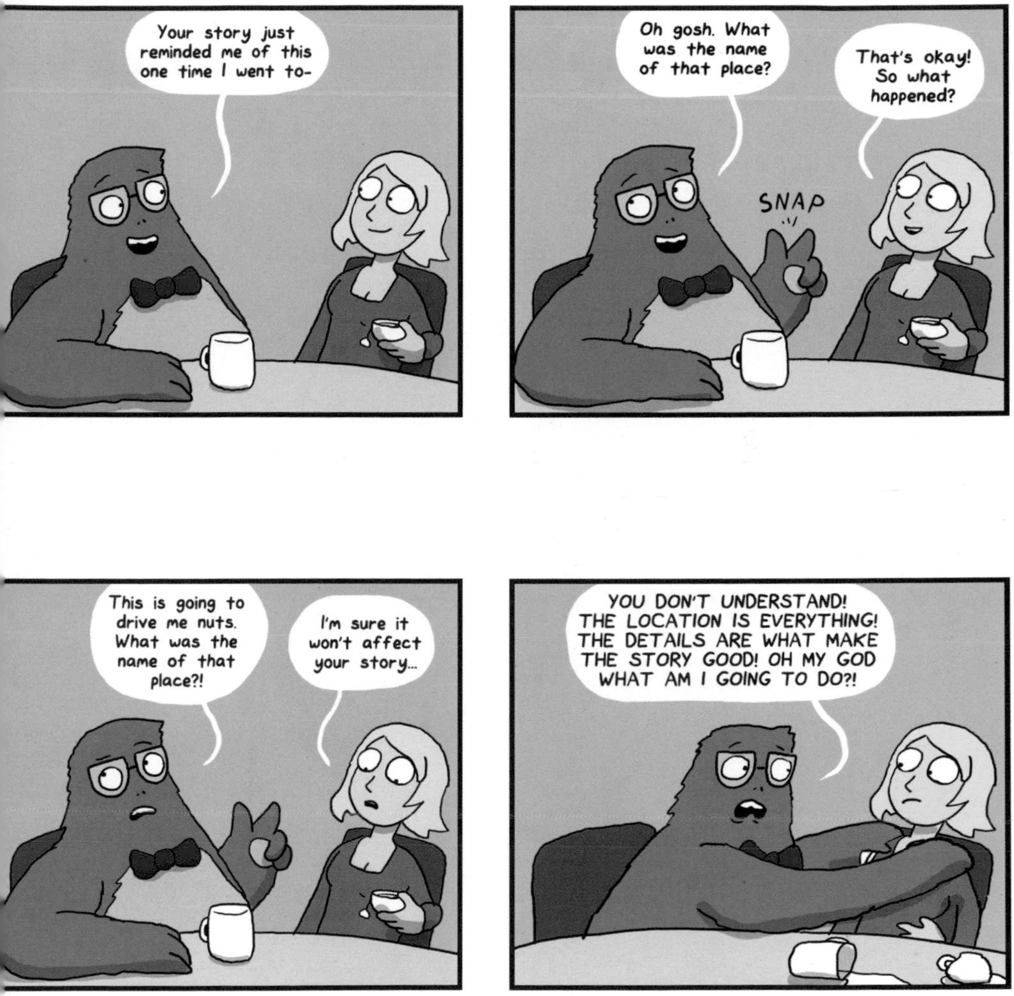

Your story just reminded me of this one time I went to-
Oh gosh. What was the name of that place?
SNAP
That's okay! So what happened?
This is going to drive me nuts. What was the name of that place?!
I'm sure it won't affect your story...
YOU DON'T UNDERSTAND! THE LOCATION IS EVERYTHING! THE DETAILS ARE WHAT MAKE THE STORY GOOD! OH MY GOD WHAT AM I GOING TO DO?!

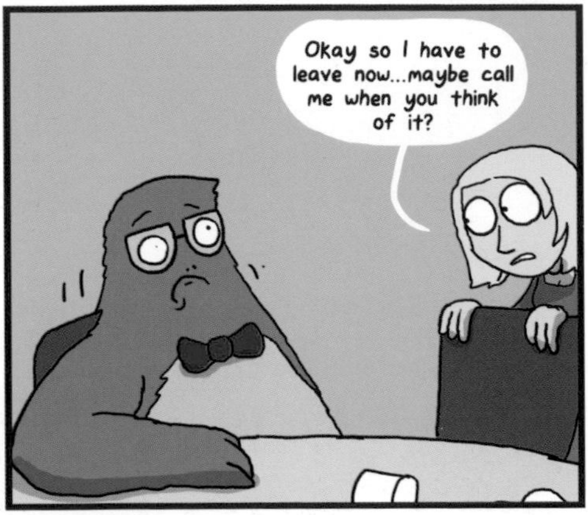
Okay so I have to leave now...maybe call me when you think of it?

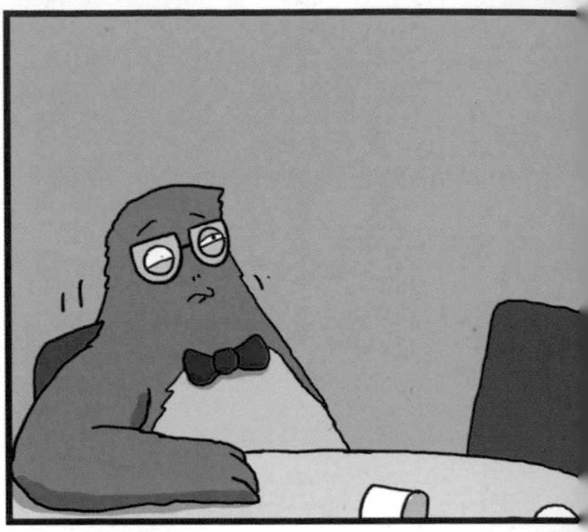

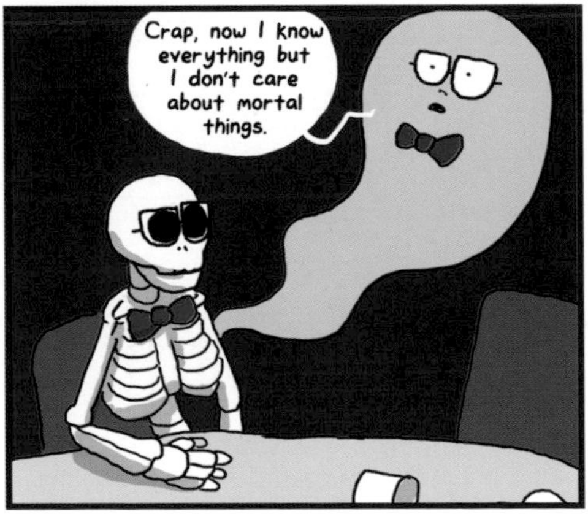
Crap, now I know everything but I don't care about mortal things.

Gamblin' Man

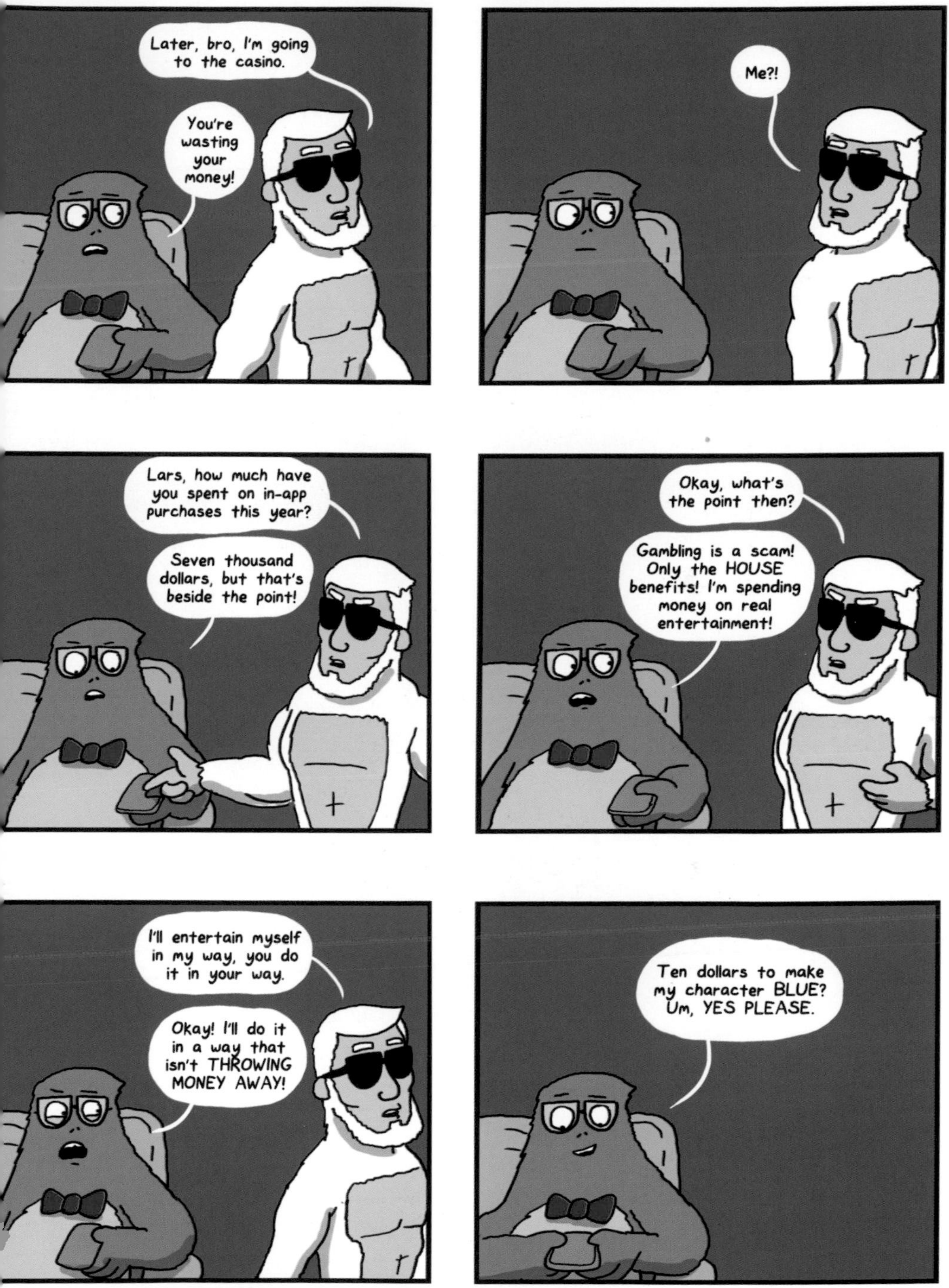
Later, bro, I'm going to the casino.
You're wasting your money!
Me?!
Lars, how much have you spent on in-app purchases this year?
Seven thousand dollars, but that's beside the point!
Okay, what's the point then?
Gambling is a scam! Only the HOUSE benefits! I'm spending money on real entertainment!
I'll entertain myself in my way, you do it in your way.
Okay! I'll do it in a way that isn't THROWING MONEY AWAY!
Ten dollars to make my character BLUE? Um, YES PLEASE.

The Ending Story

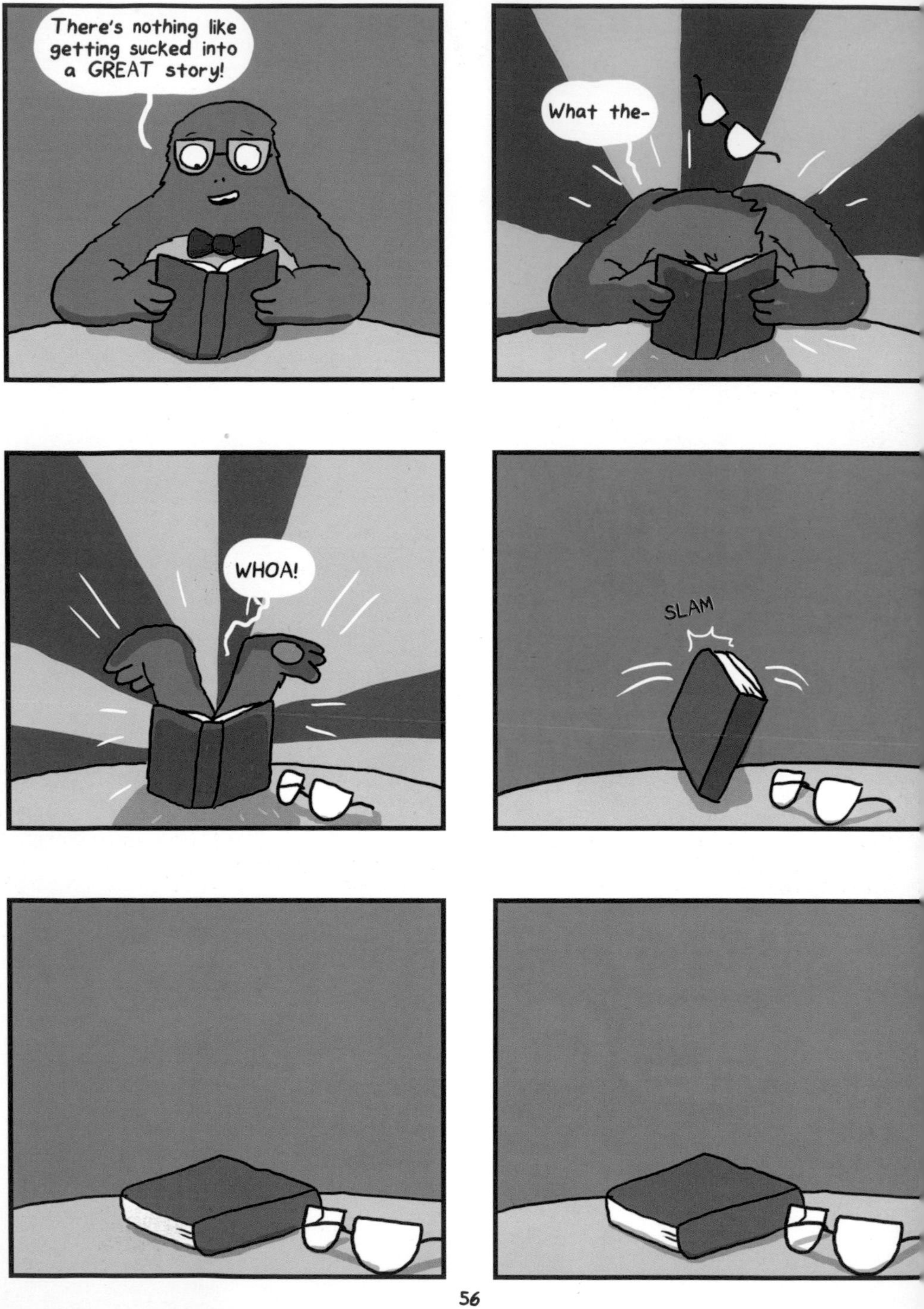
There's nothing like getting sucked into a GREAT story!
What the-
WHOA!
SLAM

Lars Orders for a Friend

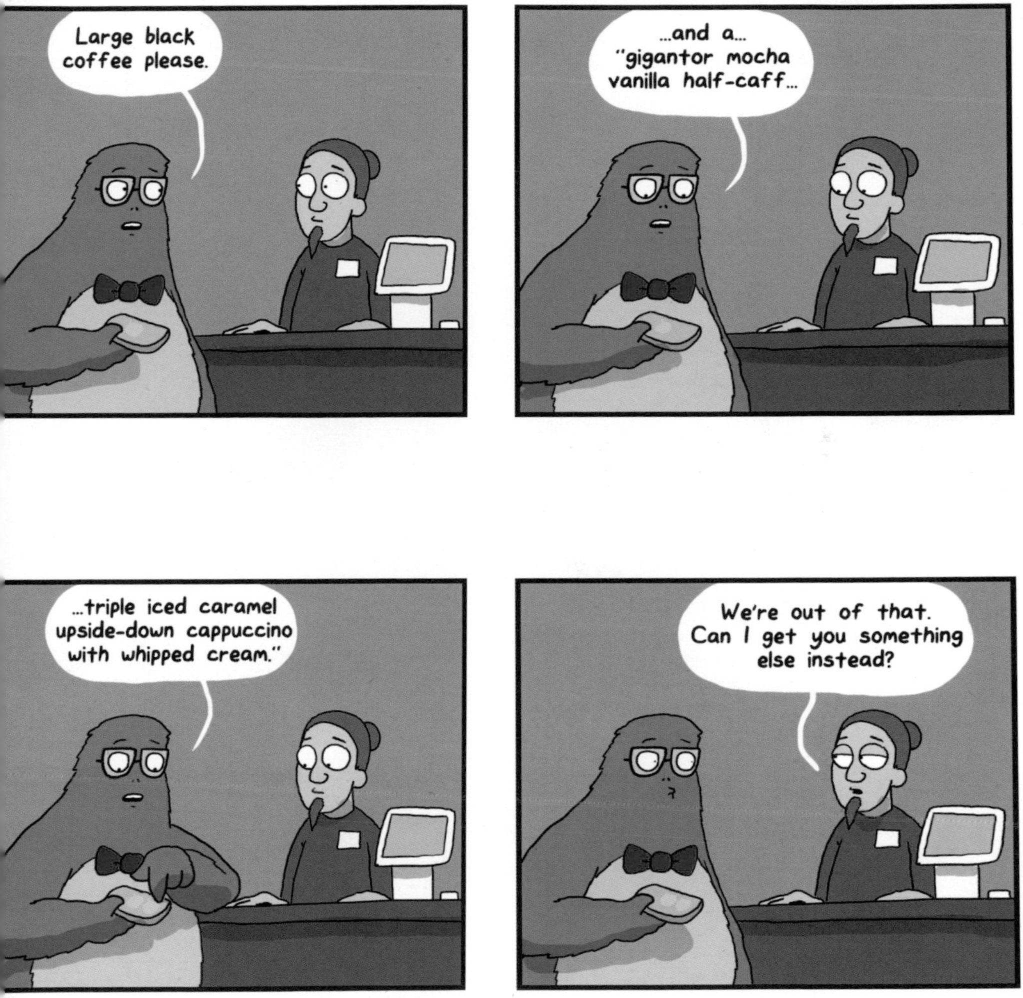
Large black coffee please.
...and a... "gigantor mocha vanilla half-caff...
...triple iced caramel upside-down cappuccino with whipped cream."
We're out of that. Can I get you something else instead?

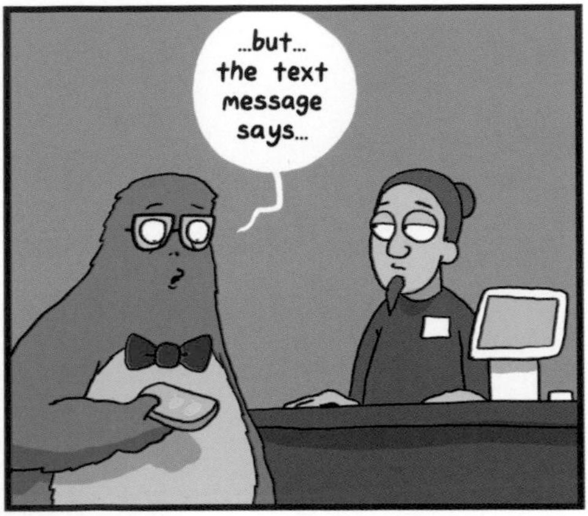
...but...
the text
message
says...

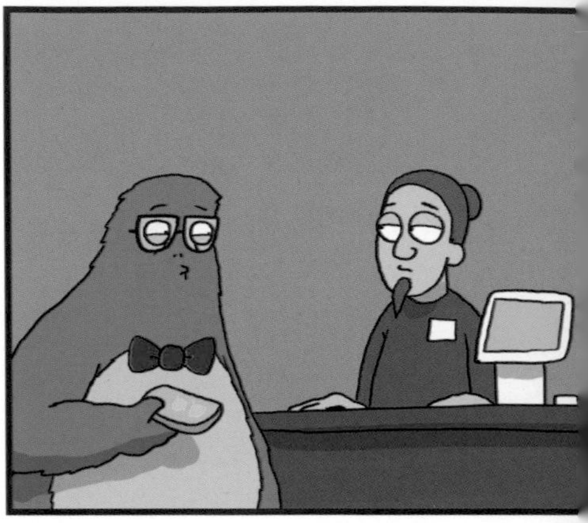

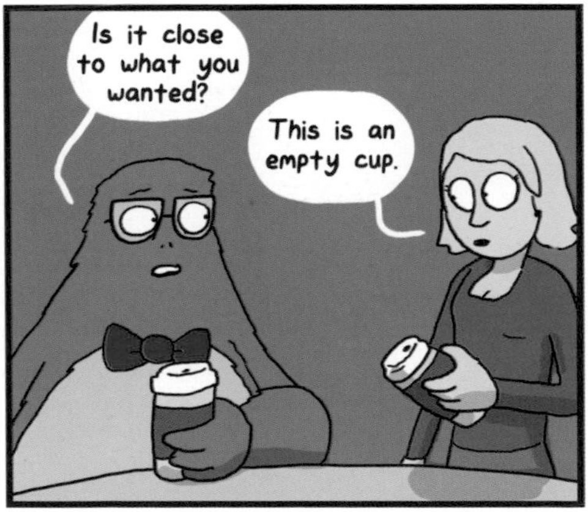
Is it close
to what you
wanted?
This is an
empty cup.

Careful What You Wish For

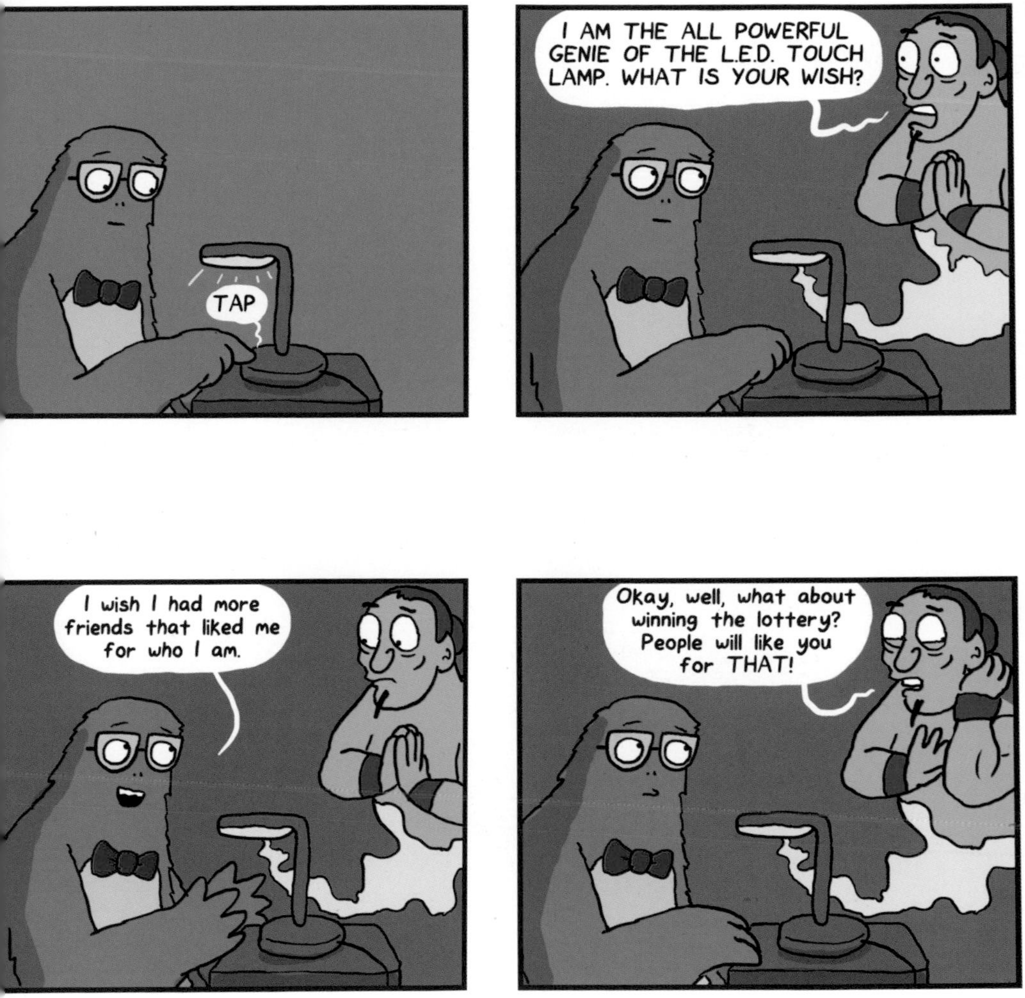
TAP
I AM THE ALL POWERFUL GENIE OF THE L.E.D. TOUCH LAMP. WHAT IS YOUR WISH?
I wish I had more friends that liked me for who I am.
Okay, well, what about winning the lottery? People will like you for THAT!

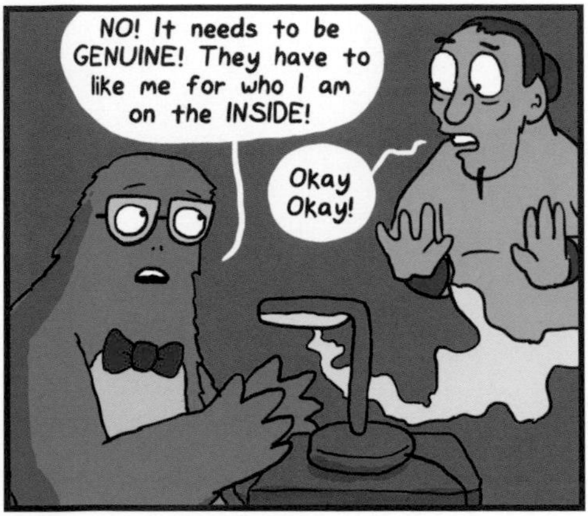
NO! It needs to be GENUINE! They have to like me for who I am on the INSIDE!
Okay Okay!

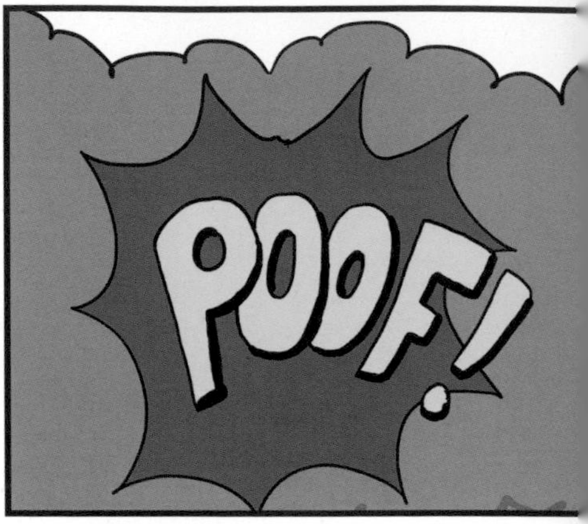
POOF!

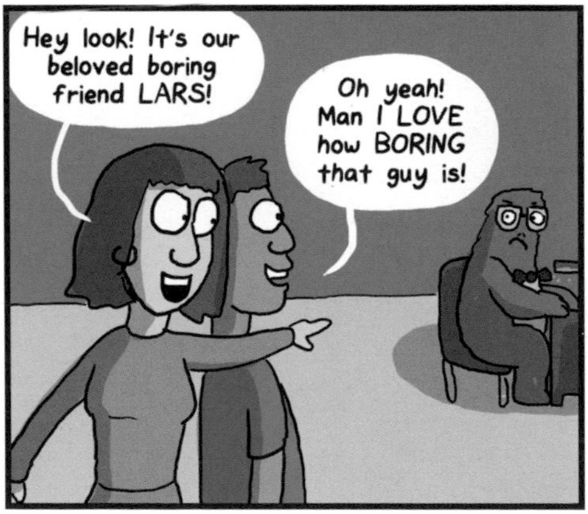
Hey look! It's our beloved boring friend LARS!
Oh yeah! Man I LOVE how BORING that guy is!

Productivity

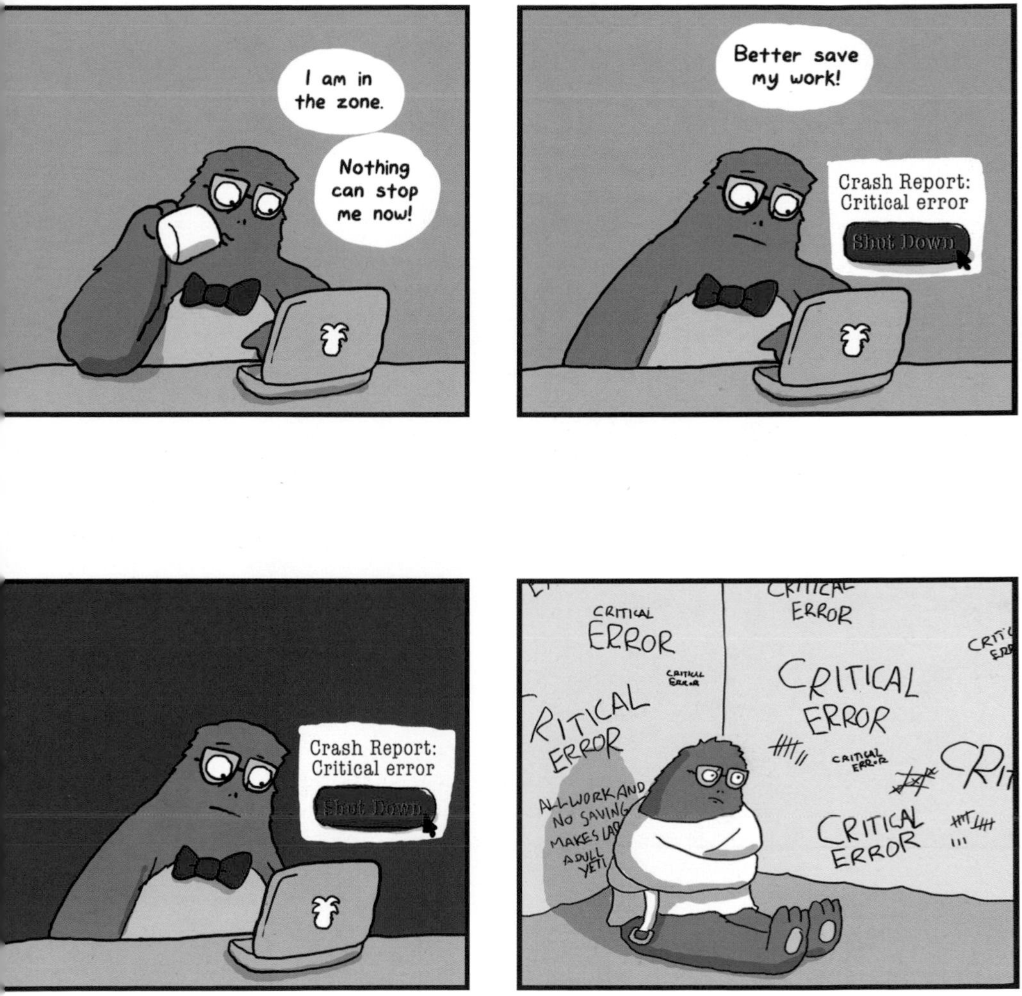

I am in the zone.
Nothing can stop me now!
Better save my work!
Crash Report: Critical error
Shut Down
Crash Report: Critical error
Shut Down
CRITICAL ERROR
CRITICAL ERROR
CRITICAL ERROR
CRITICAL ERROR
CRITICAL ERROR
CRITICAL ERROR

Lars Nails Another Interview

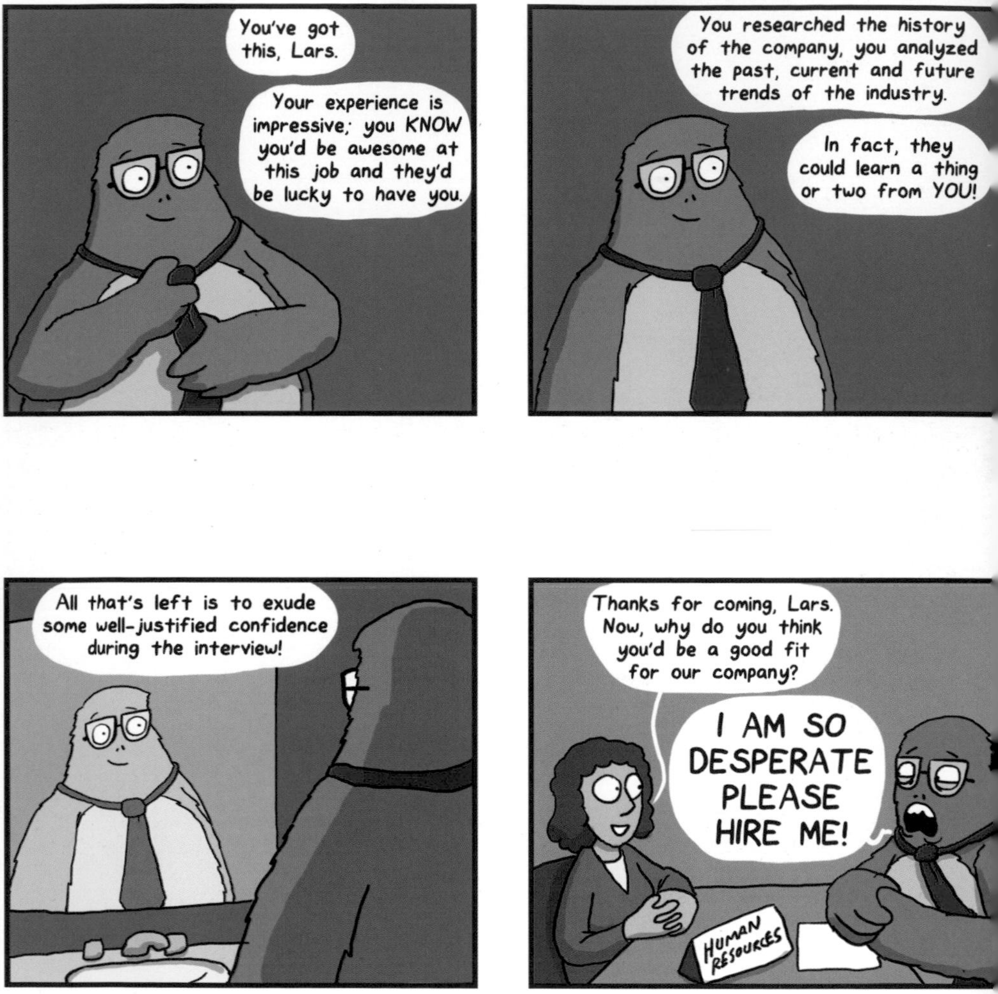

You've got this, Lars.
Your experience is impressive; you KNOW you'd be awesome at this job and they'd be lucky to have you.
You researched the history of the company, you analyzed the past, current and future trends of the industry.
In fact, they could learn a thing or two from YOU!
All that's left is to exude some well-justified confidence during the interview!
Thanks for coming, Lars. Now, why do you think you'd be a good fit for our company?
I AM SO DESPERATE PLEASE HIRE ME!
HUMAN RESOURCES

Bird's Pep Talk

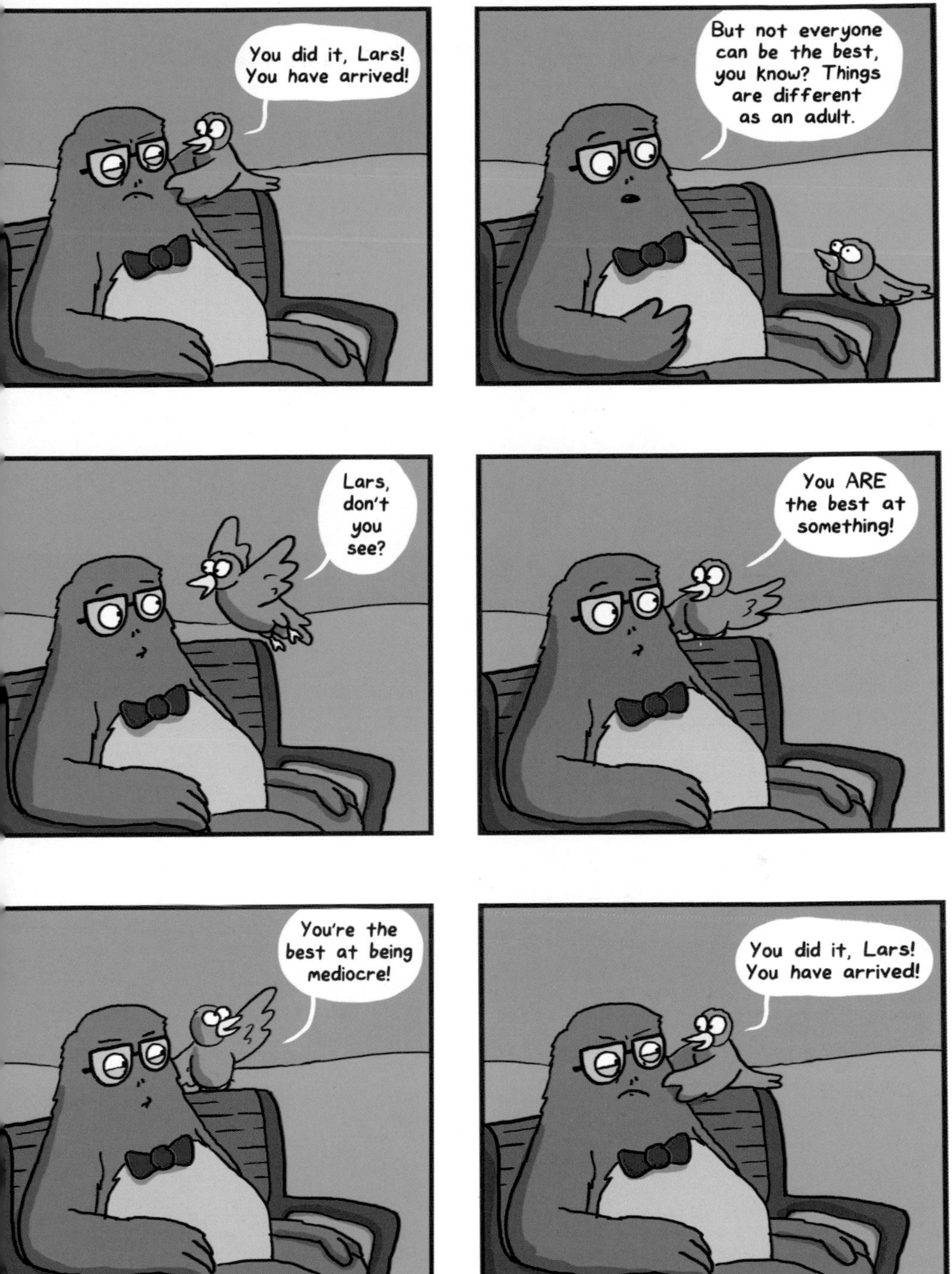
You did it, Lars! You have arrived!
But not everyone can be the best, you know? Things are different as an adult.
Lars, don't you see?
You ARE the best at something!
You're the best at being mediocre!
You did it, Lars! You have arrived!

Biker

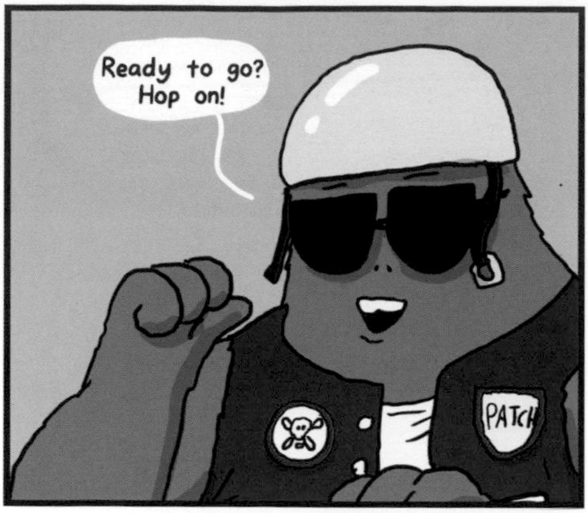
Ready to go? Hop on!
PATCH

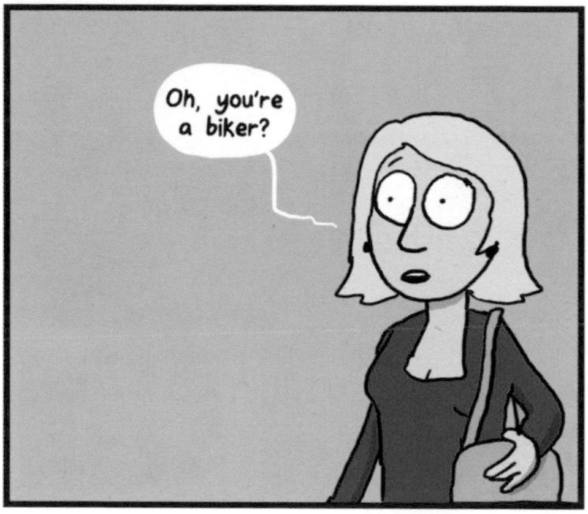
Oh, you're a biker?

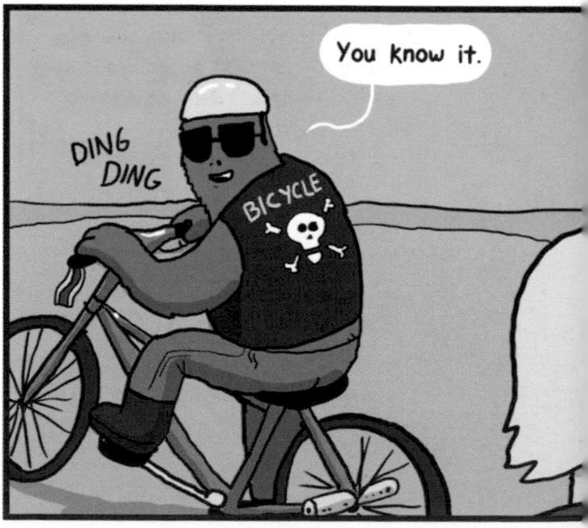
You know it.
DING DING
BICYCLE

Gratuity

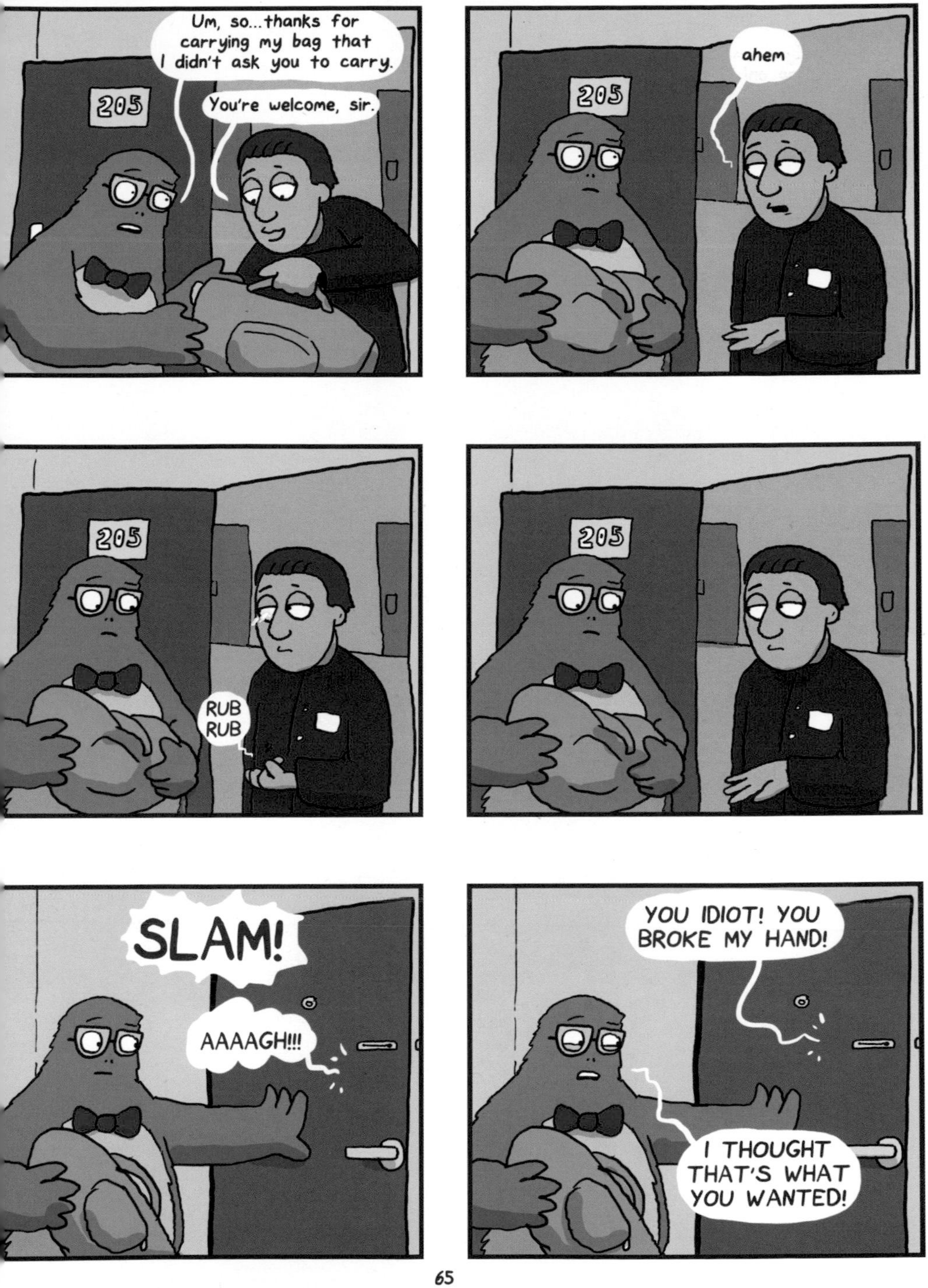
Um, so...thanks for carrying my bag that I didn't ask you to carry.
You're welcome, sir.
205
ahem
205
RUB RUB
205
SLAM!
AAAAGH!!!
YOU IDIOT! YOU BROKE MY HAND!
I THOUGHT THAT'S WHAT YOU WANTED!

Feeling of Accomplishment

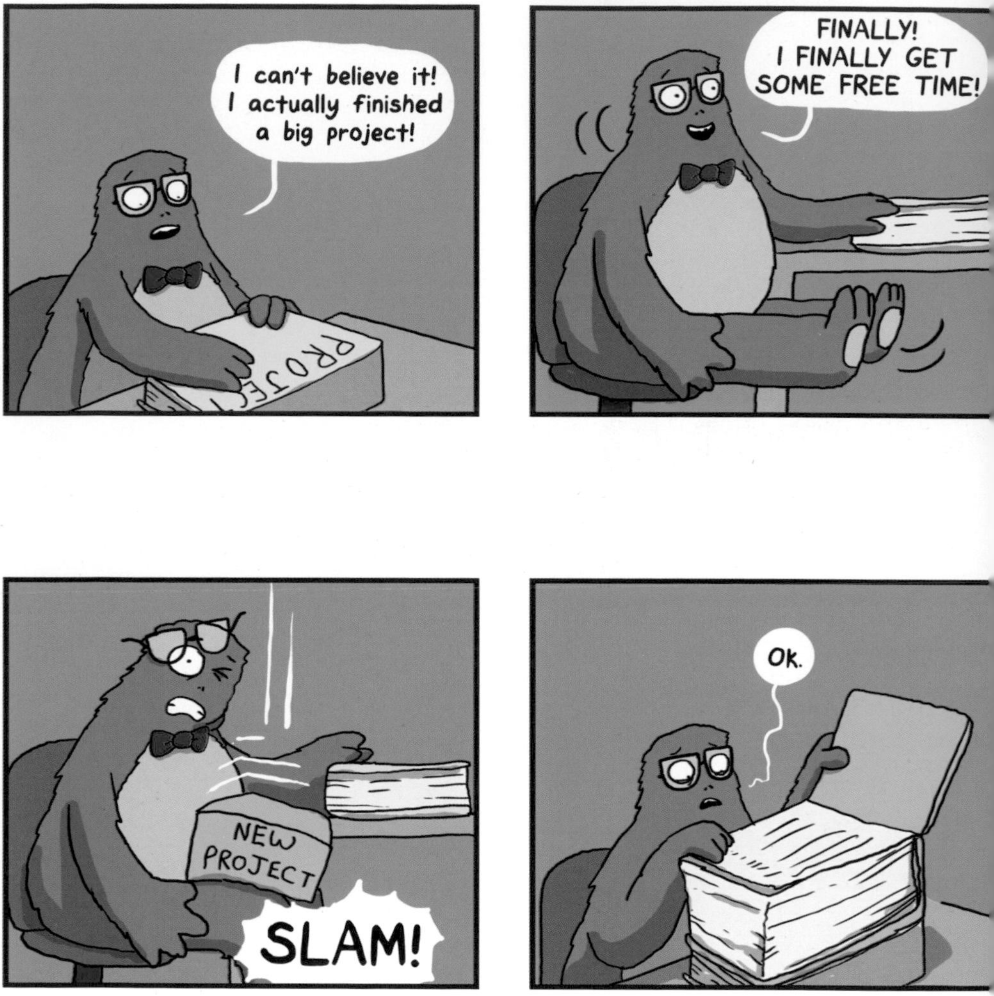
I can't believe it! I actually finished a big project!
PROJECT
FINALLY! I FINALLY GET SOME FREE TIME!
NEW PROJECT
SLAM!
Ok.

The Stranger

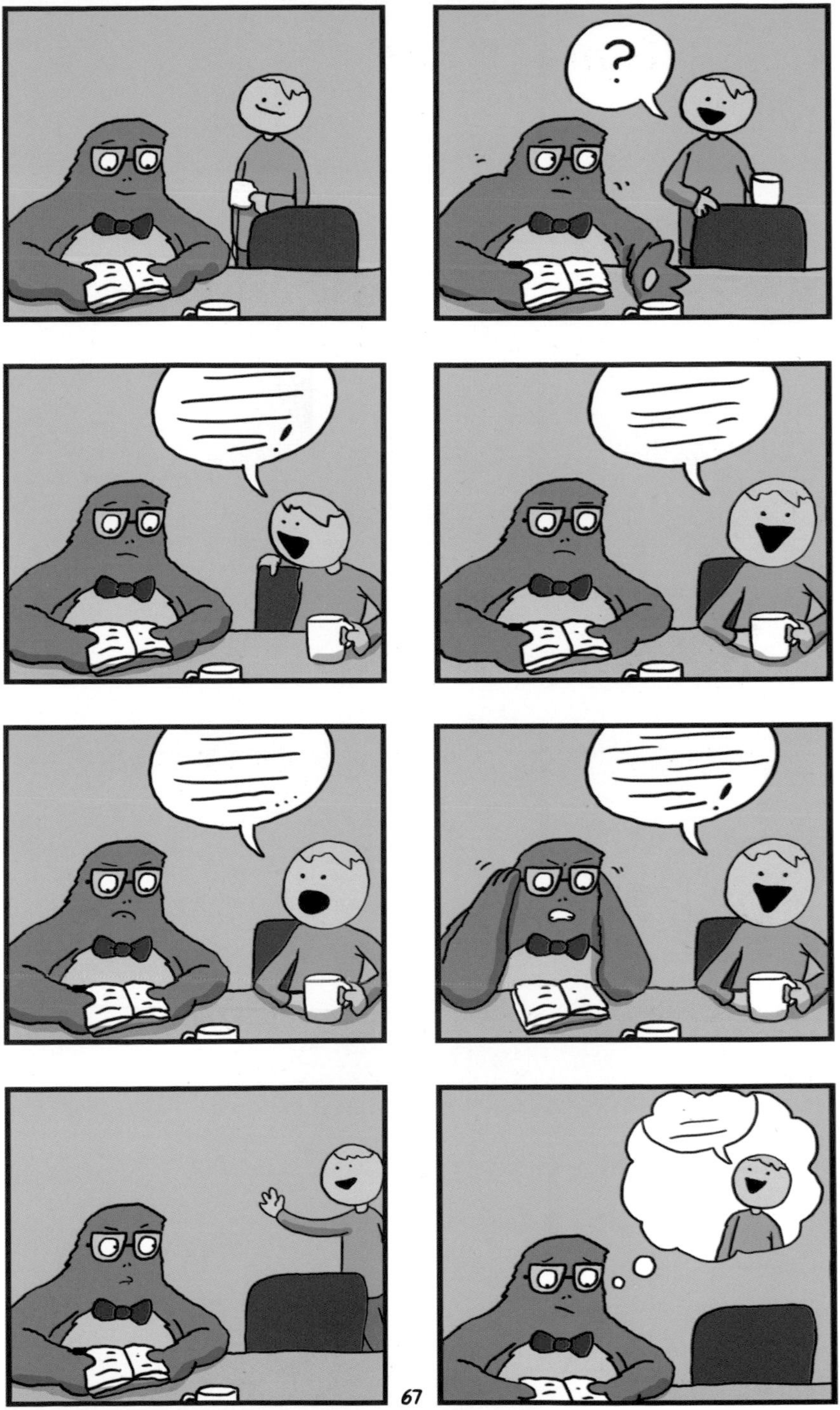
?

The Salad

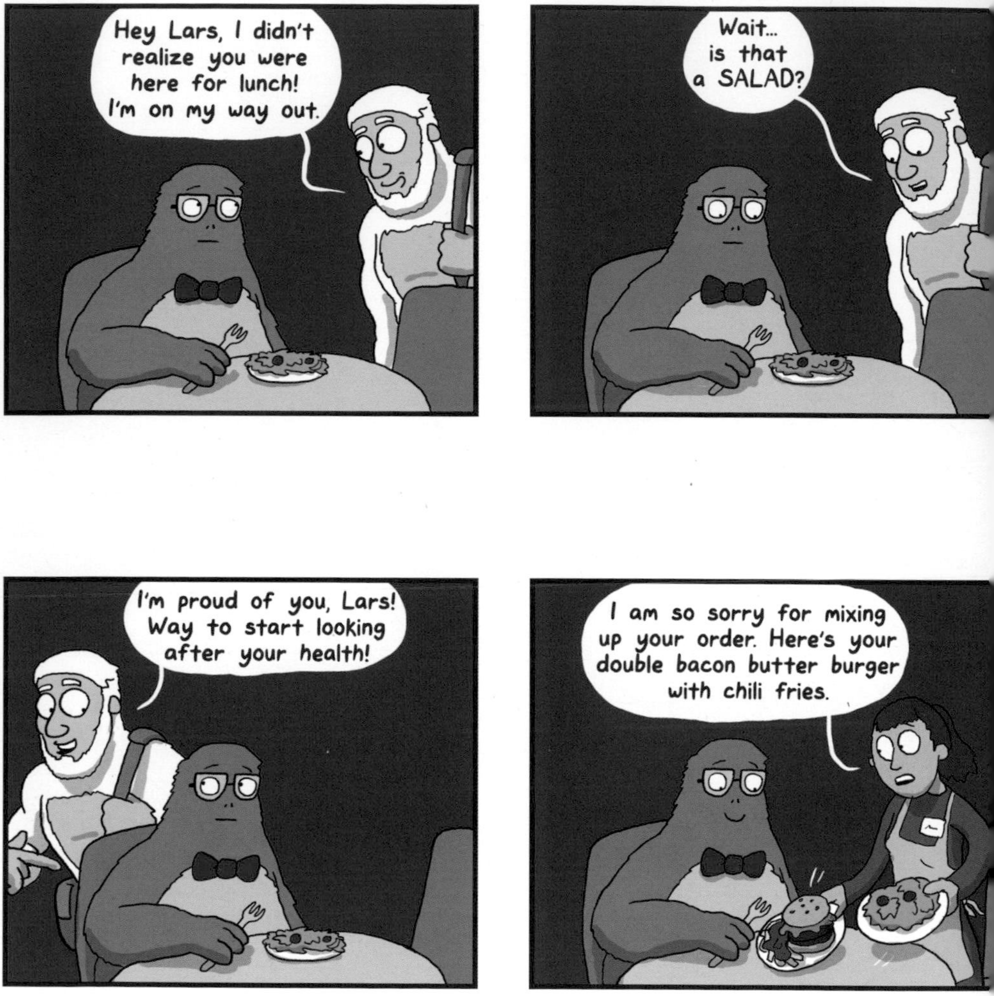
Hey Lars, I didn't realize you were here for lunch! I'm on my way out.
Wait... is that a SALAD?
I'm proud of you, Lars! Way to start looking after your health!
I am so sorry for mixing up your order. Here's your double bacon butter burger with chili fries.

Lungs' Cry for Help

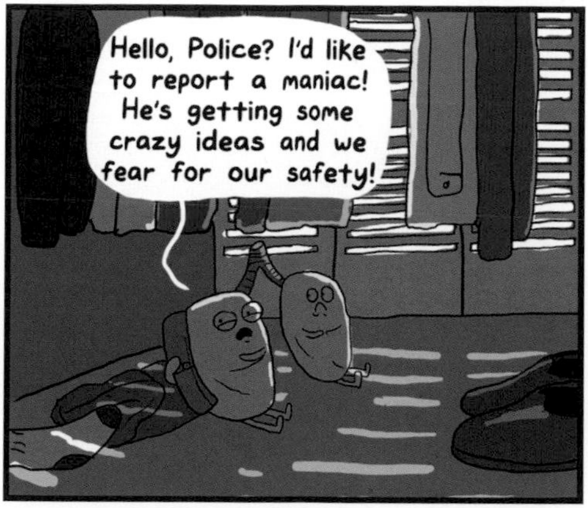
Hello, Police? I'd like to report a maniac! He's getting some crazy ideas and we fear for our safety!

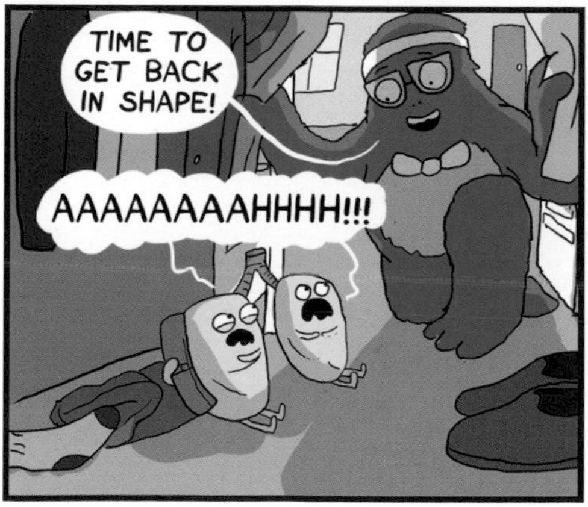
TIME TO GET BACK IN SHAPE!
AAAAAAAAHHHH!!!

Runner's High

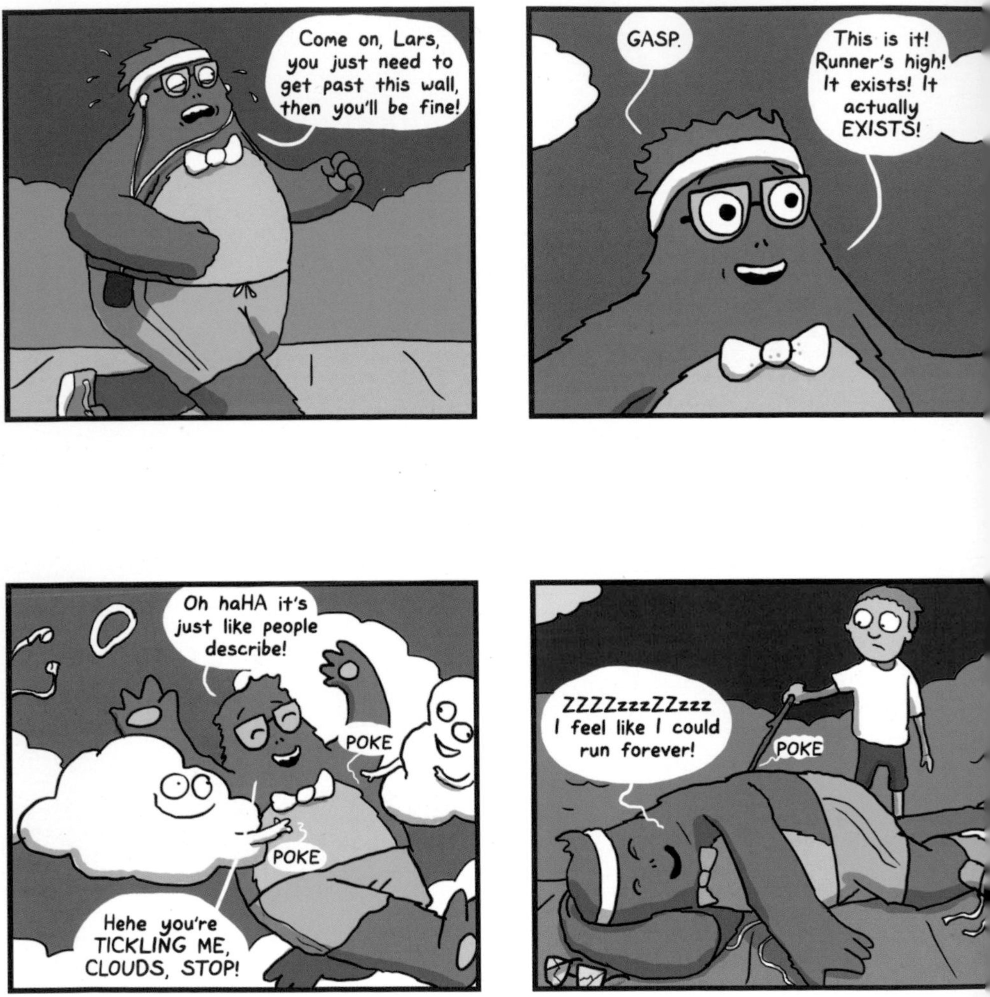
Come on, Lars, you just need to get past this wall, then you'll be fine!
GASP.
This is it! Runner's high! It exists! It actually EXISTS!
Oh haHA it's just like people describe!
POKE
POKE
Hehe you're TICKLING ME, CLOUDS, STOP!
ZZZZzzzZZzzz I feel like I could run forever!
POKE

Depression

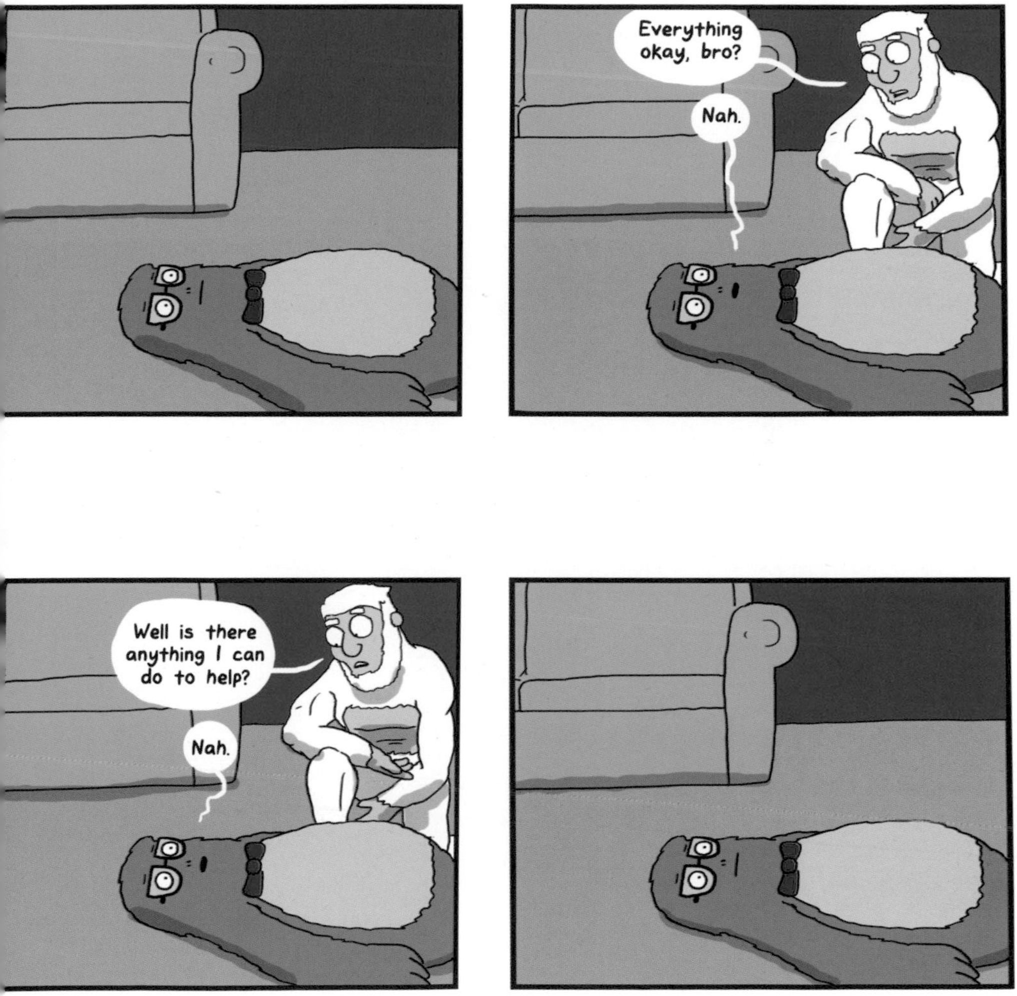
Everything okay, bro?
Nah.
Well is there anything I can do to help?
Nah.

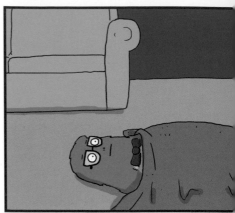
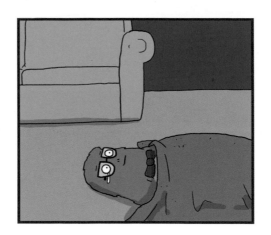

The Free Sample

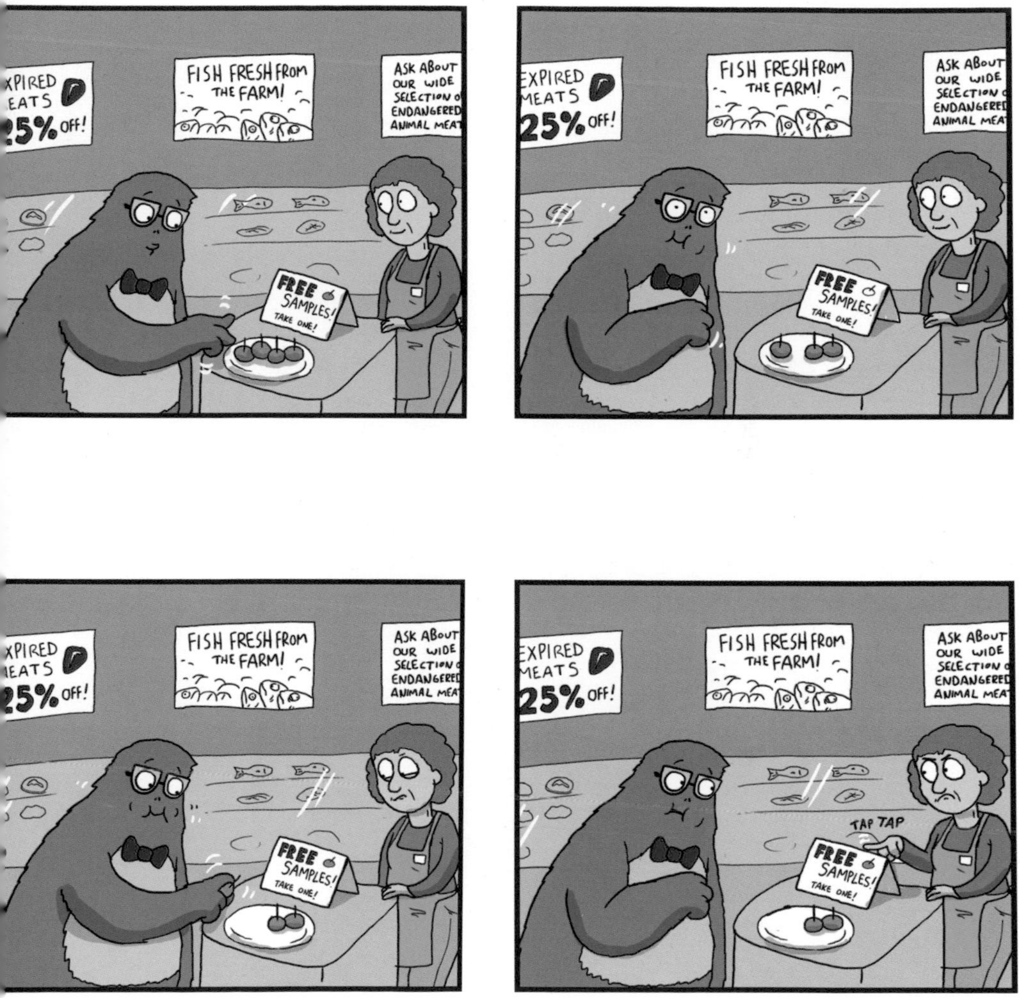

XPIRED EATS 25% OFF!
FISH FRESH FROM THE FARM!
ASK ABOUT OUR WIDE SELECTION O ENDANGERED ANIMAL MEAT
FREE SAMPLES! TAKE ONE!
TAP TAP

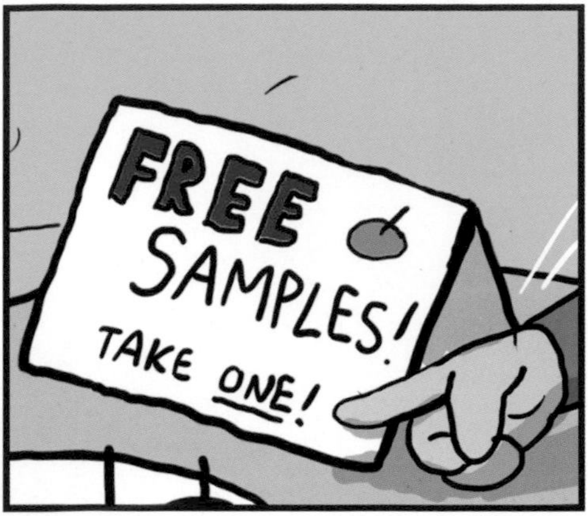
FREE
SAMPLES!
TAKE ONE!

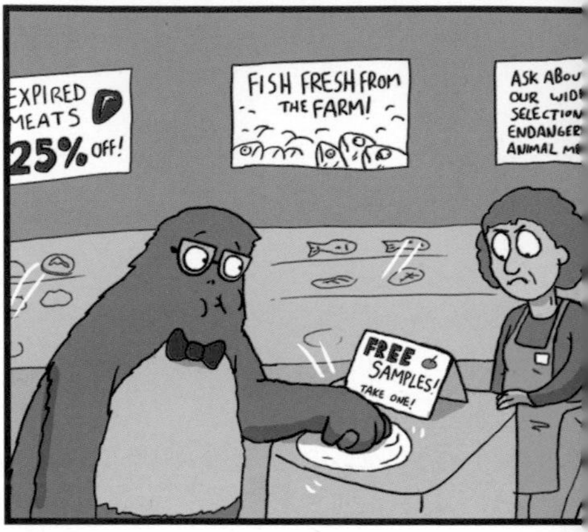
EXPIRED
MEATS
25% OFF!
FISH FRESH FROM
THE FARM!
ASK ABOU
OUR WID
SELECTION
ENDANGER
ANIMAL M
FREE
SAMPLES!
TAKE ONE!

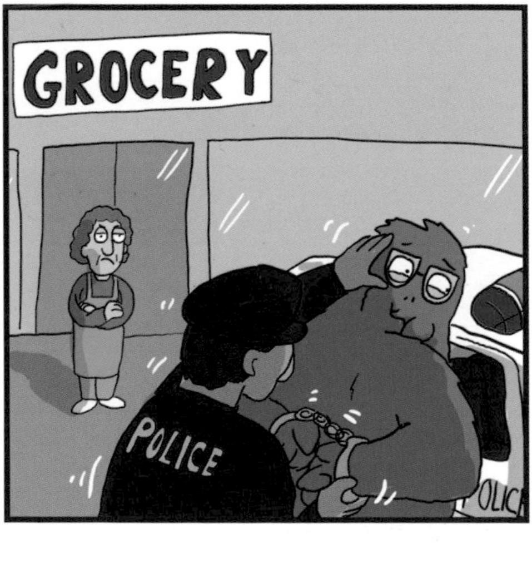
GROCERY
POLICE
POLIC

Motivation to Live

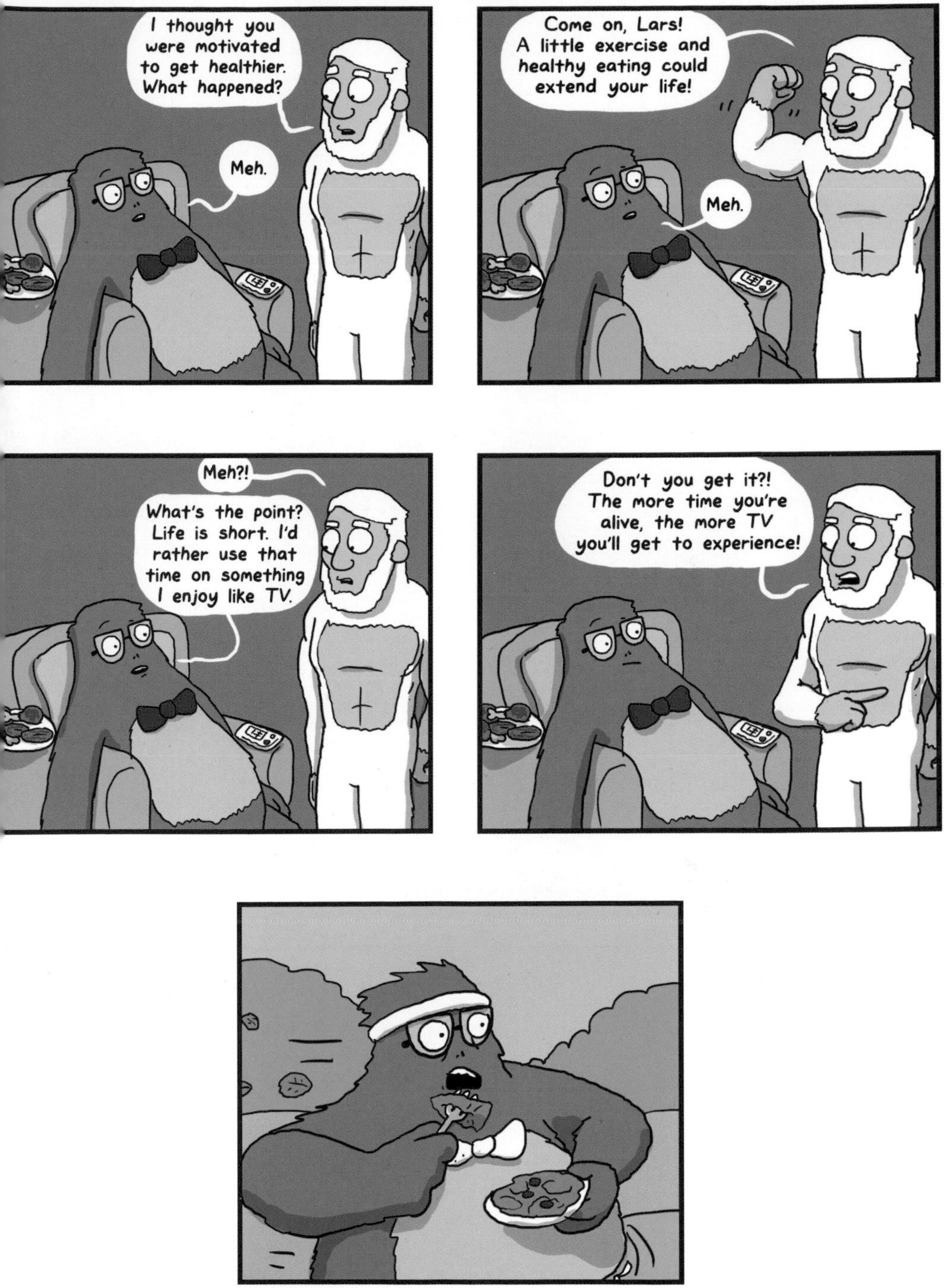

I thought you were motivated to get healthier. What happened?
Meh.
Come on, Lars! A little exercise and healthy eating could extend your life!
Meh.
Meh?!
What's the point? Life is short. I'd rather use that time on something I enjoy like TV.
Don't you get it?! The more time you're alive, the more TV you'll get to experience!

Life on Other Planets

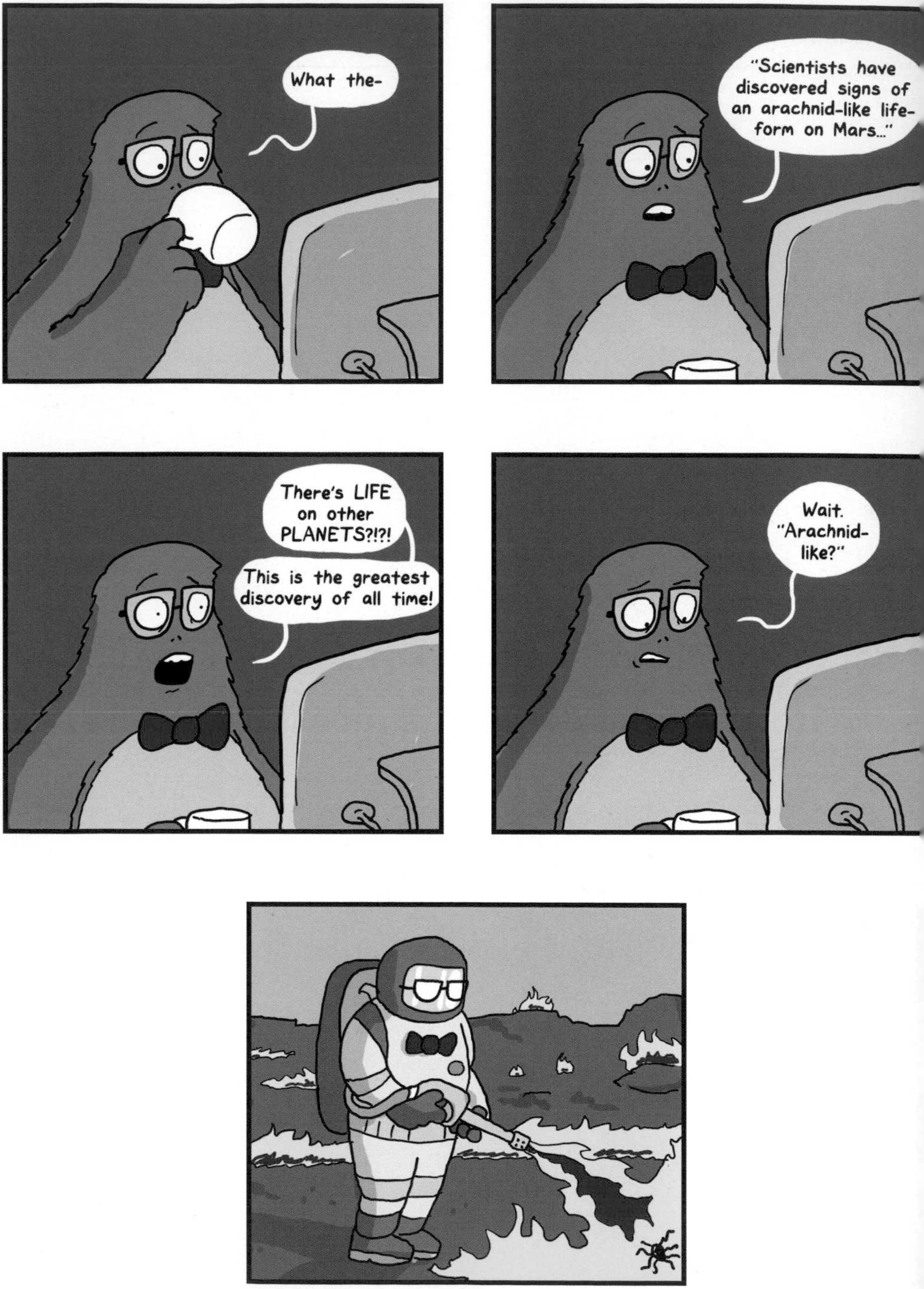

What the-
"Scientists have discovered signs of an arachnid-like life-form on Mars..."
There's LIFE on other PLANETS?!?!
This is the greatest discovery of all time!
Wait. "Arachnid-like?"

A New Day

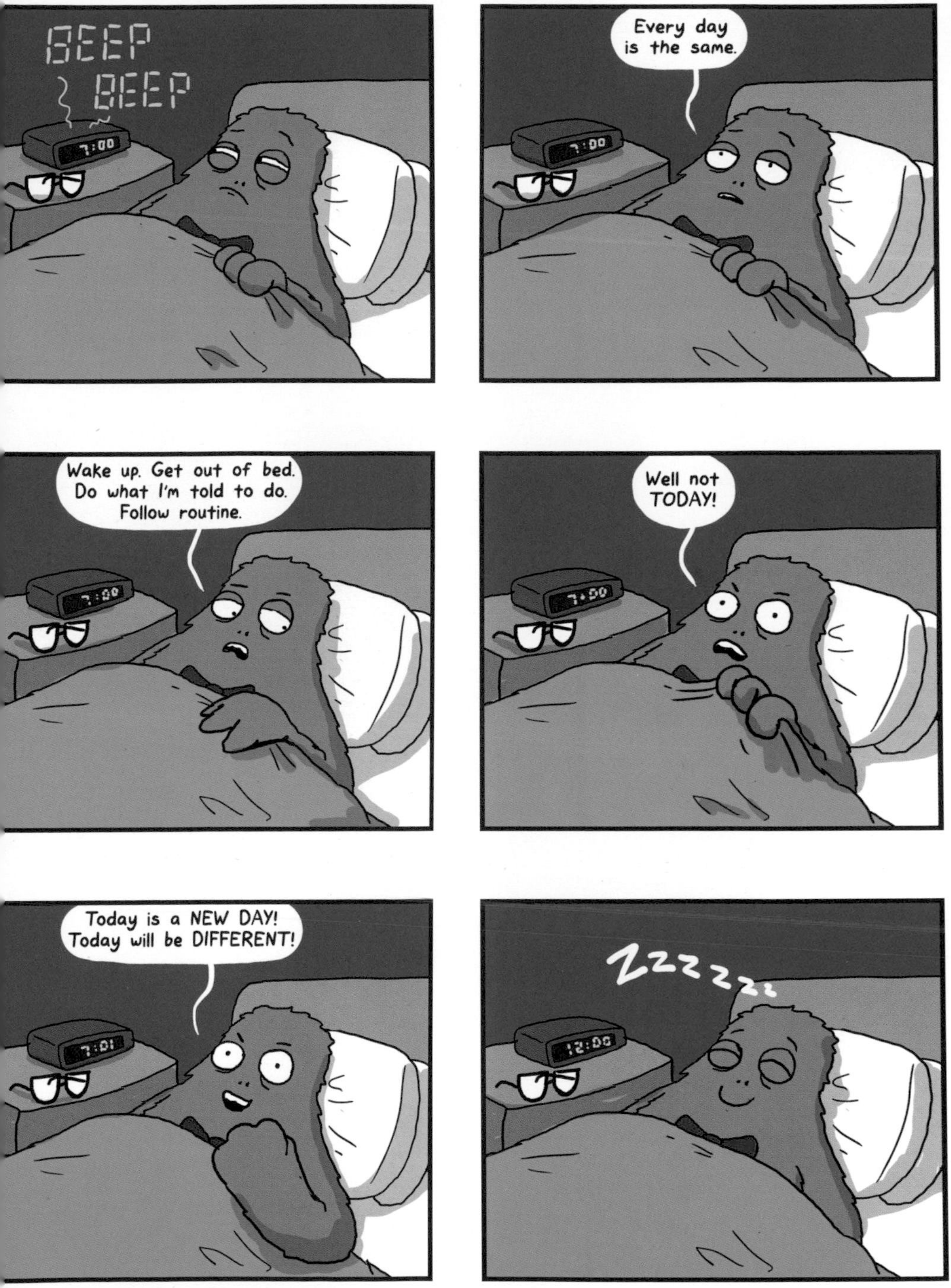
BEEP
BEEP
Every day is the same.
Wake up. Get out of bed. Do what I'm told to do. Follow routine.
Well not TODAY!
Today is a NEW DAY! Today will be DIFFERENT!
ZZZZZZZ

Virtual Training

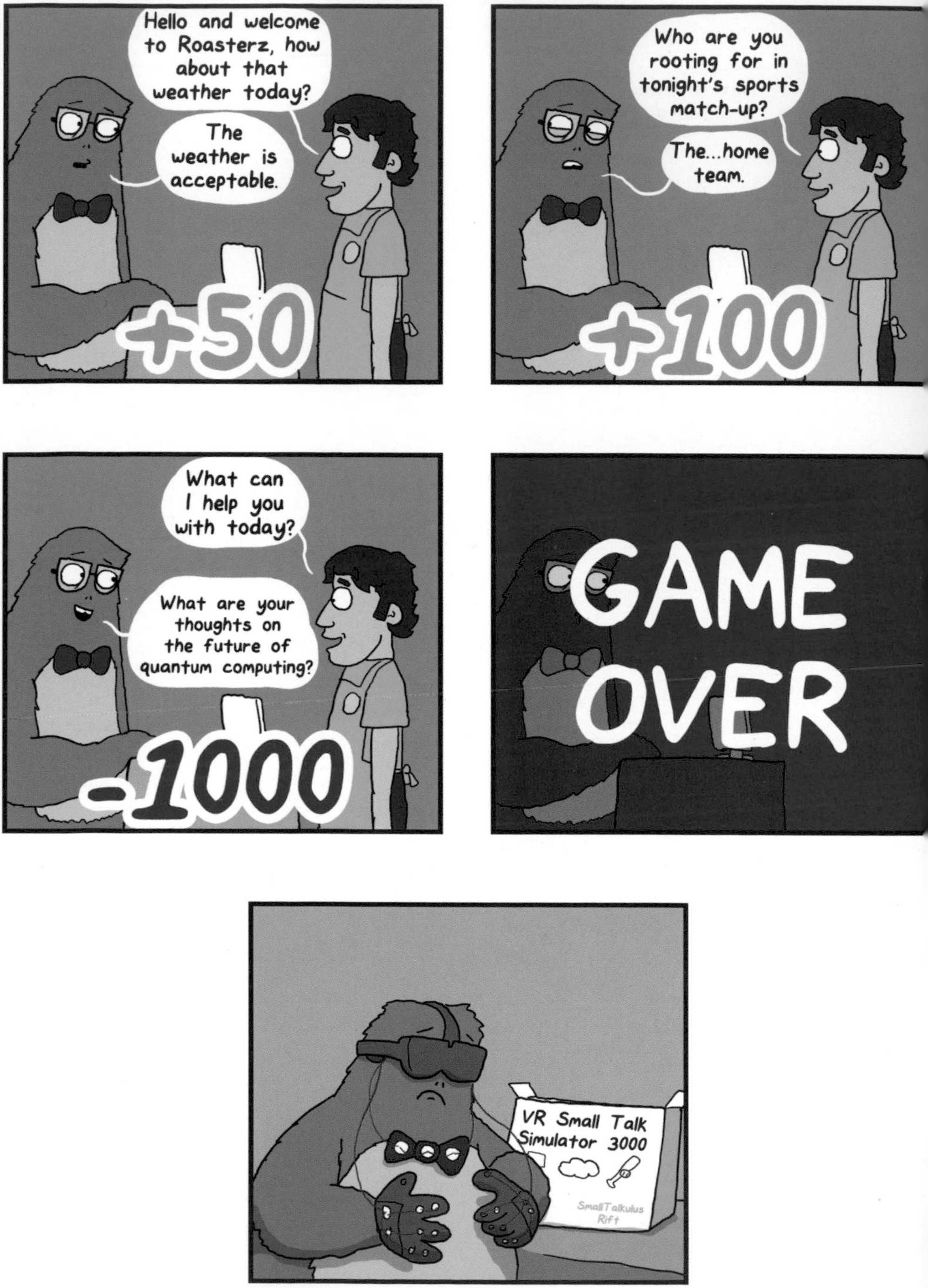
Hello and welcome to Roasterz, how about that weather today?
The weather is acceptable.
+50
Who are you rooting for in tonight's sports match-up?
The...home team.
+100
What can I help you with today?
What are your thoughts on the future of quantum computing?
-1000
GAME OVER
VR Small Talk Simulator 3000
SmallTalkulus Rift

Define "Diet"

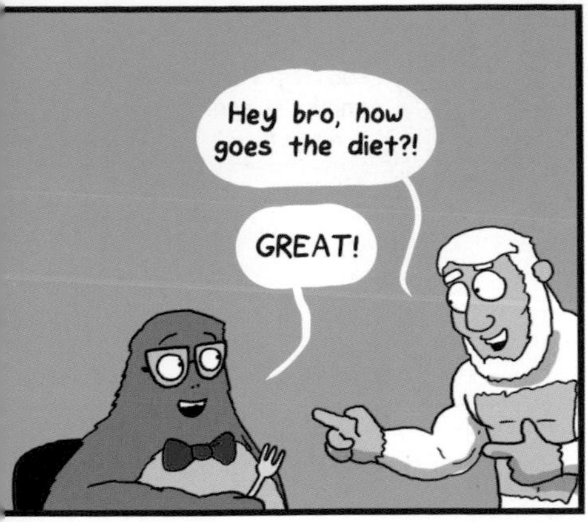

Hey bro, how goes the diet?!
GREAT!

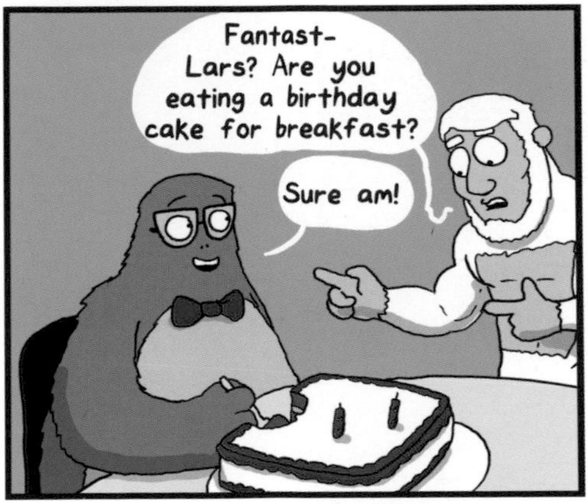

Fantast- Lars? Are you eating a birthday cake for breakfast?
Sure am!

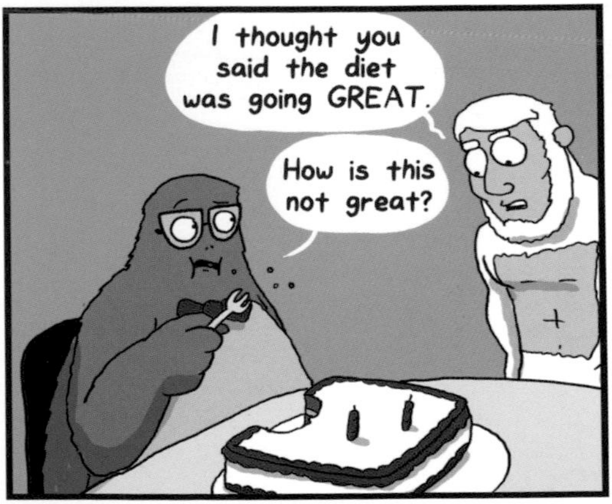

I thought you said the diet was going GREAT.
How is this not great?

Self-Fulfilling

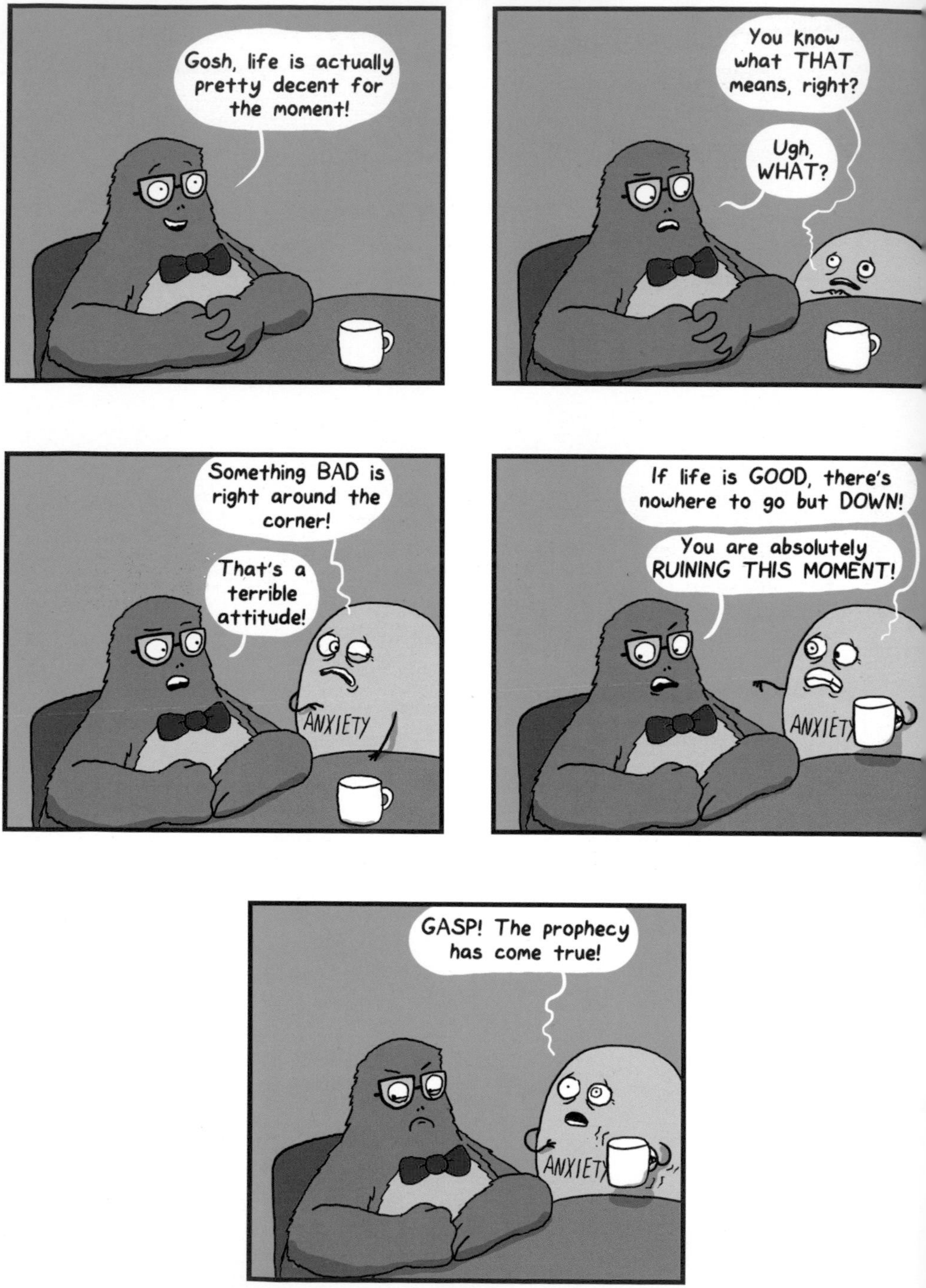

Gosh, life is actually pretty decent for the moment!
You know what THAT means, right?
Ugh, WHAT?
Something BAD is right around the corner!
That's a terrible attitude!
ANXIETY
If life is GOOD, there's nowhere to go but DOWN!
You are absolutely RUINING THIS MOMENT!
ANXIETY
GASP! The prophecy has come true!
ANXIETY

Living with Anxiety

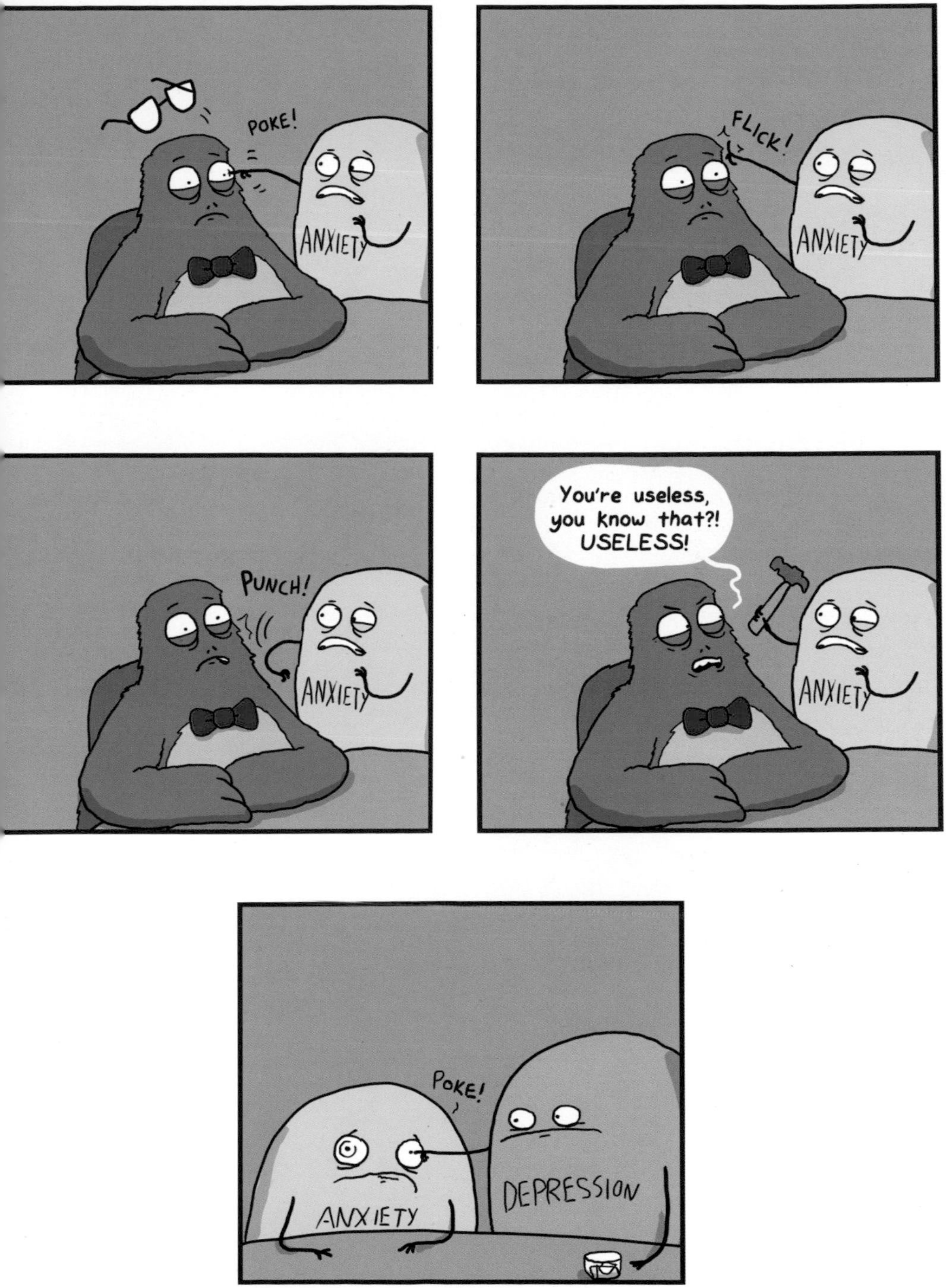
POKE!
ANXIETY
FLICK!
ANXIETY
PUNCH!
ANXIETY
You're useless, you know that?! USELESS!
ANXIETY
POKE!
ANXIETY
DEPRESSION

The Bill

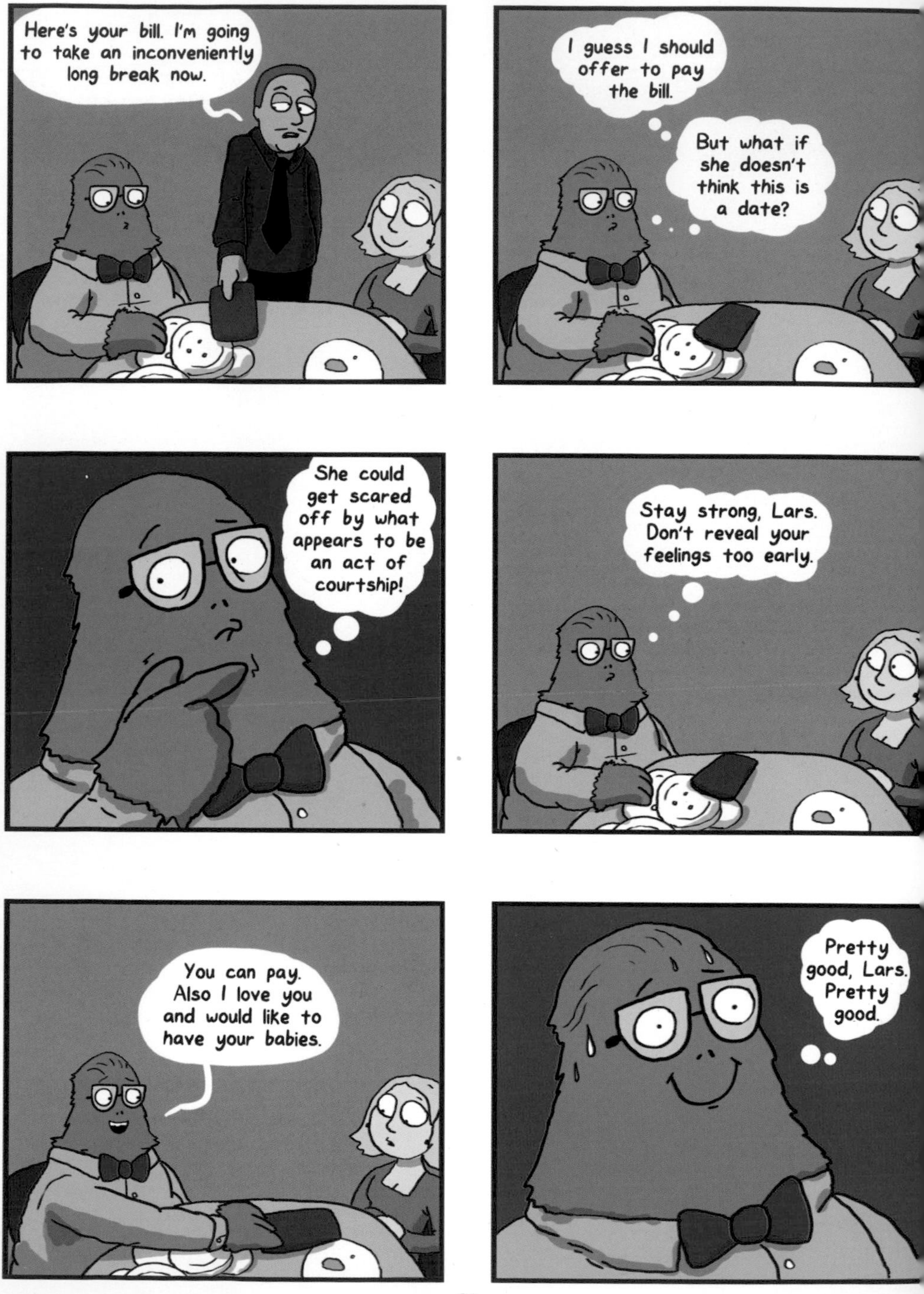
Here's your bill. I'm going to take an inconveniently long break now.
I guess I should offer to pay the bill.
But what if she doesn't think this is a date?
She could get scared off by what appears to be an act of courtship!
Stay strong, Lars. Don't reveal your feelings too early.
You can pay. Also I love you and would like to have your babies.
Pretty good, Lars. Pretty good.

Around the Corner

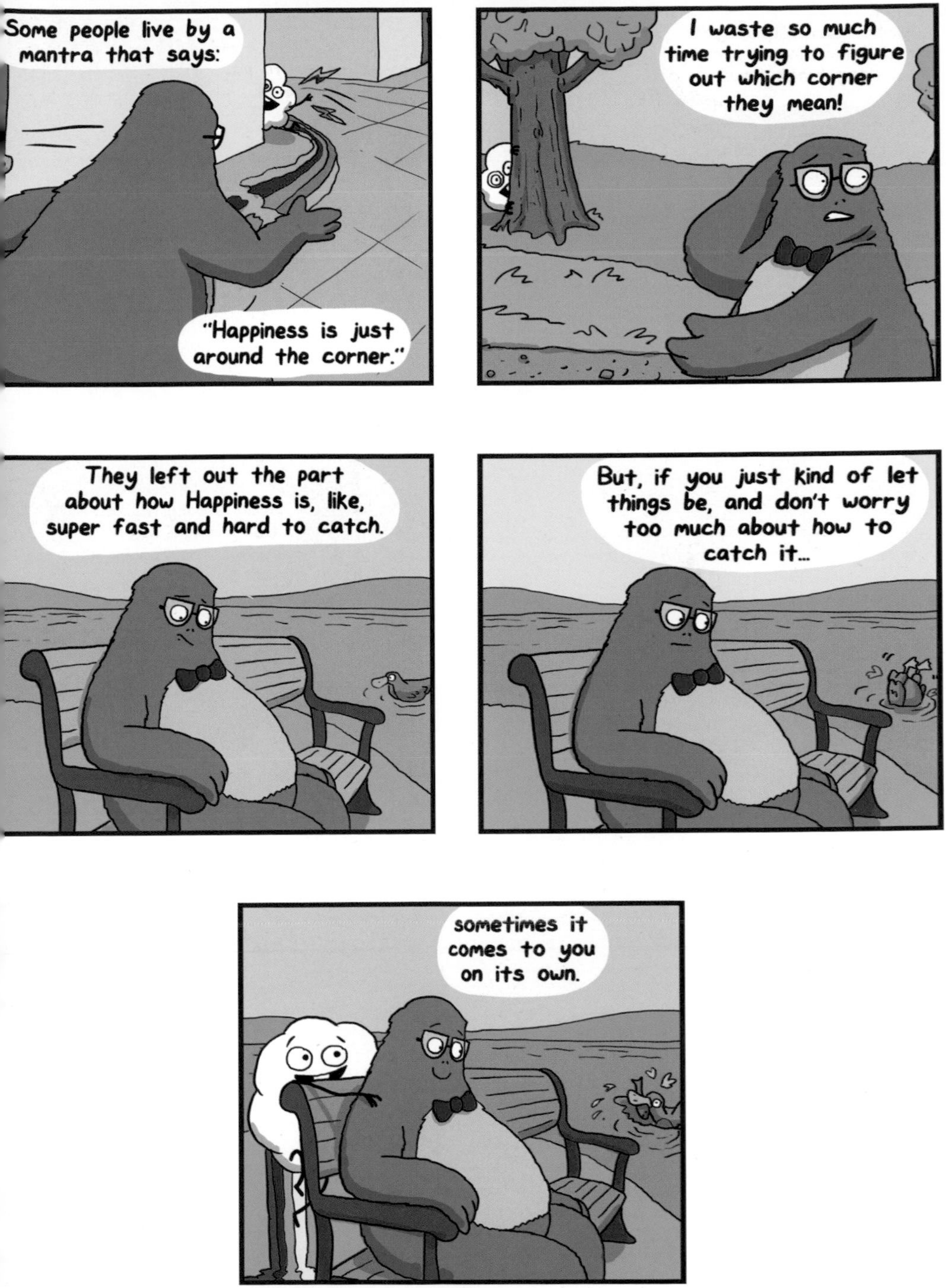

Some people live by a mantra that says:
"Happiness is just around the corner."
I waste so much time trying to figure out which corner they mean!
They left out the part about how Happiness is, like, super fast and hard to catch.
But, if you just kind of let things be, and don't worry too much about how to catch it...
sometimes it comes to you on its own.

The Early Bird Gets the Worm

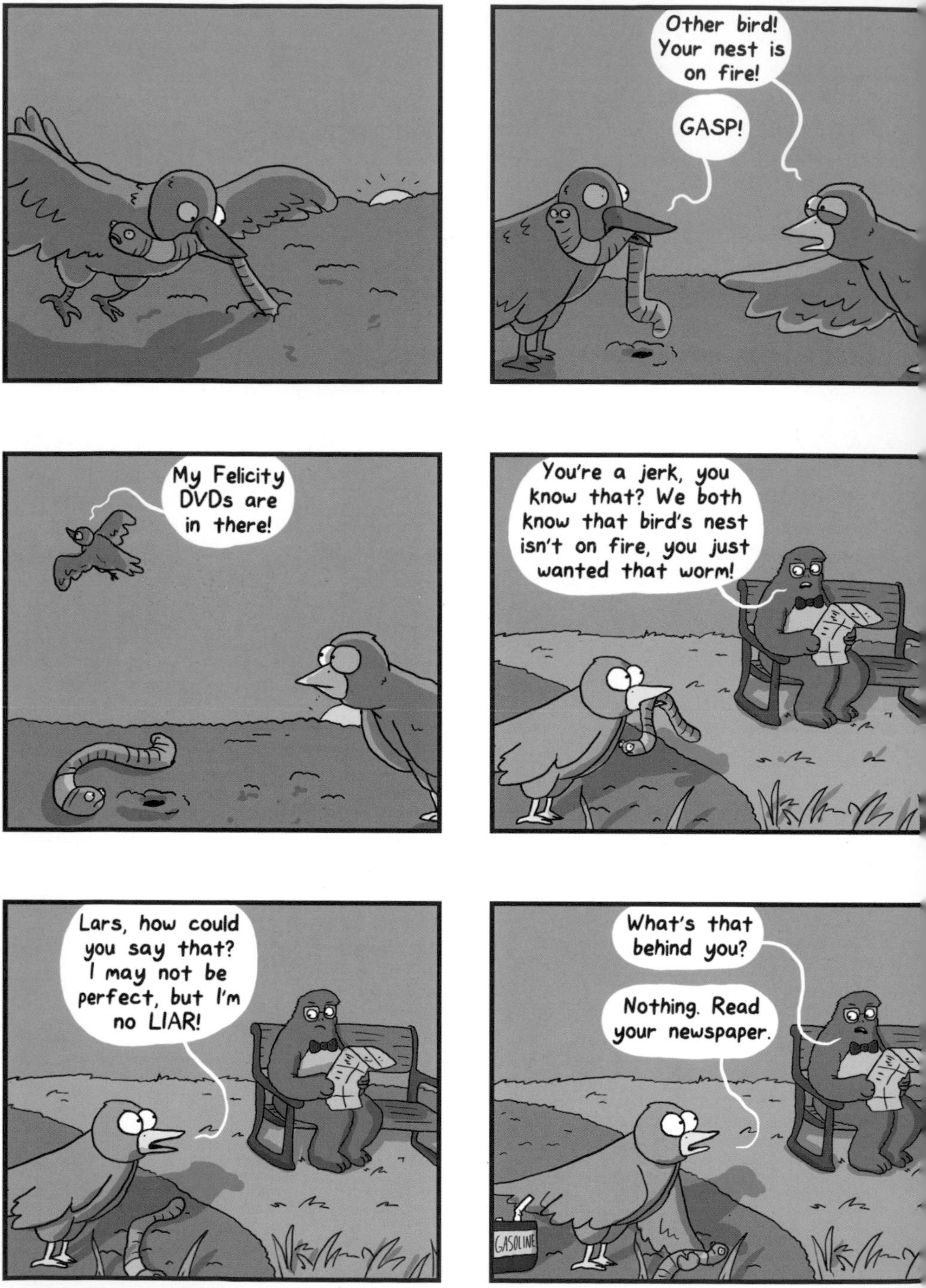
Other bird! Your nest is on fire!
GASP!
My Felicity DVDs are in there!
You're a jerk, you know that? We both know that bird's nest isn't on fire, you just wanted that worm!
Lars, how could you say that? I may not be perfect, but I'm no LIAR!
What's that behind you?
Nothing. Read your newspaper.
GASOLINE

The Line

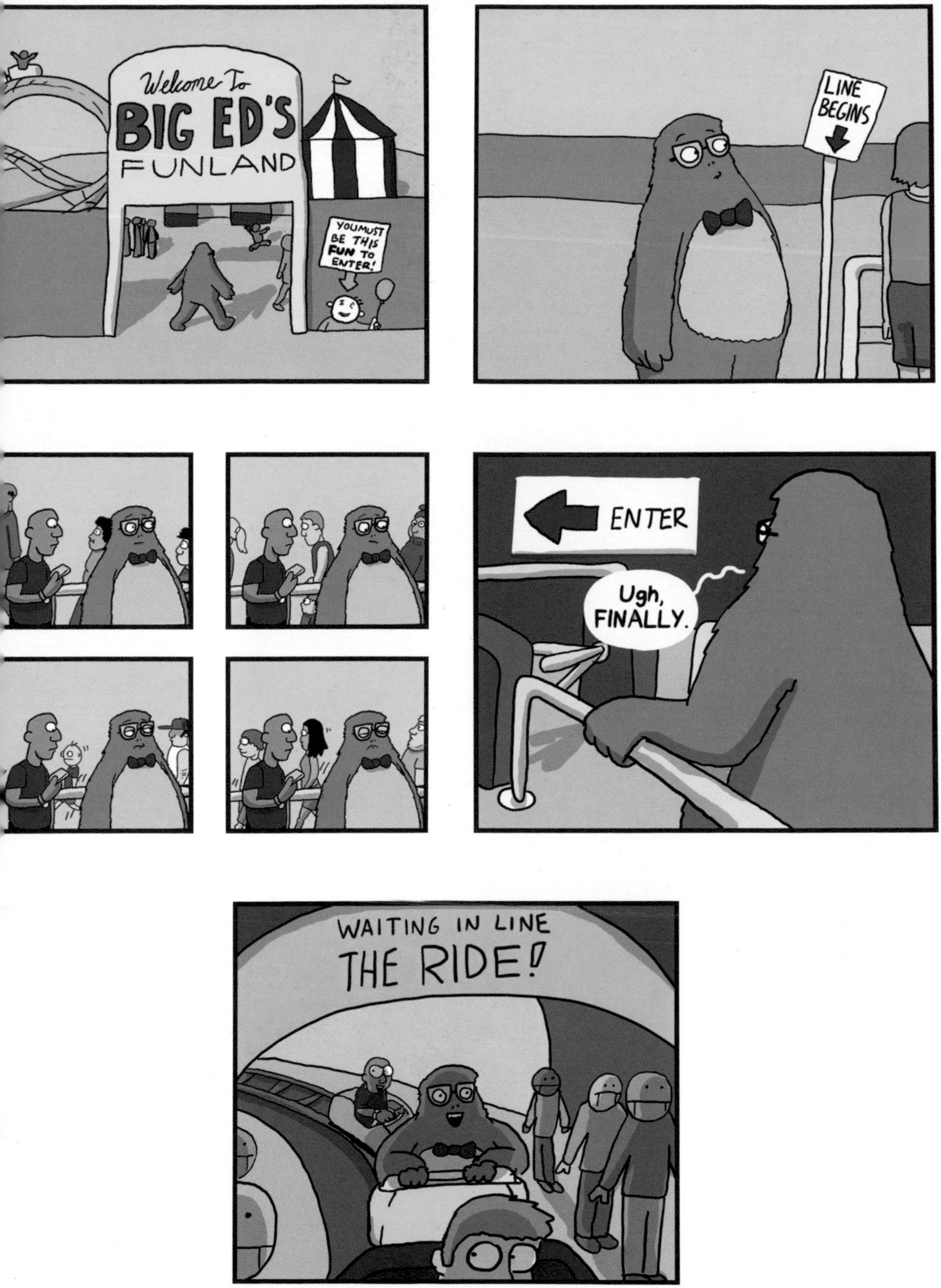
Welcome To
BIG ED'S
FUNLAND
YOUMUST BE THIS FUN TO ENTER!
LINE BEGINS
ENTER
Ugh, FINALLY.
WAITING IN LINE
THE RIDE!

Serenity Now

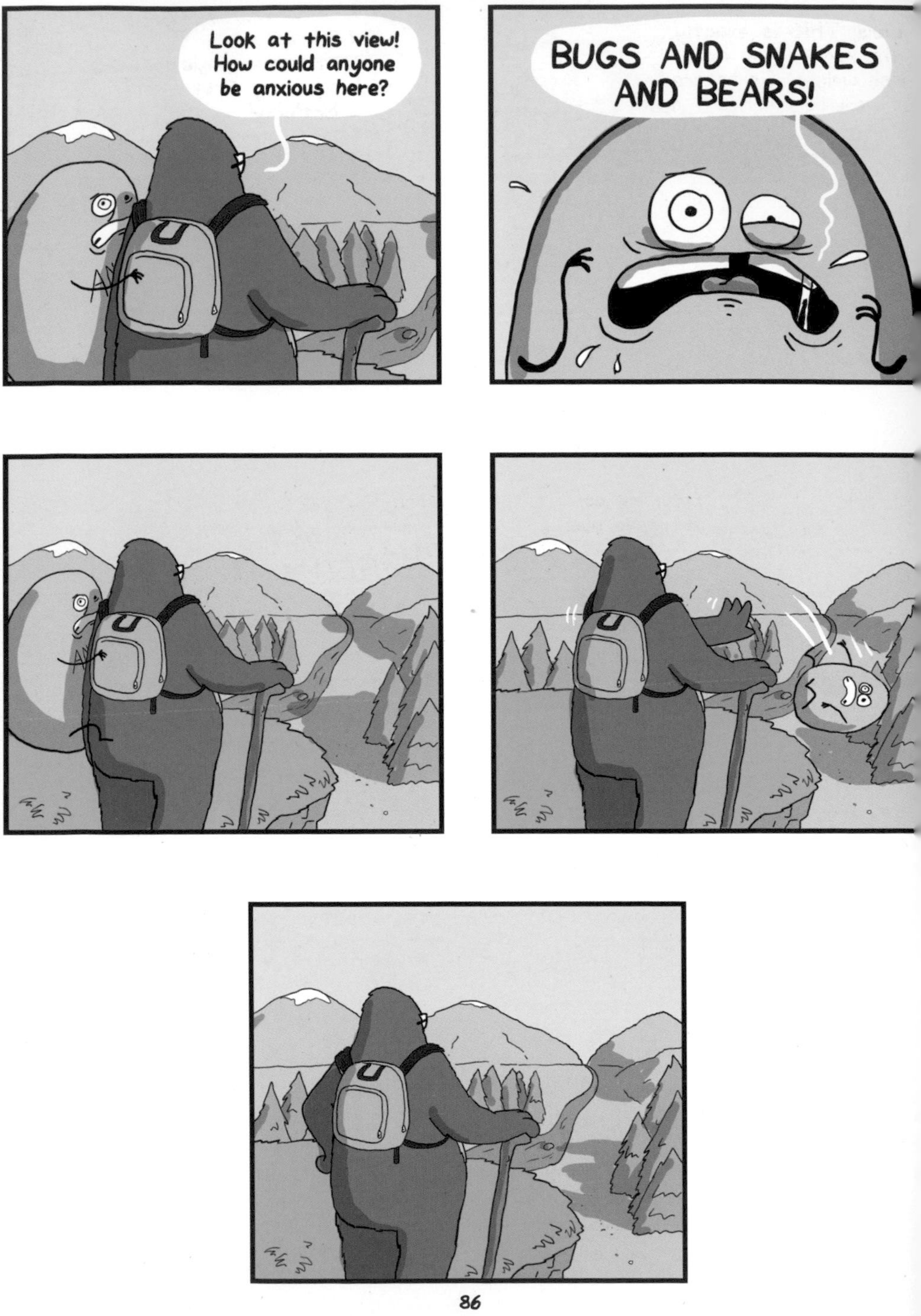

Look at this view! How could anyone be anxious here?
BUGS AND SNAKES AND BEARS!

Carbs vs Abs

Lars, THIS is exactly the reason you never lose weight! Carbs are empty calories!
Look at me. I haven't had a single carb since my first birthday!
Even my abs' abs have abs.
HOOOOORRRRRRK
LARS you got carbs all over my 258-pack!

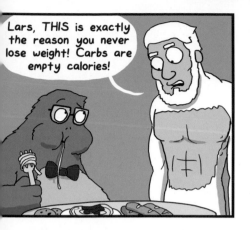

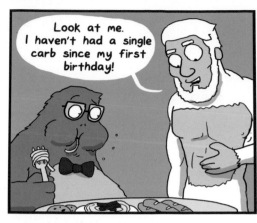

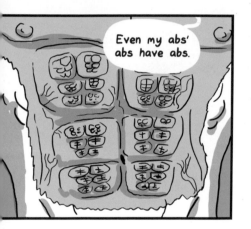

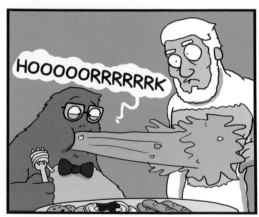

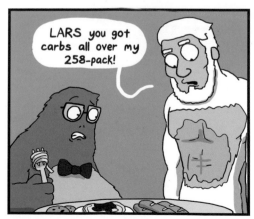

Depression vs Happiness

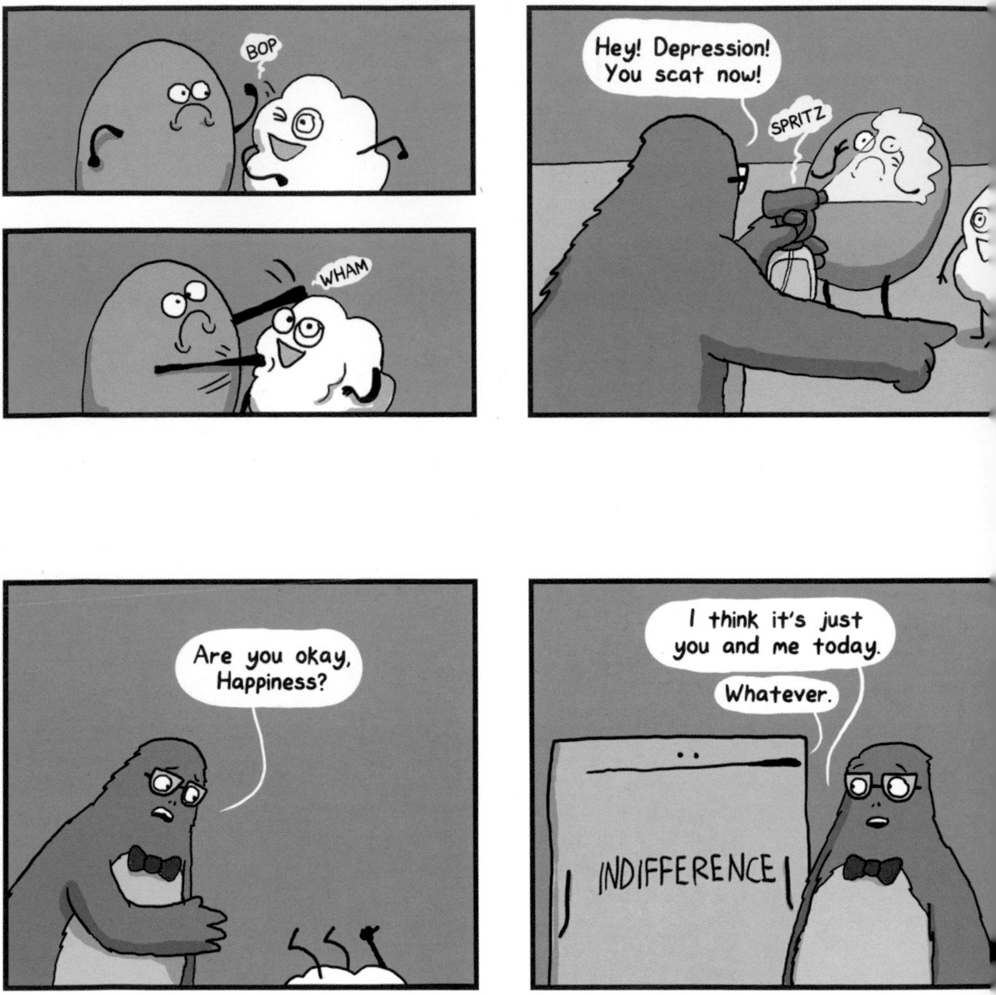
BOP
WHAM
Hey! Depression! You scat now!
SPRITZ
Are you okay, Happiness?
I think it's just you and me today.
Whatever.
INDIFFERENCE

Lars Tries to Joke on Social Media

LARS:
Broccoli? More like YUCKoli!

POKEMAN01 REPLIED:
Bury yourself alive in a garden
FARMS4LYFE REPLIED:
#BroccoliLivesMatter
BROCCOLILUVR REPLIED:
I hope a piece of broccoli becomes sentient and gives you a bad stock tip that eventually bankrupts you, loser!

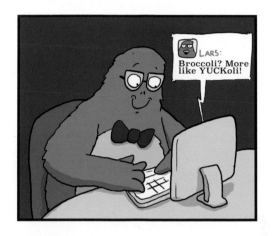

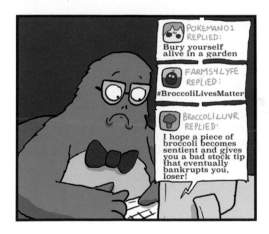

Lars and the Special Brownie

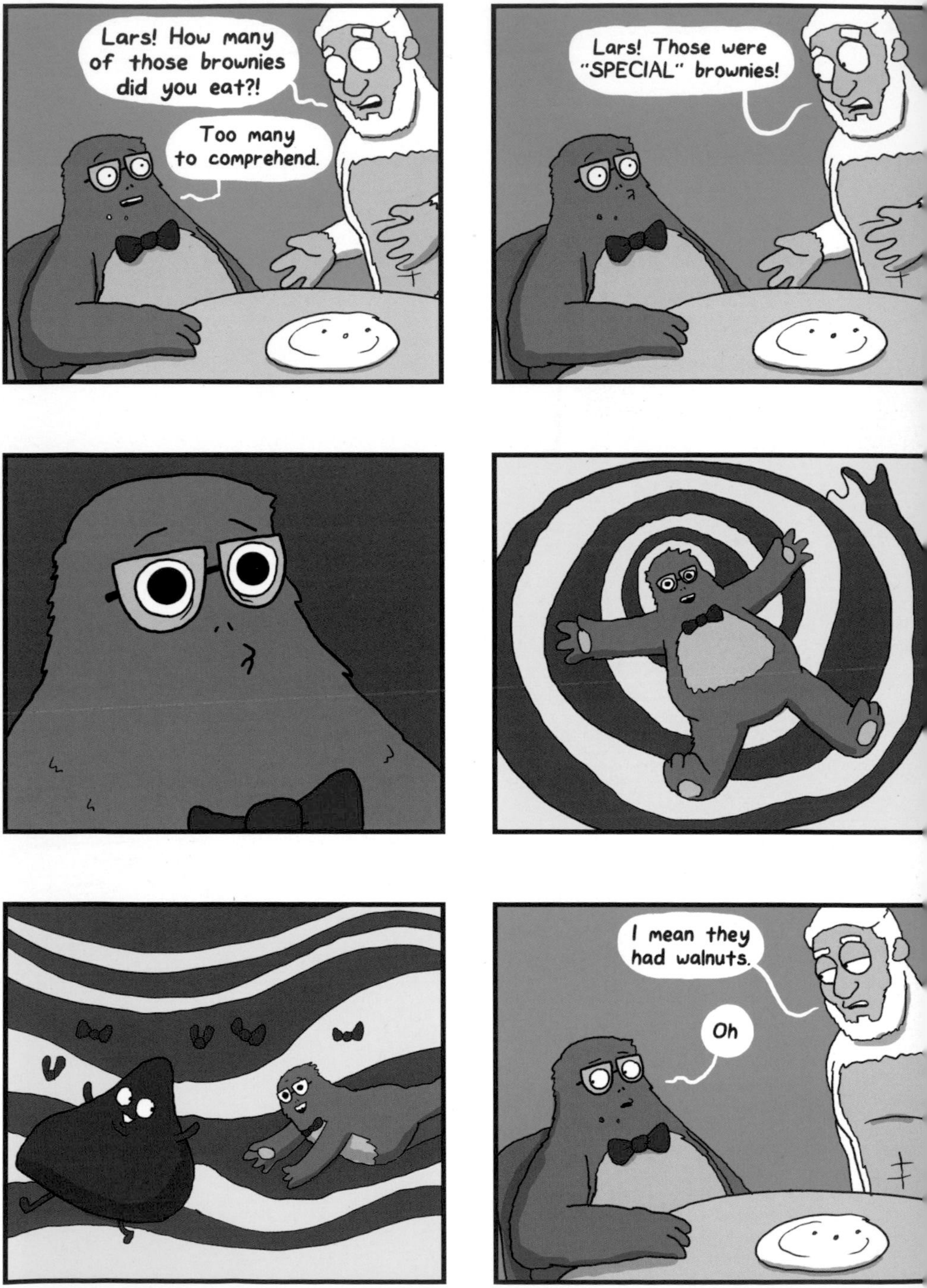
Lars! How many of those brownies did you eat?!
Too many to comprehend.
Lars! Those were "SPECIAL" brownies!
I mean they had walnuts.
Oh

The Boost

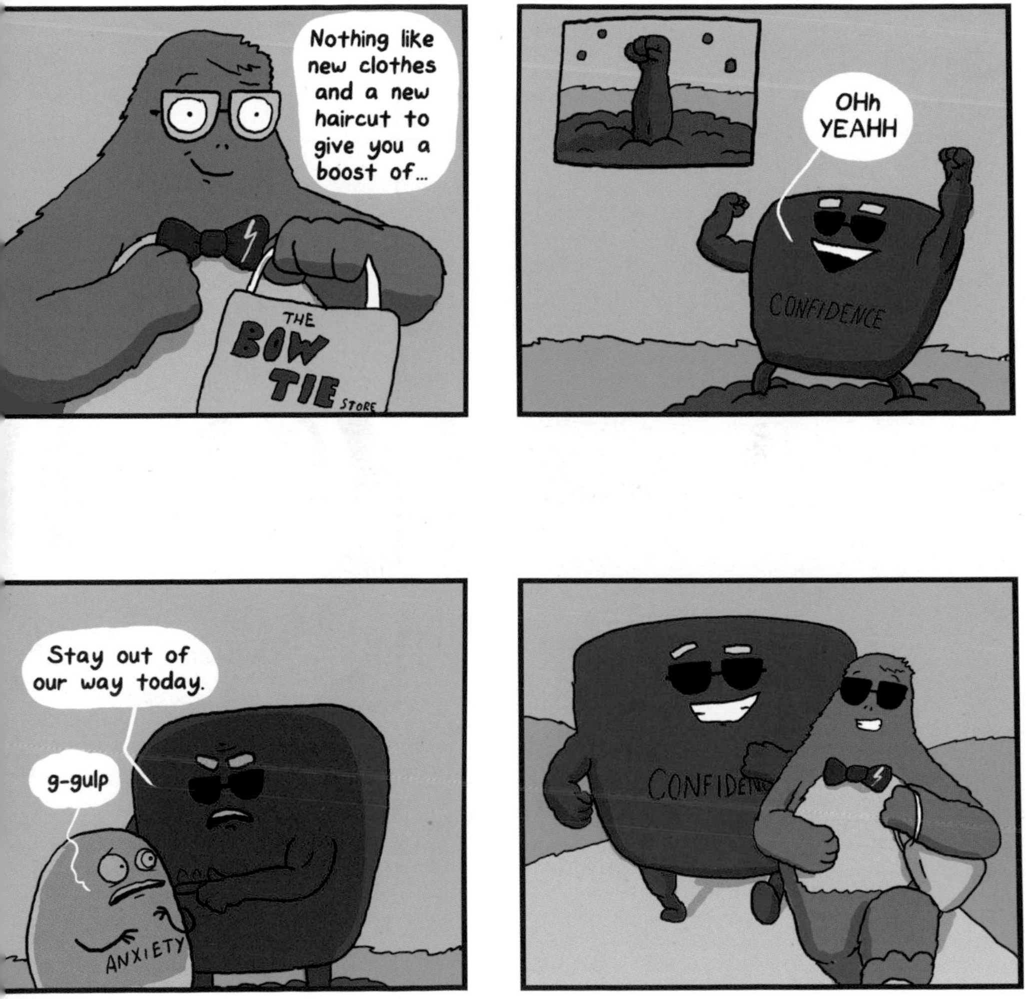
Nothing like new clothes and a new haircut to give you a boost of...
THE BOW TIE STORE
OHh YEAHH
CONFIDENCE
Stay out of our way today.
g-gulp
ANXIETY
CONFIDENC

Letting Go

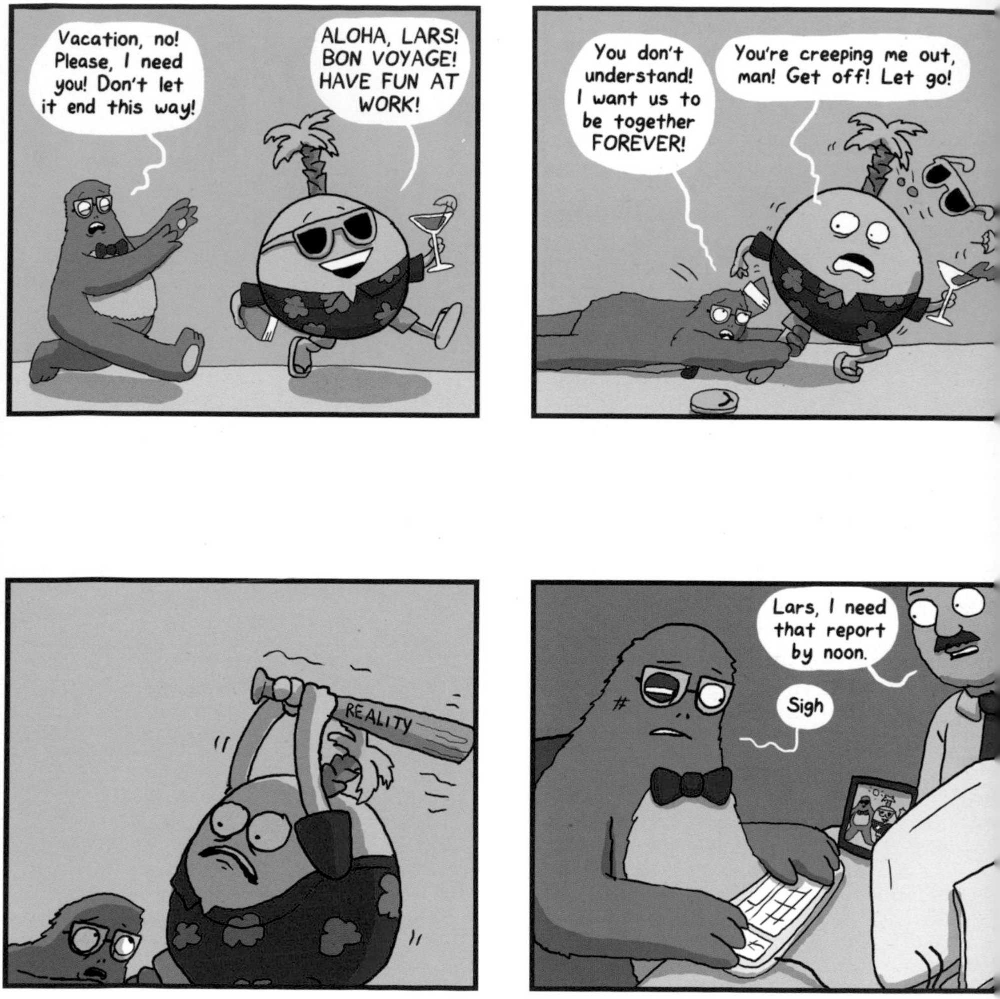

Vacation, no! Please, I need you! Don't let it end this way!
ALOHA, LARS! BON VOYAGE! HAVE FUN AT WORK!
You don't understand! I want us to be together FOREVER!
You're creeping me out, man! Get off! Let go!
REALITY
Lars, I need that report by noon.
Sigh

Return of the One-Upper

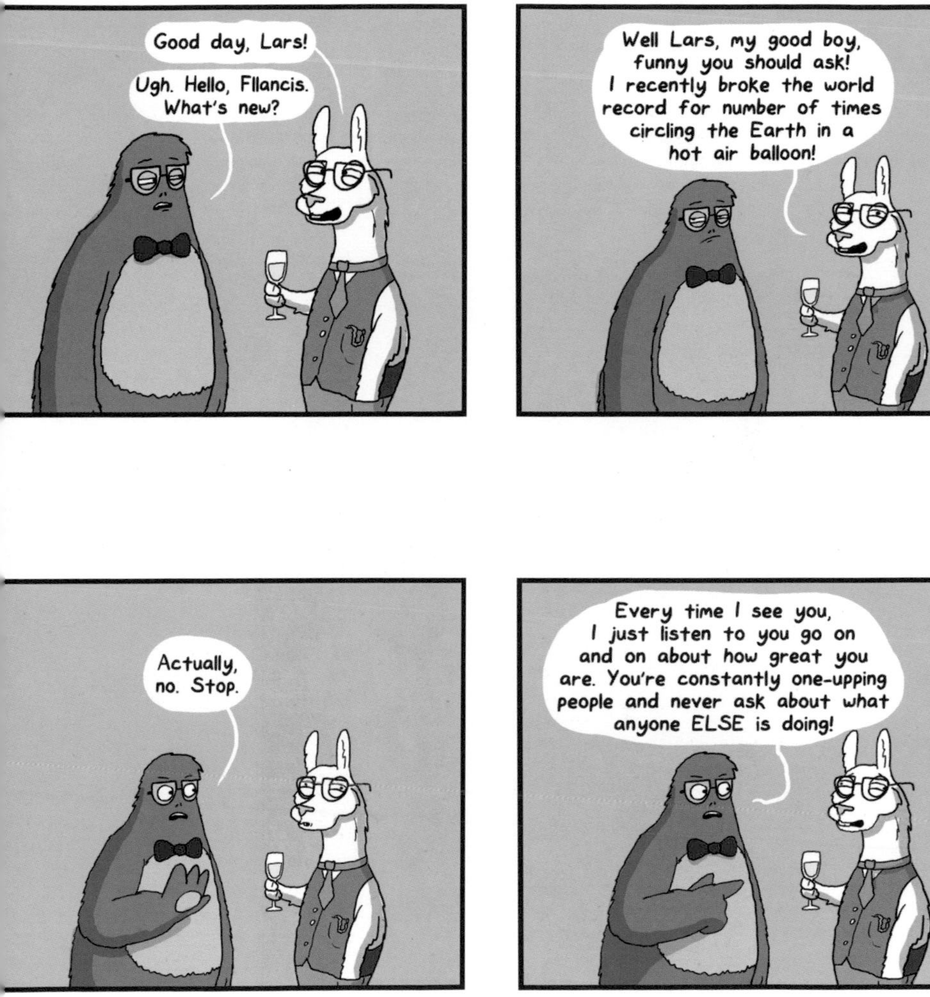

Good day, Lars!
Ugh. Hello, Fllancis. What's new?
Well Lars, my good boy, funny you should ask! I recently broke the world record for number of times circling the Earth in a hot air balloon!
Actually, no. Stop.
Every time I see you, I just listen to you go on and on about how great you are. You're constantly one-upping people and never ask about what anyone ELSE is doing!

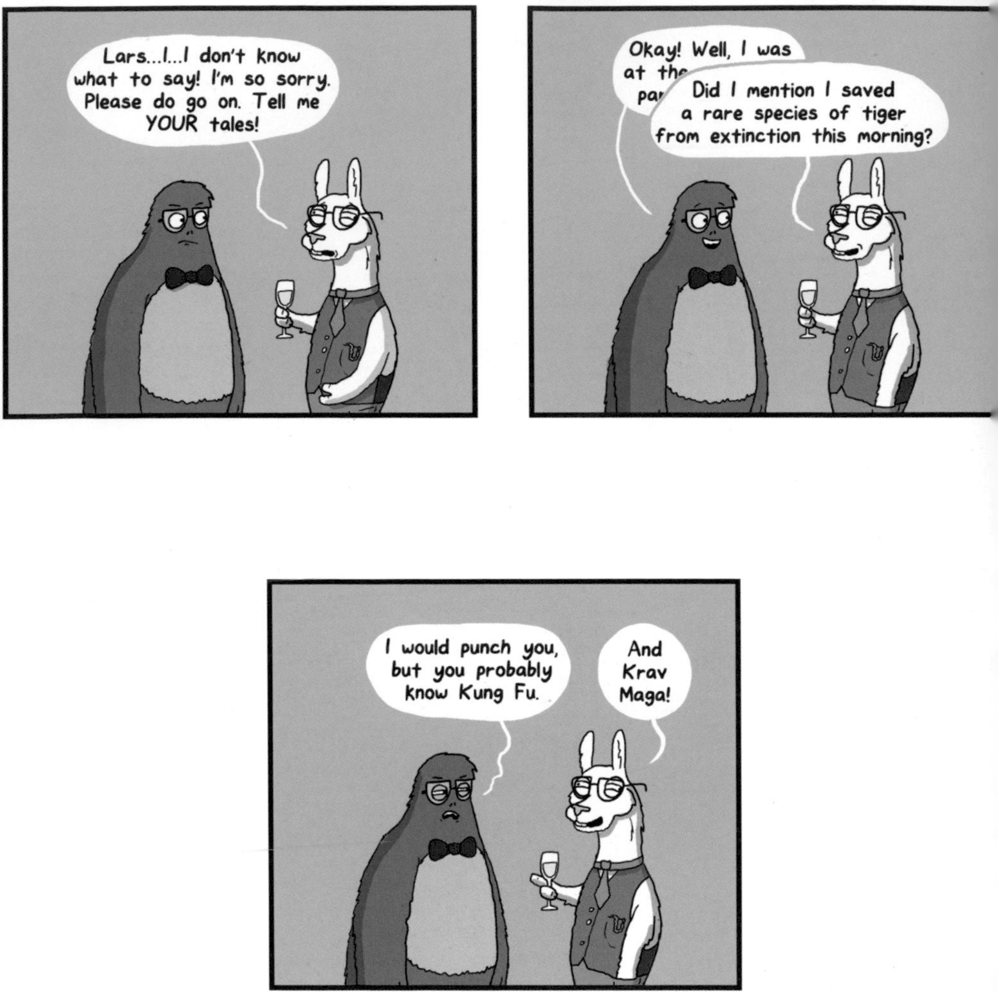
Lars...I...I don't know what to say! I'm so sorry. Please do go on. Tell me YOUR tales!
Okay! Well, I was
Did I mention I saved a rare species of tiger from extinction this morning?
I would punch you, but you probably know Kung Fu.
And Krav Maga!

Politics

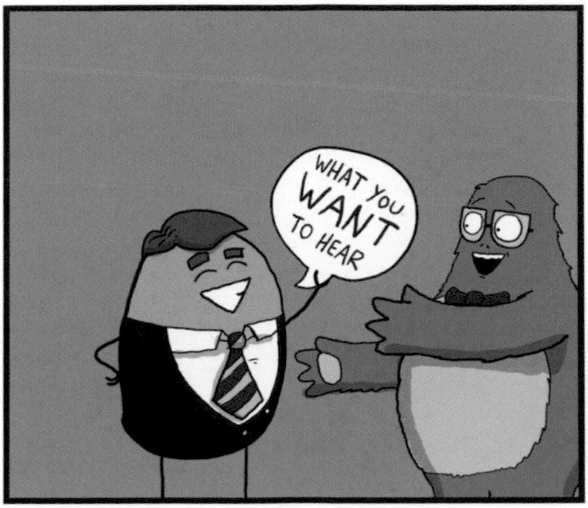
WHAT YOU WANT TO HEAR

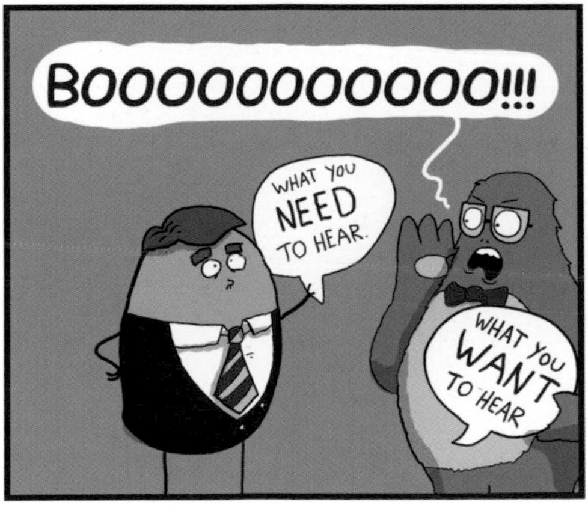
BOOOOOOOOOOO!!!
WHAT YOU NEED TO HEAR.
WHAT YOU WANT TO HEAR

Revenge of the Book Nerds

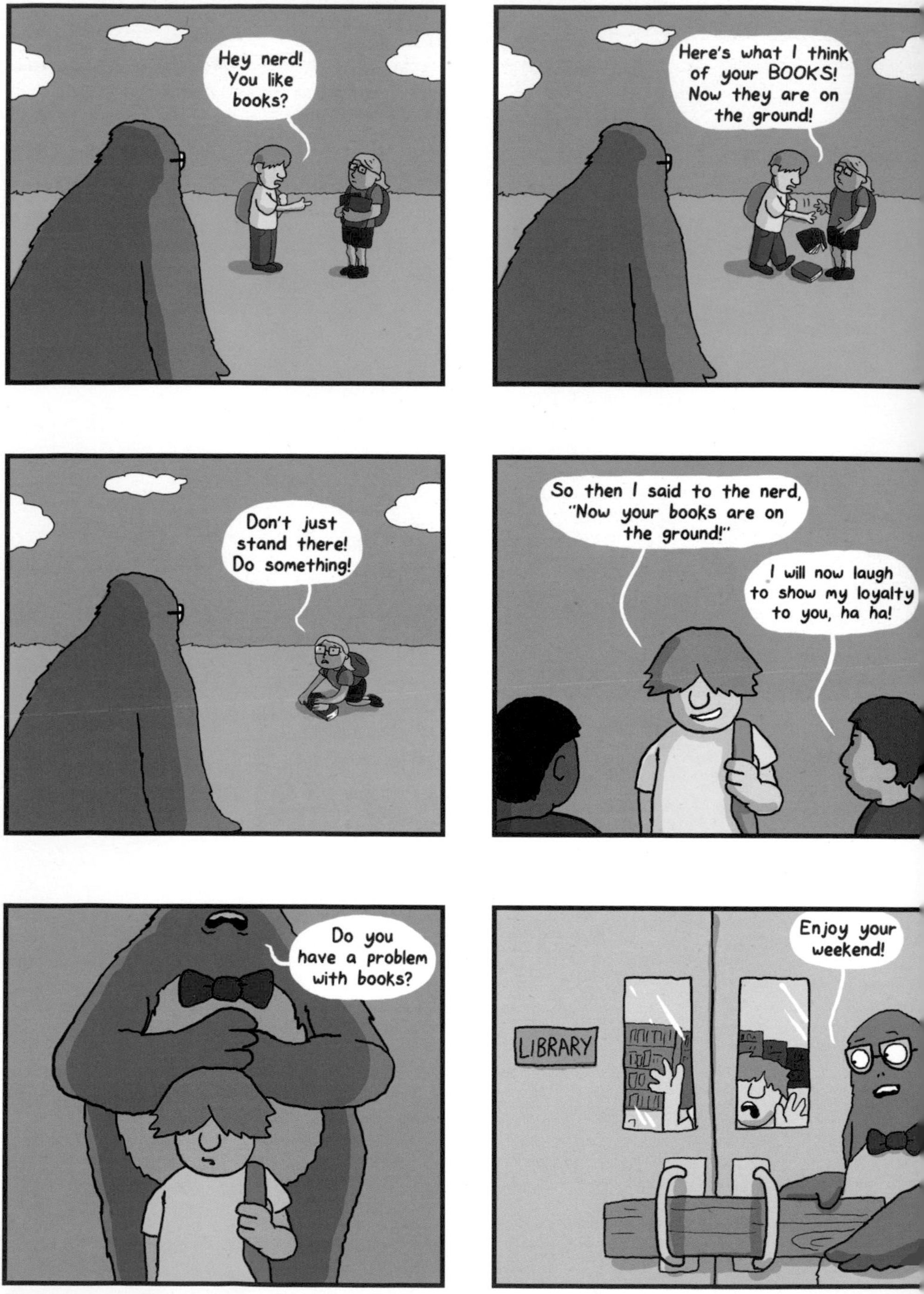
Hey nerd! You like books?
Here's what I think of your BOOKS! Now they are on the ground!
Don't just stand there! Do something!
So then I said to the nerd, "Now your books are on the ground!"
I will now laugh to show my loyalty to you, ha ha!
Do you have a problem with books?
LIBRARY
Enjoy your weekend!

Awklars

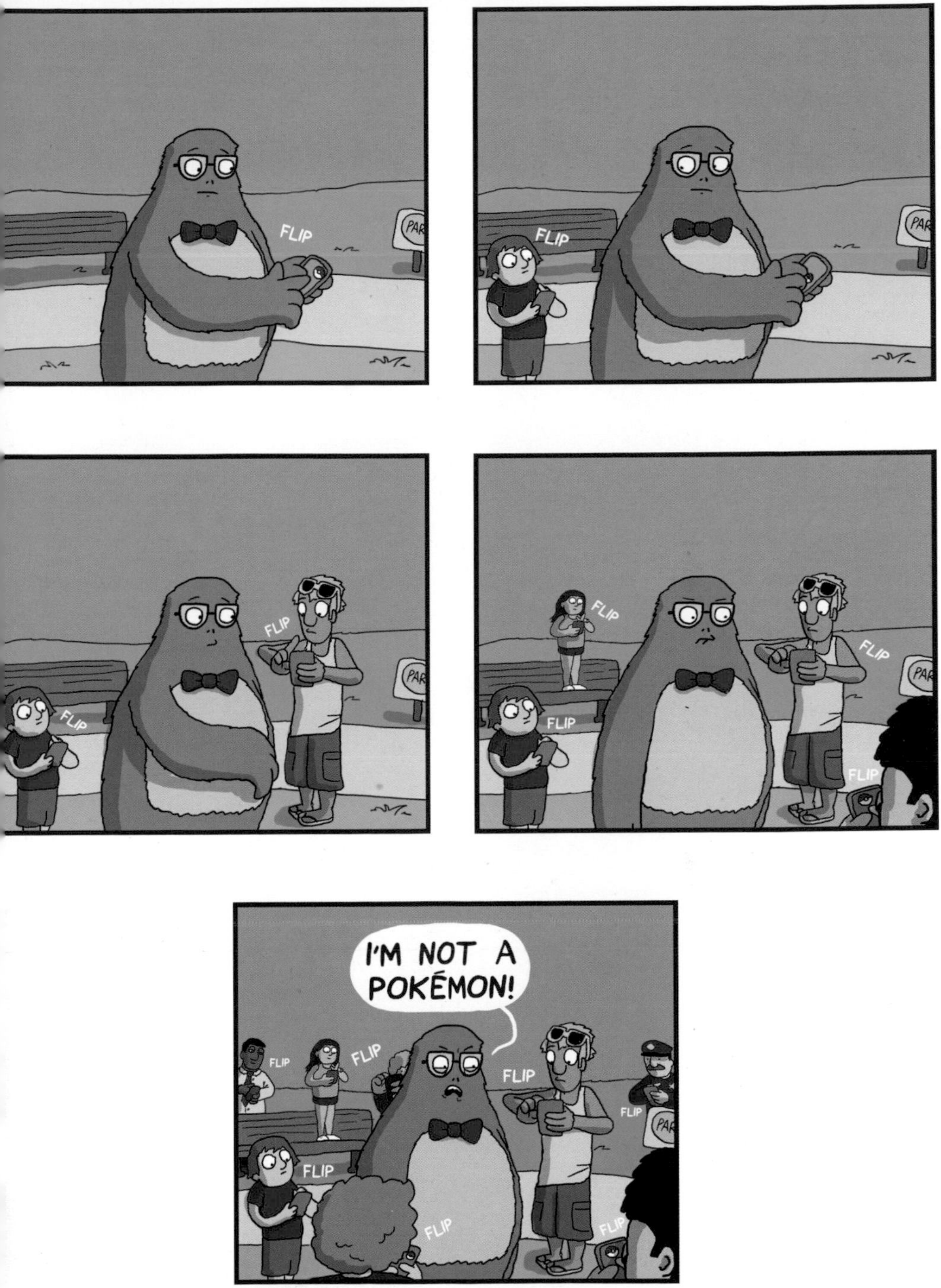
FLIP
PAR
FLIP
FLIP
PAR
FLIP
FLIP
PAR
FLIP
FLIP
FLIP
PAR
FLIP
I'M NOT A POKÉMON!
FLIP
FLIP
FLIP
FLIP
FLIP
PAR
FLIP
FLIP

Vices

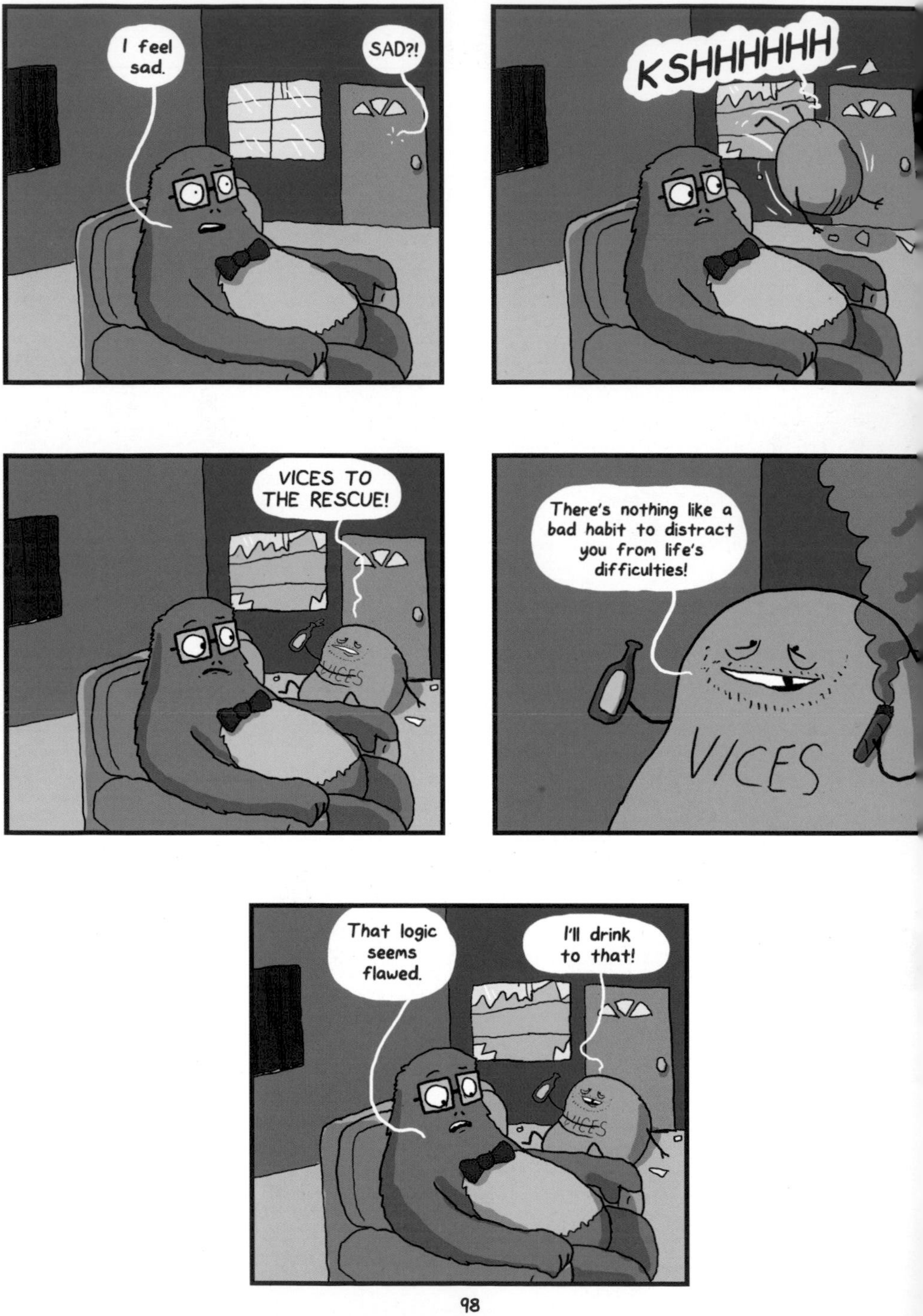
I feel sad.
SAD?!
KSHHHHHH
VICES TO THE RESCUE!
VICES
There's nothing like a bad habit to distract you from life's difficulties!
VICES
That logic seems flawed.
I'll drink to that!
VICES

Appreciation

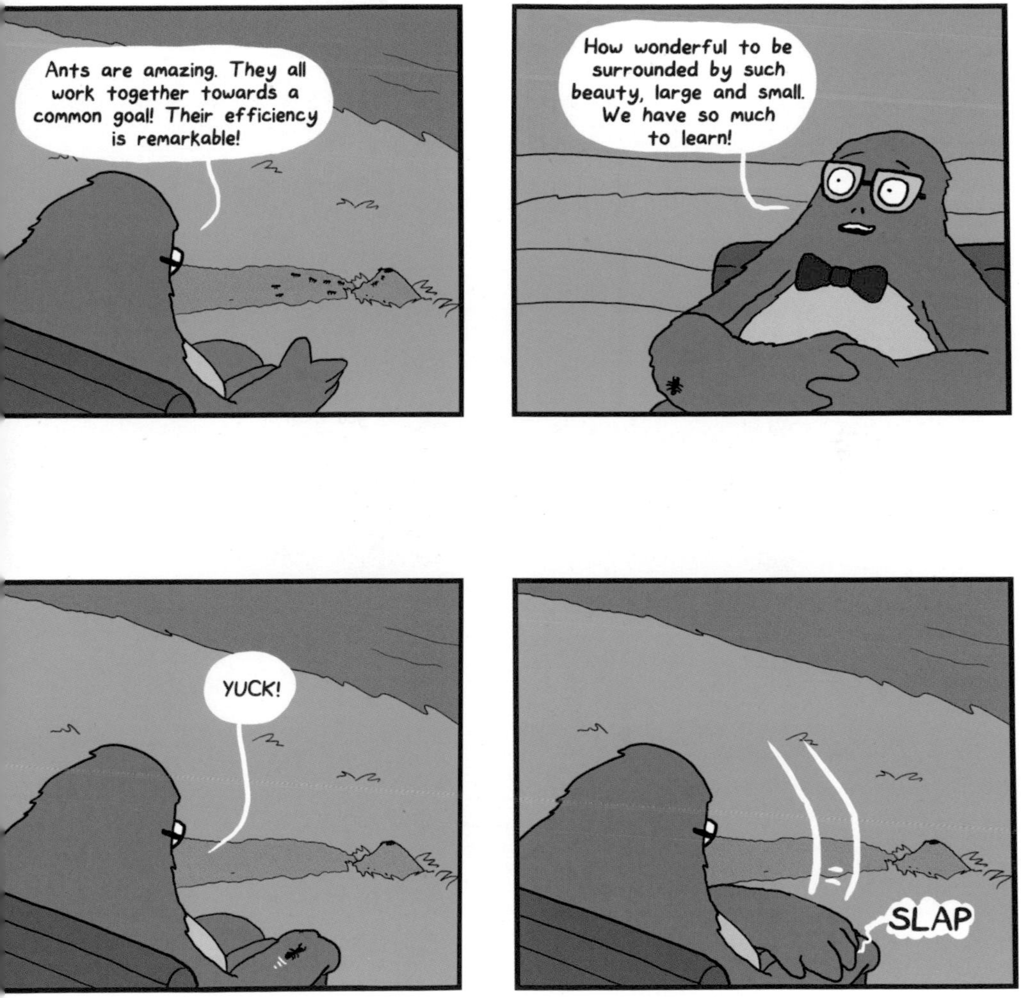
Ants are amazing. They all work together towards a common goal! Their efficiency is remarkable!
How wonderful to be surrounded by such beauty, large and small. We have so much to learn!
YUCK!
SLAP

Olympian

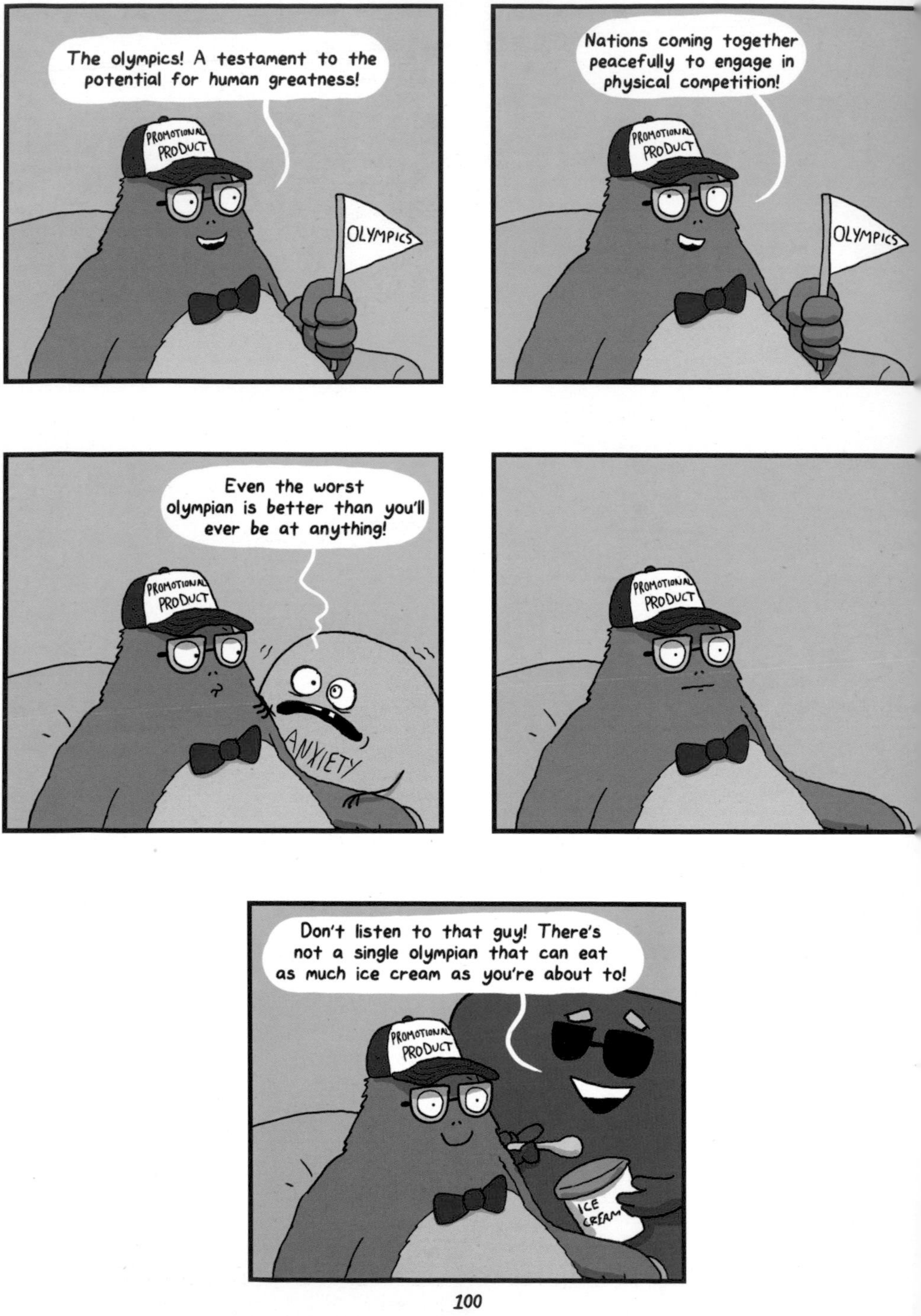
The olympics! A testament to the potential for human greatness!
PROMOTIONAL PRODUCT
OLYMPICS
Nations coming together peacefully to engage in physical competition!
PROMOTIONAL PRODUCT
OLYMPICS
Even the worst olympian is better than you'll ever be at anything!
PROMOTIONAL PRODUCT
ANXIETY
PROMOTIONAL PRODUCT
Don't listen to that guy! There's not a single olympian that can eat as much ice cream as you're about to!
PROMOTIONAL PRODUCT
ICE CREAM

Mortality

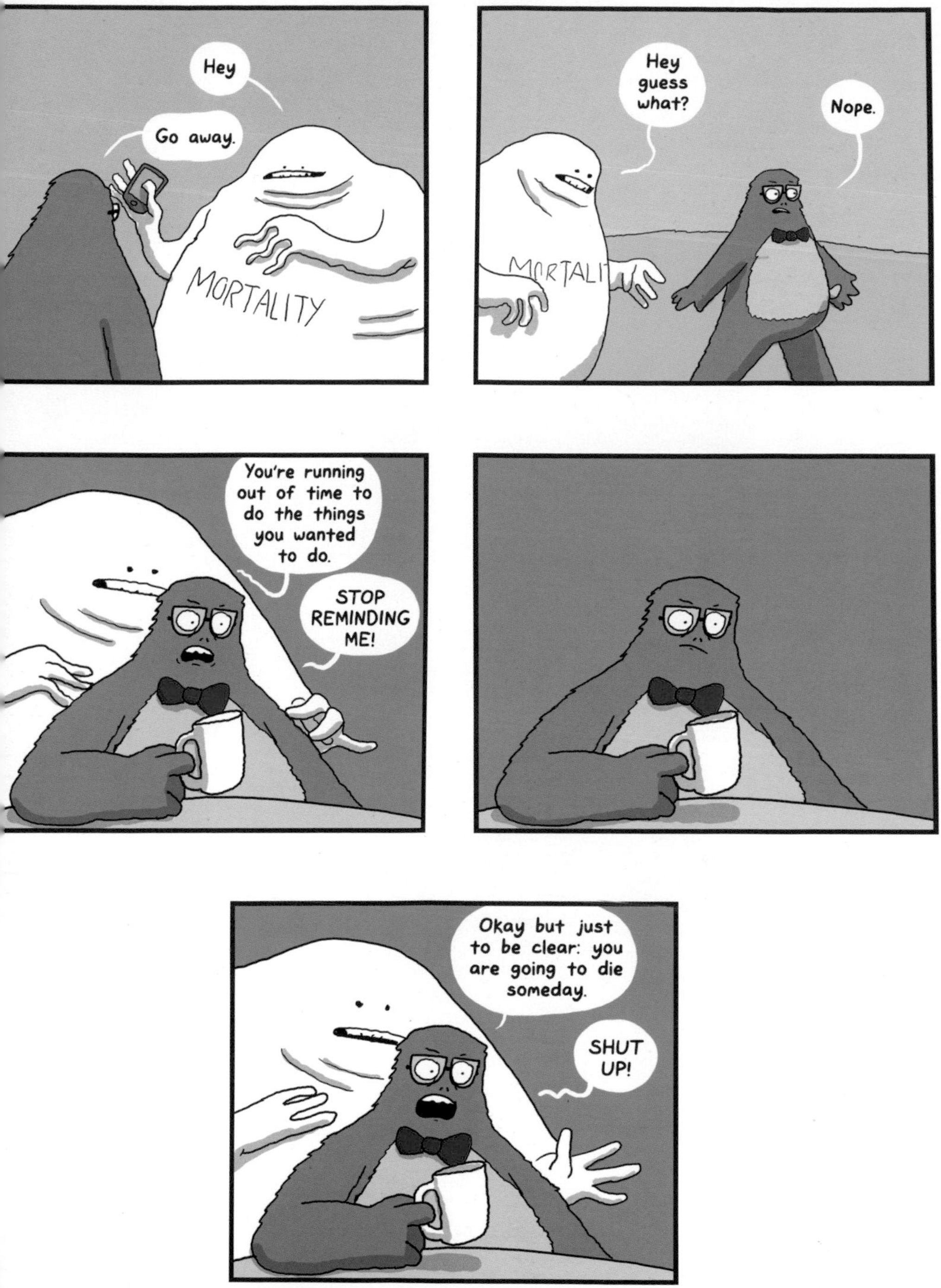
Hey
Go away.
MORTALITY
Hey guess what?
Nope.
You're running out of time to do the things you wanted to do.
STOP REMINDING ME!
Okay but just to be clear: you are going to die someday.
SHUT UP!

Mortality Part 2

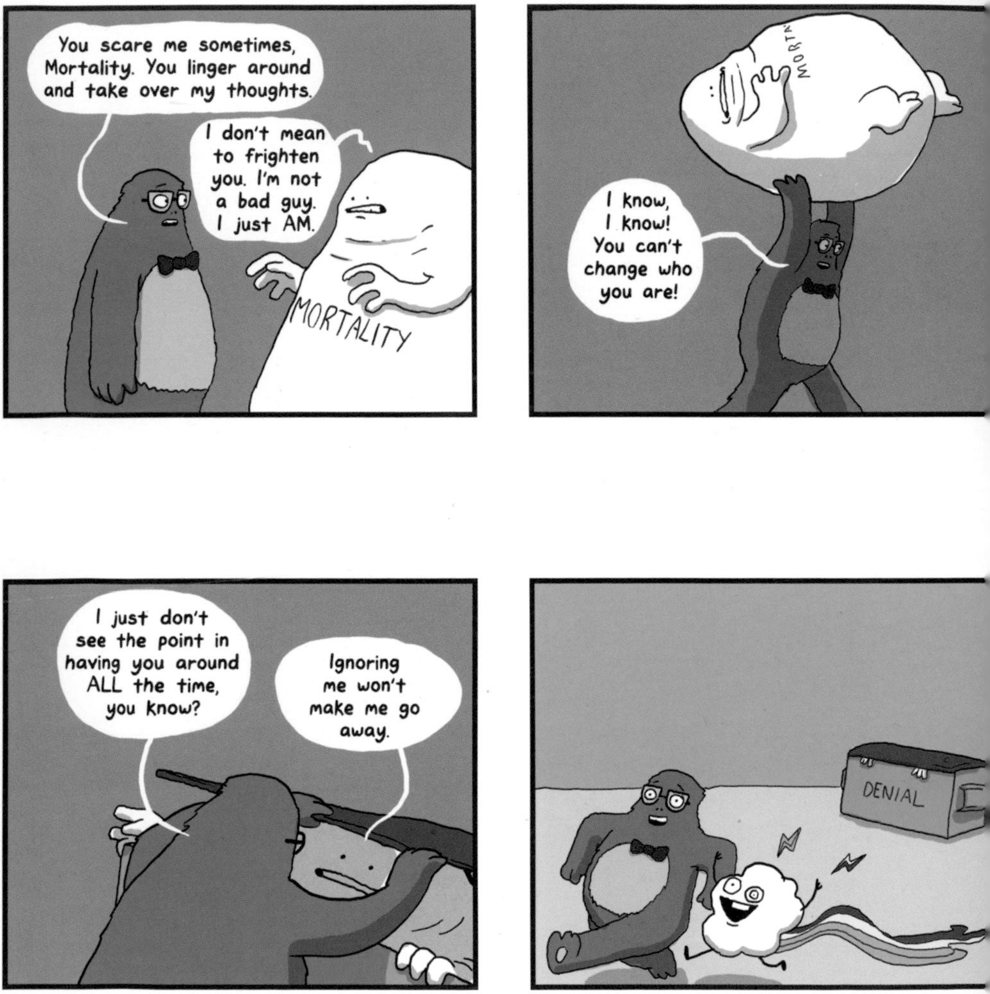
You scare me sometimes, Mortality. You linger around and take over my thoughts.
I don't mean to frighten you. I'm not a bad guy. I just AM.
MORTALITY
I know, I know! You can't change who you are!
I just don't see the point in having you around ALL the time, you know?
Ignoring me won't make me go away.
DENIAL

Relatively Problematic

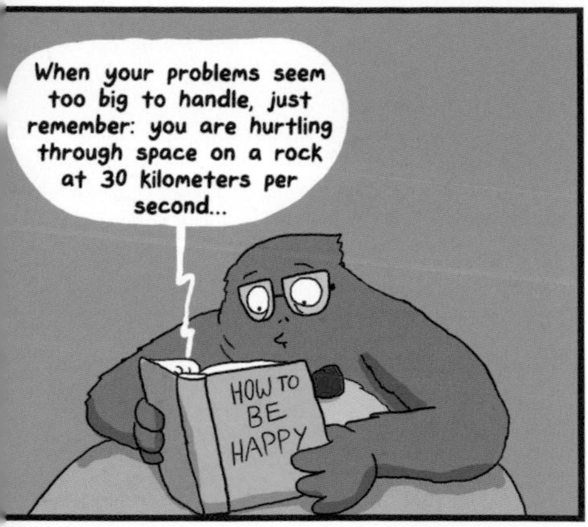
When your problems seem too big to handle, just remember: you are hurtling through space on a rock at 30 kilometers per second...
HOW TO BE HAPPY

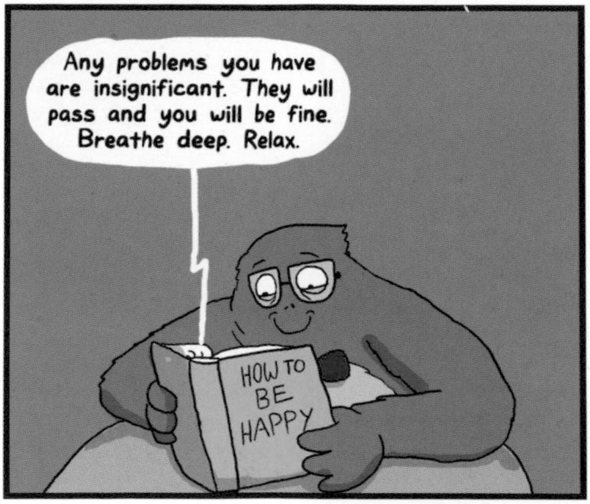
Any problems you have are insignificant. They will pass and you will be fine. Breathe deep. Relax.
HOW TO BE HAPPY

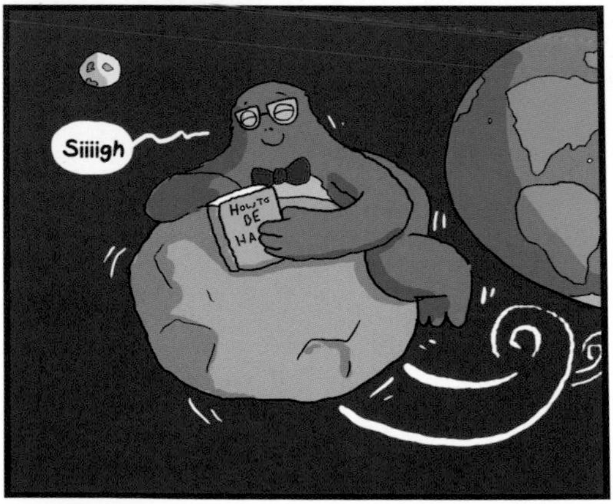
Siiiigh

The Nutritious Breakfast Crew!

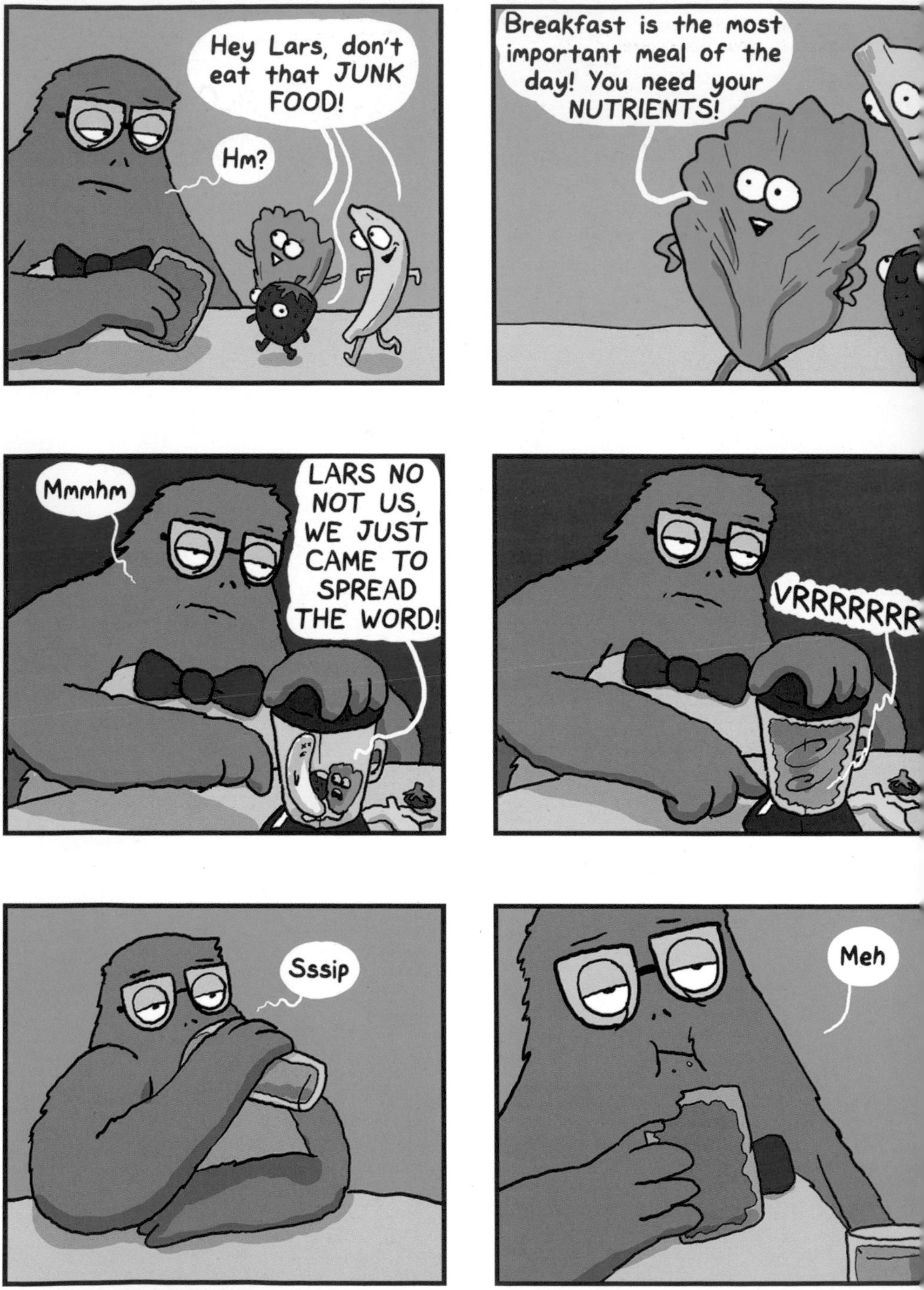

Hey Lars, don't eat that JUNK FOOD!
Hm?
Breakfast is the most important meal of the day! You need your NUTRIENTS!
Mmmhm
LARS NO NOT US, WE JUST CAME TO SPREAD THE WORD!
VRRRRRRR
Sssip
Meh

New Tricks

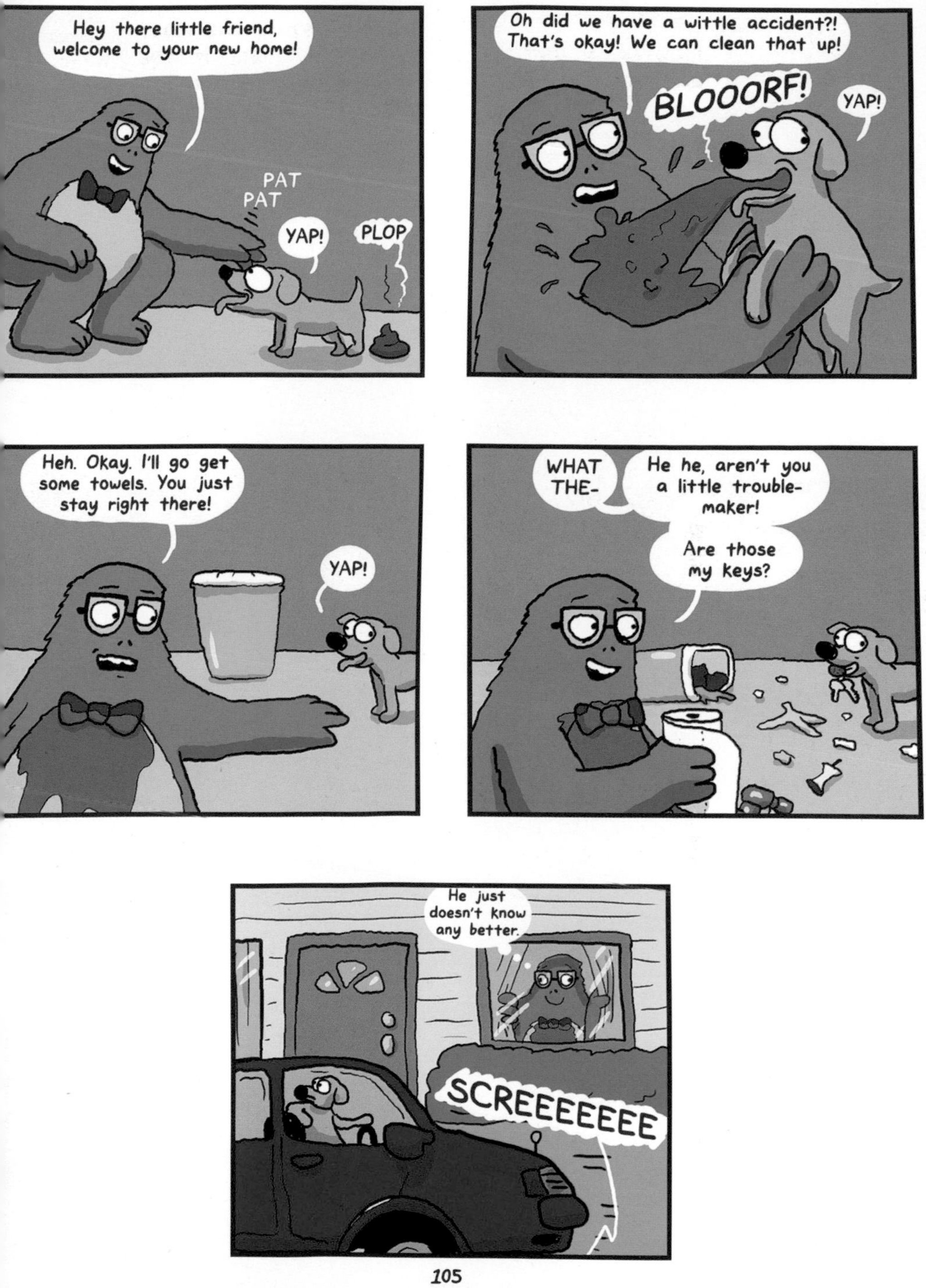
Hey there little friend, welcome to your new home!
PAT PAT
YAP!
PLOP
Oh did we have a wittle accident?! That's okay! We can clean that up!
BLOOORF!
YAP!
Heh. Okay. I'll go get some towels. You just stay right there!
YAP!
WHAT THE-
He he, aren't you a little trouble-maker!
Are those my keys?
He just doesn't know any better.
SCREEEEEEEE

New Friends

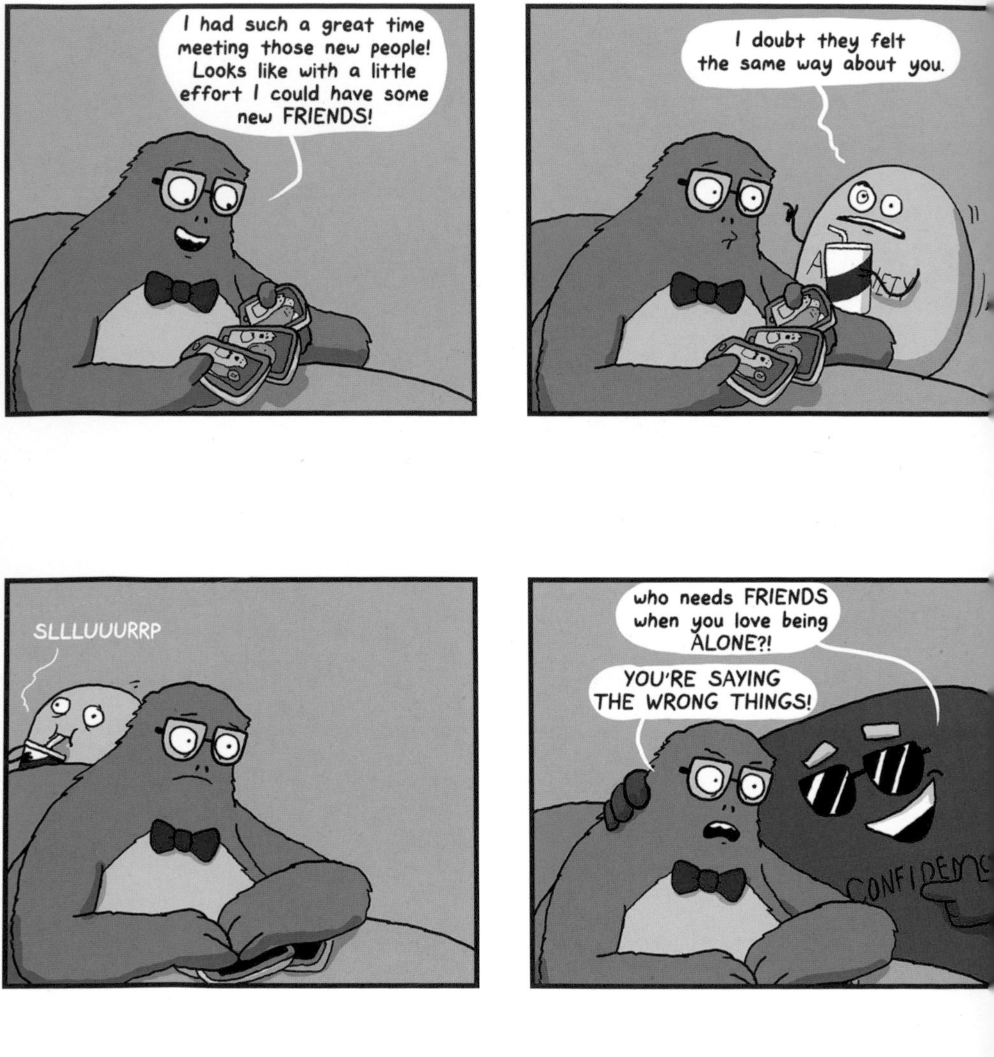
I had such a great time meeting those new people! Looks like with a little effort I could have some new FRIENDS!
I doubt they felt the same way about you.
SLLLUUURRP
who needs FRIENDS when you love being ALONE?!
YOU'RE SAYING THE WRONG THINGS!

Successfully Envied

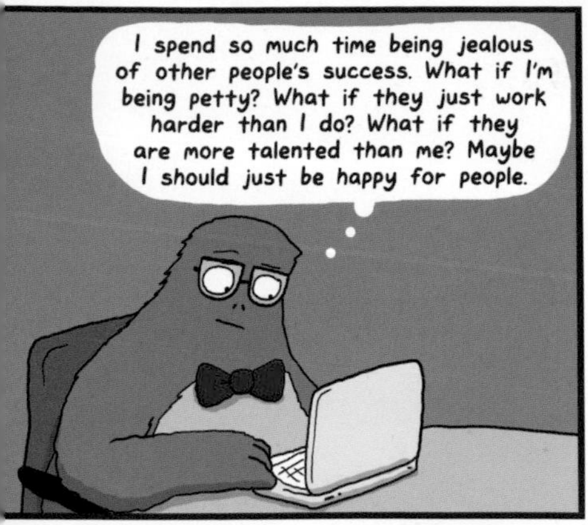
I spend so much time being jealous of other people's success. What if I'm being petty? What if they just work harder than I do? What if they are more talented than me? Maybe I should just be happy for people.

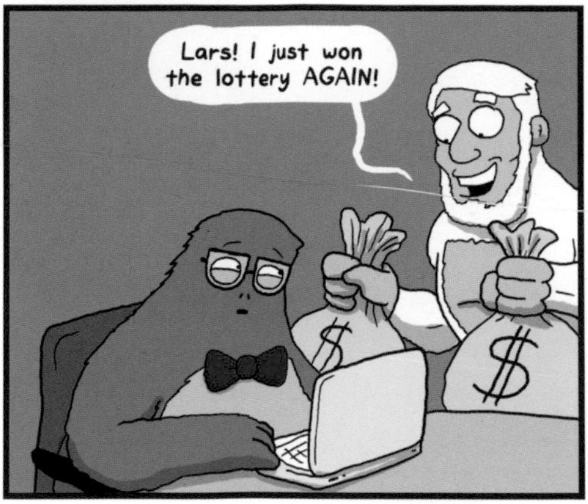
Lars! I just won the lottery AGAIN!

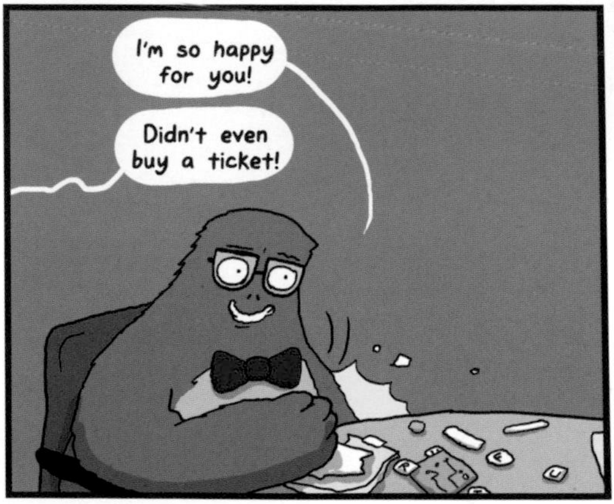
I'm so happy for you!
Didn't even buy a ticket!

Orange You Glad

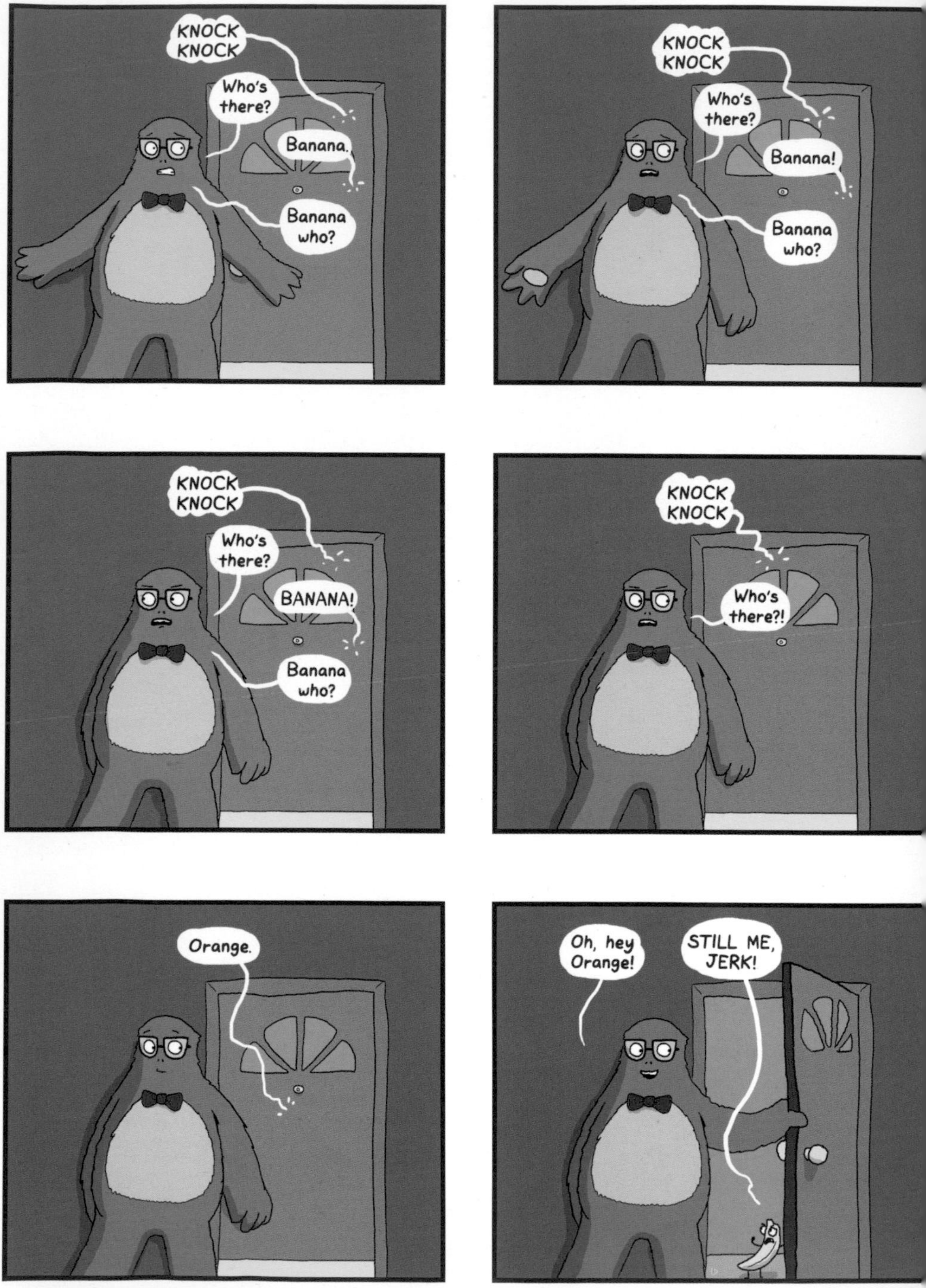
KNOCK KNOCK
Who's there?
Banana.
Banana who?
KNOCK KNOCK
Who's there?
Banana!
Banana who?
KNOCK KNOCK
Who's there?
BANANA!
Banana who?
KNOCK KNOCK
Who's there?!
Orange.
Oh, hey Orange!
STILL ME, JERK!

Surprise!

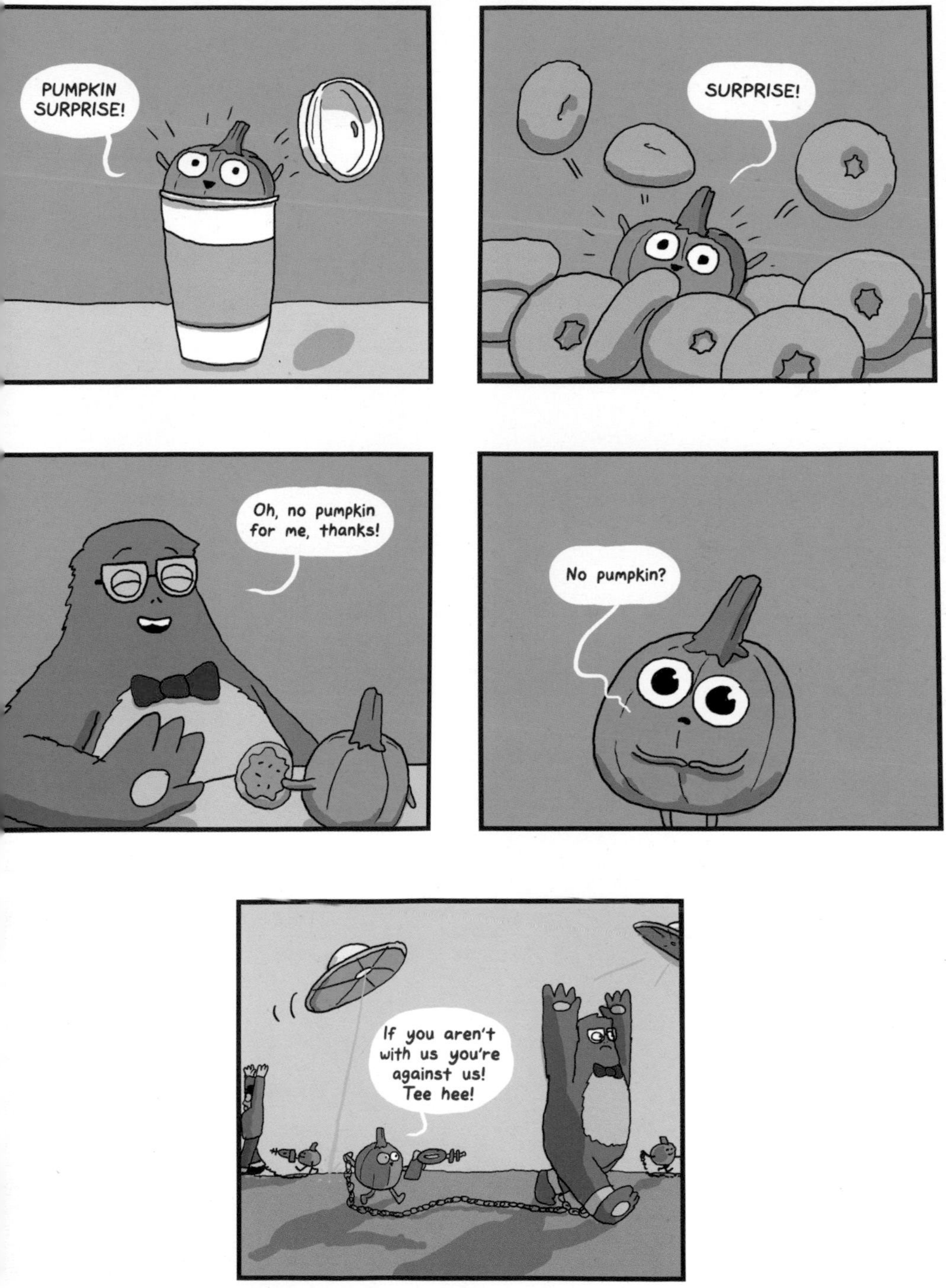
PUMPKIN SURPRISE!
SURPRISE!
Oh, no pumpkin for me, thanks!
No pumpkin?
If you aren't with us you're against us! Tee hee!

Use as Directed

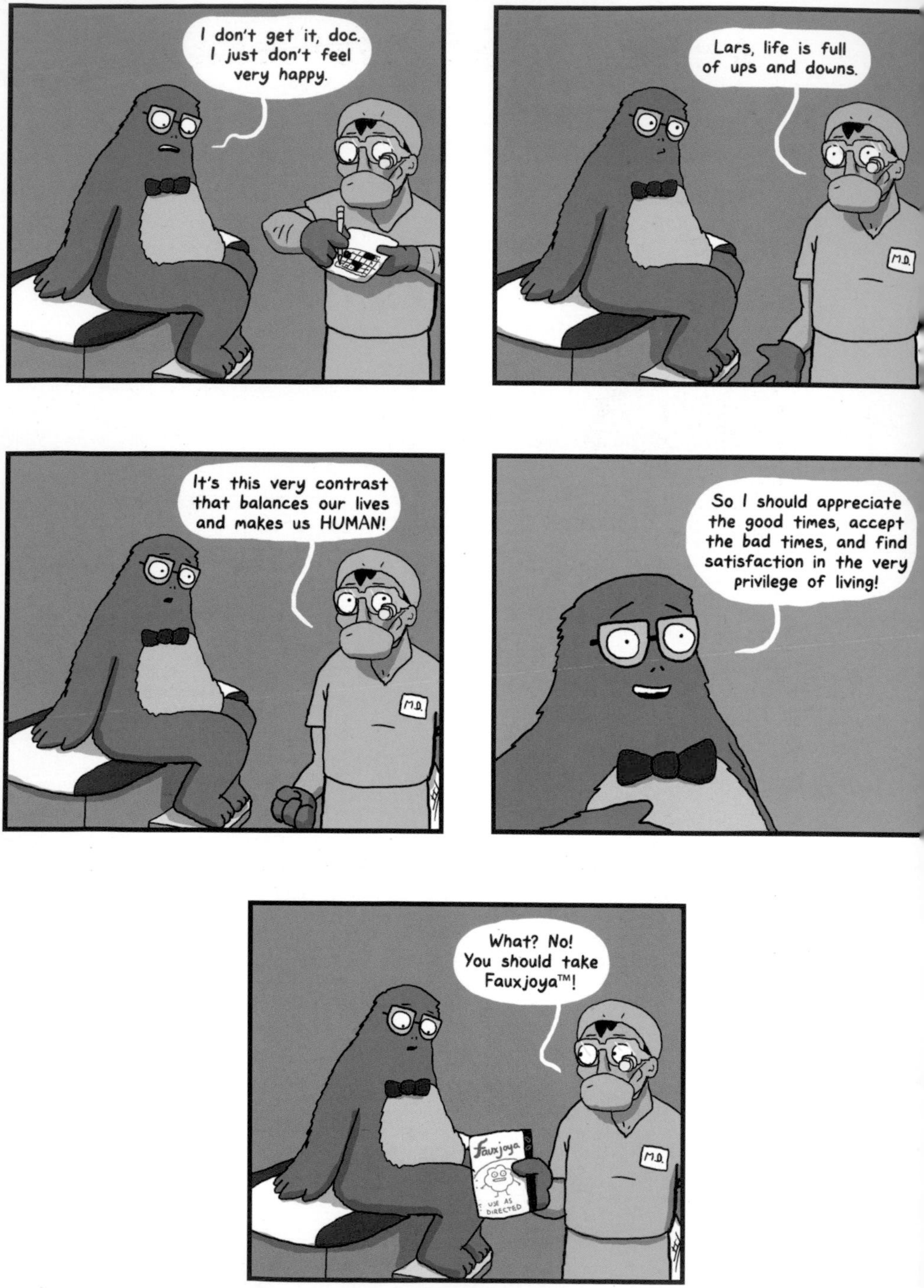
I don't get it, doc. I just don't feel very happy.
Lars, life is full of ups and downs.
It's this very contrast that balances our lives and makes us HUMAN!
So I should appreciate the good times, accept the bad times, and find satisfaction in the very privilege of living!
What? No! You should take Fauxjoya™!
Fauxjoya
USE AS DIRECTED

A Message From Lars to Humans

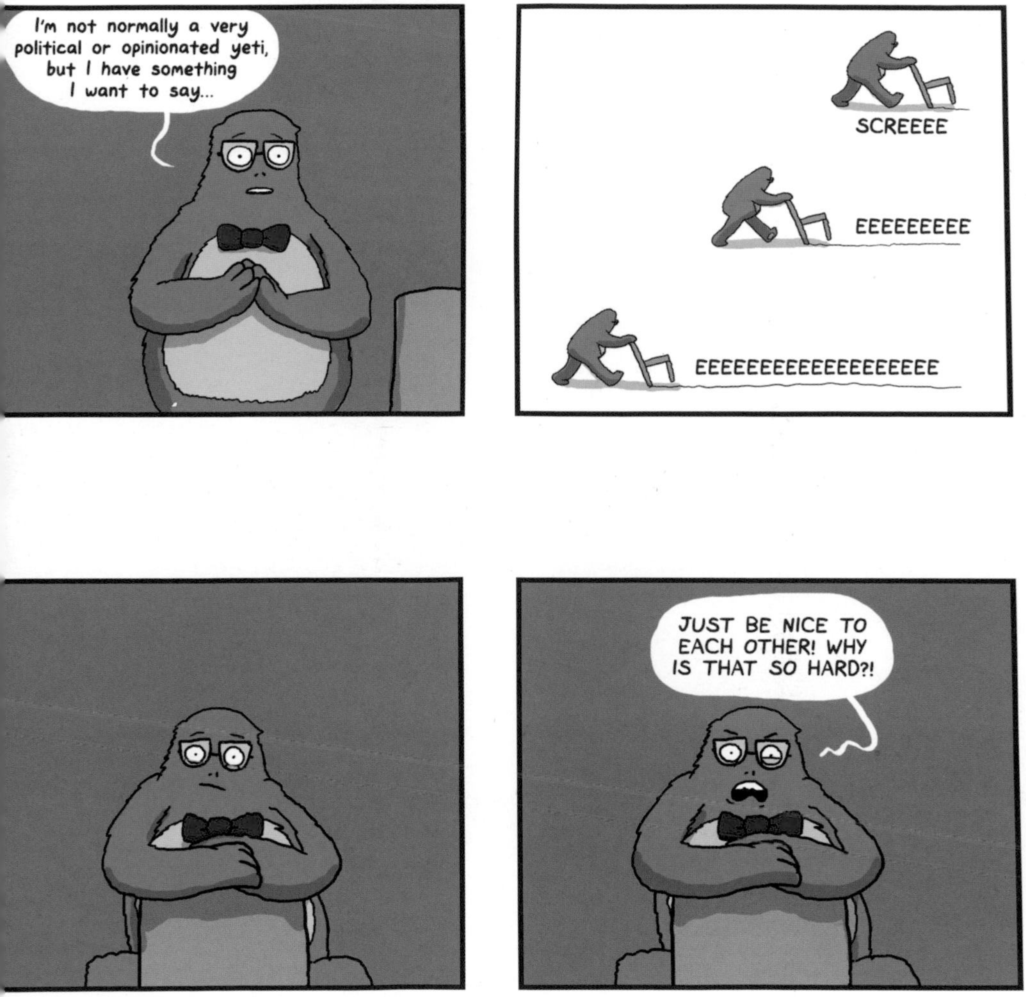
I'm not normally a very political or opinionated yeti, but I have something I want to say...
SCREEEE
EEEEEEEEE
EEEEEEEEEEEEEEEEEE
JUST BE NICE TO EACH OTHER! WHY IS THAT SO HARD?!

Seasons Change

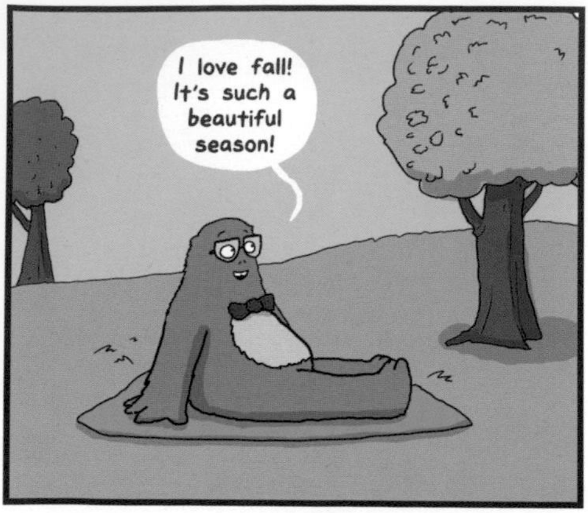
I love fall! It's such a beautiful season!

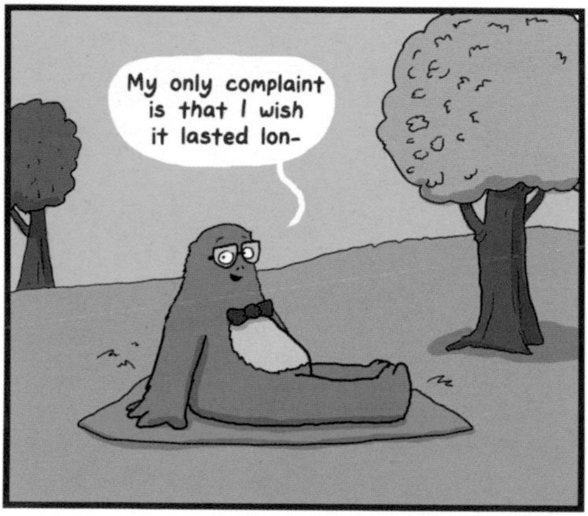
My only complaint is that I wish it lasted lon-

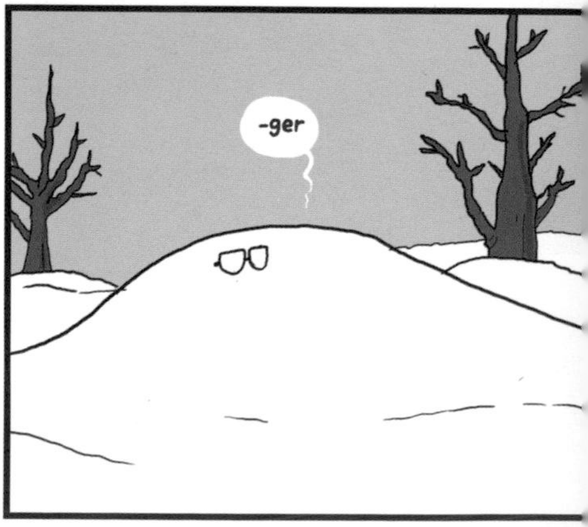
-ger

Affected

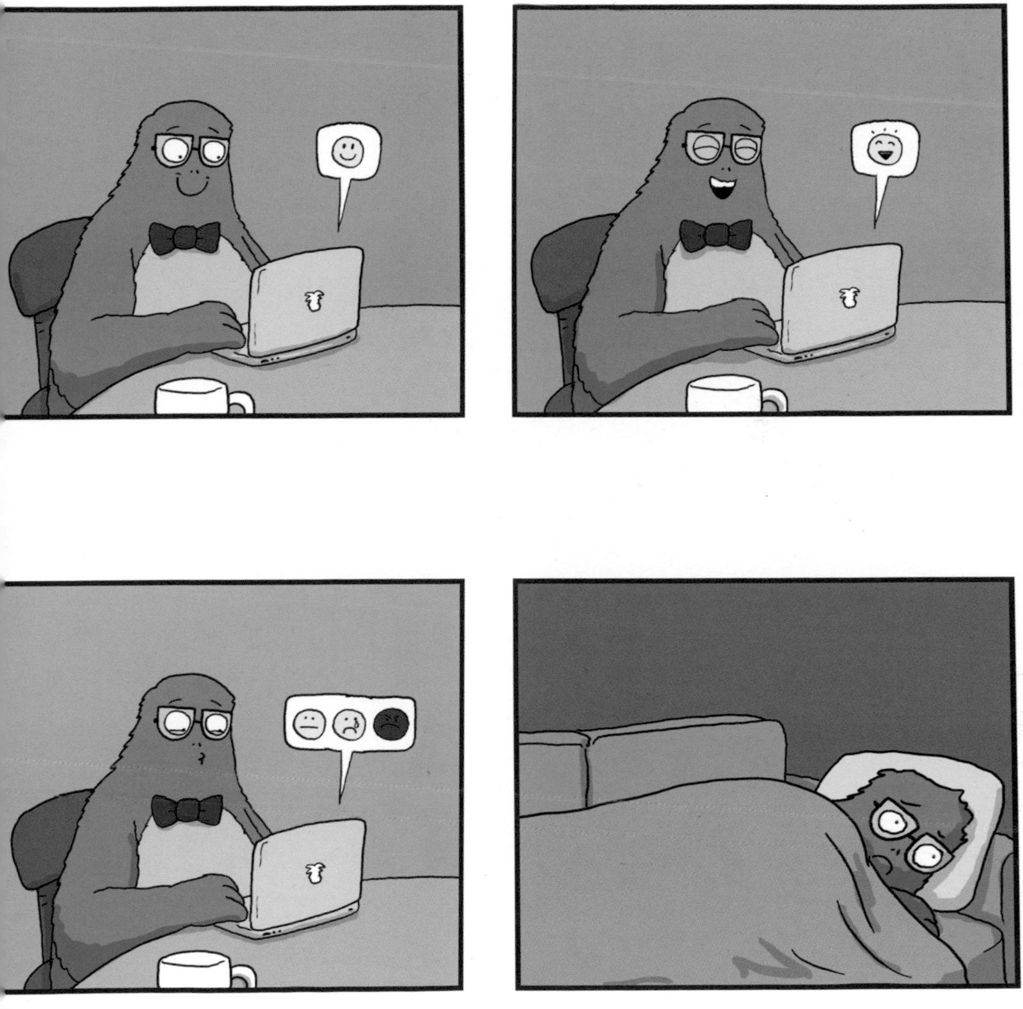

Sharing Music

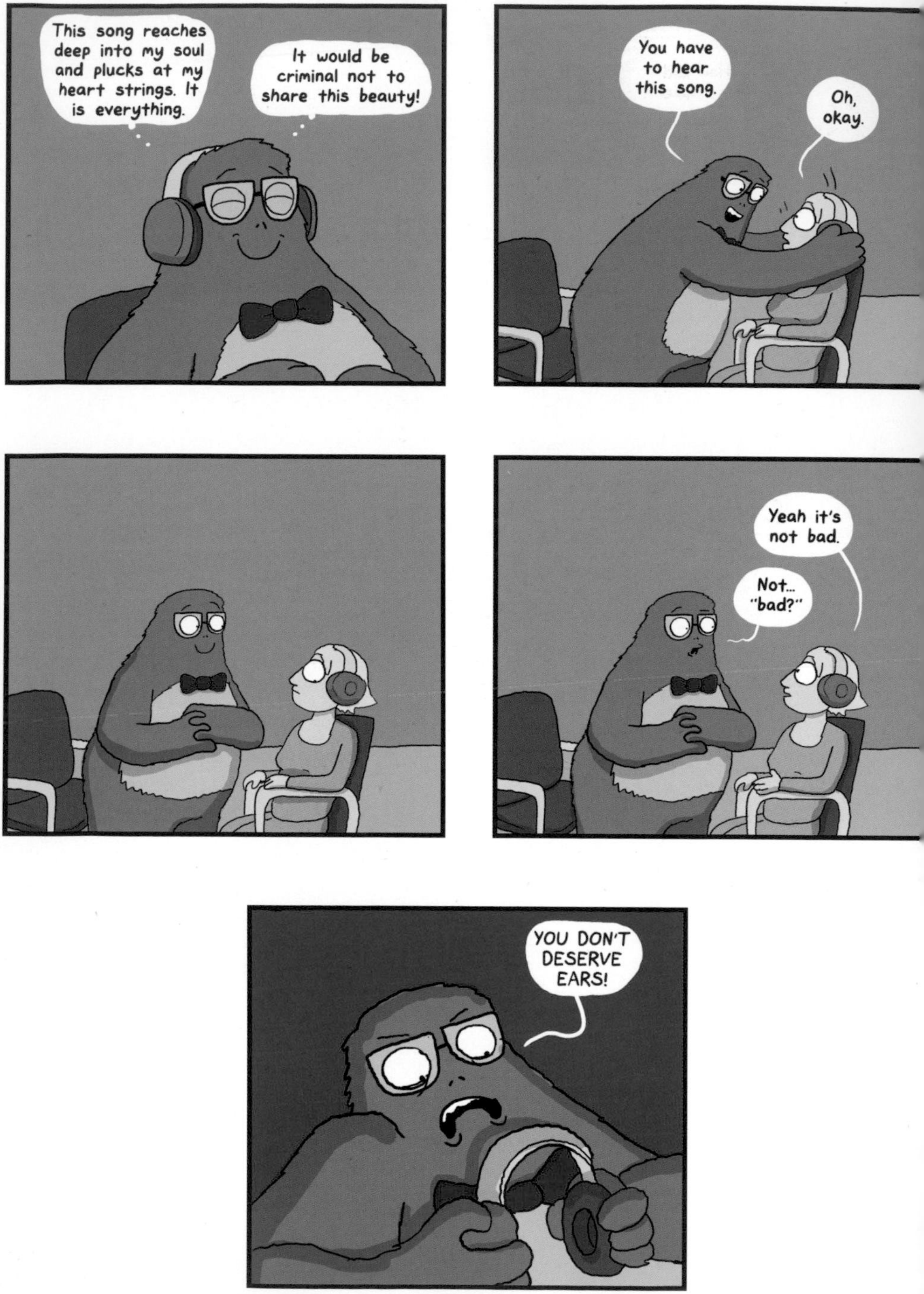
This song reaches deep into my soul and plucks at my heart strings. It is everything.
It would be criminal not to share this beauty!
You have to hear this song.
Oh, okay.
Yeah it's not bad.
Not... "bad?"
YOU DON'T DESERVE EARS!

Financial Amnesia

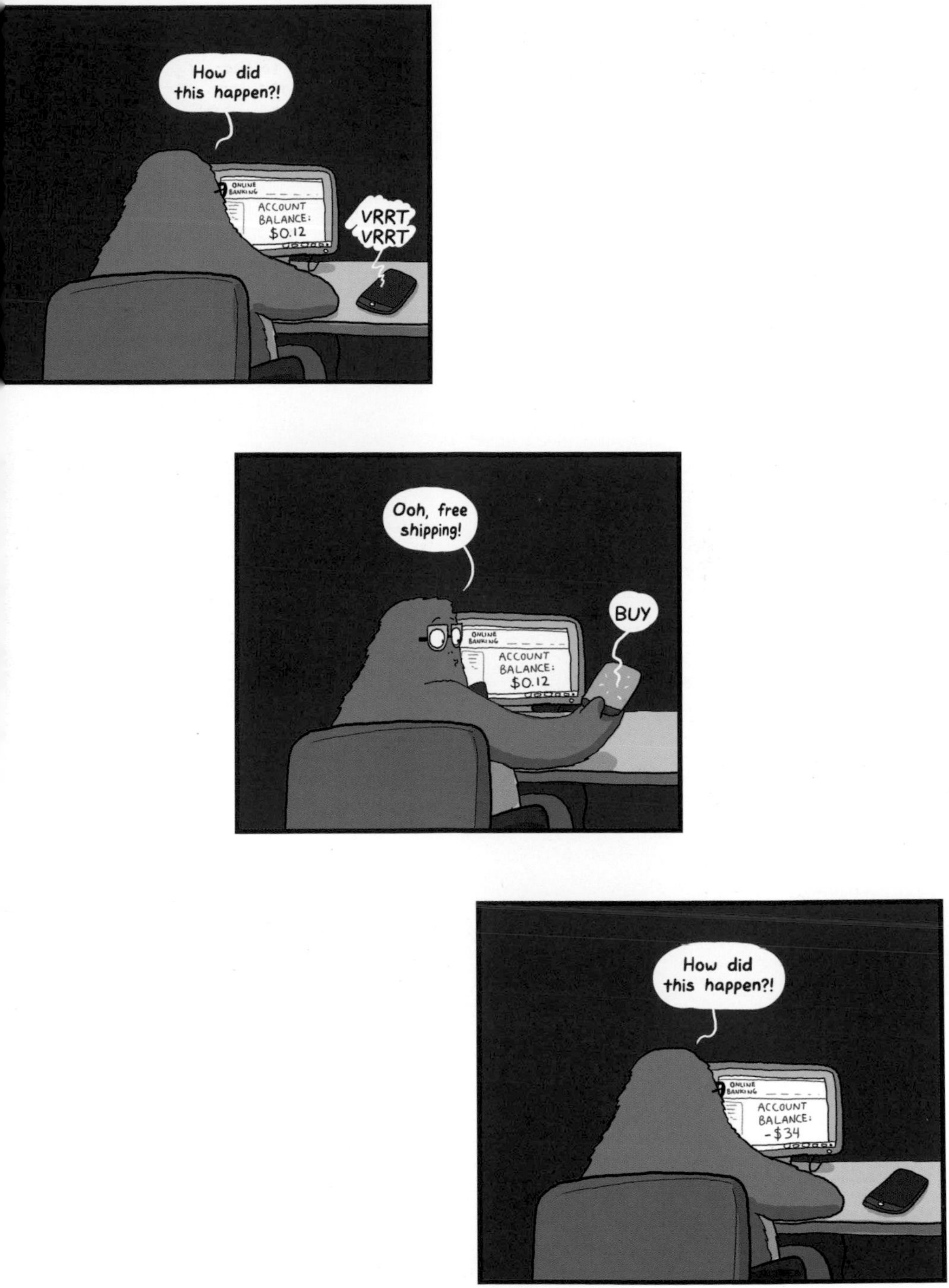
How did this happen?!
ONLINE BANKING
ACCOUNT BALANCE: $0.12
VRRT VRRT
Ooh, free shipping!
ONLINE BANKING
ACCOUNT BALANCE: $0.12
BUY
How did this happen?!
ONLINE BANKING
ACCOUNT BALANCE: -$34

Cold Months

Oops! Summer is over and I forgot to consider getting in shape.

Lars, buddy, don't worry about all that! You're about to go into HIBERNATION!
Hibernation?

Crawl into your cave and gain all of the weight you want! Nobody will ever know!
Yay!

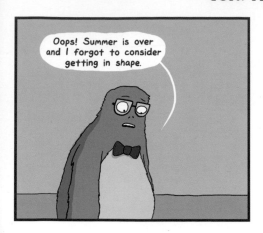

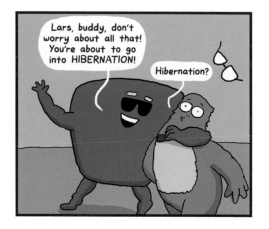

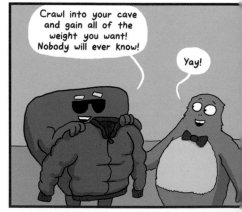

Good Advice

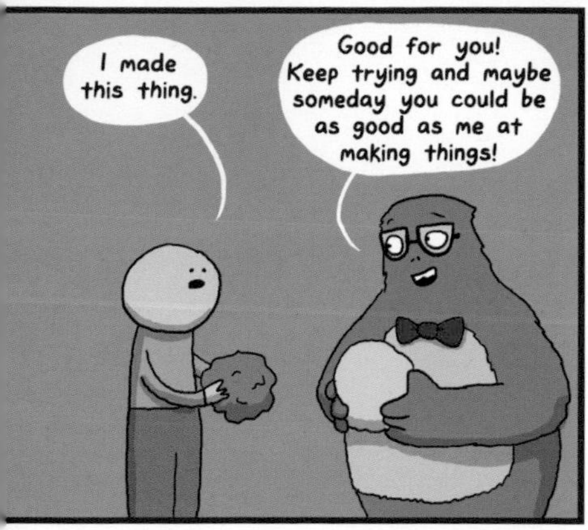

I made this thing.
Good for you! Keep trying and maybe someday you could be as good as me at making things!

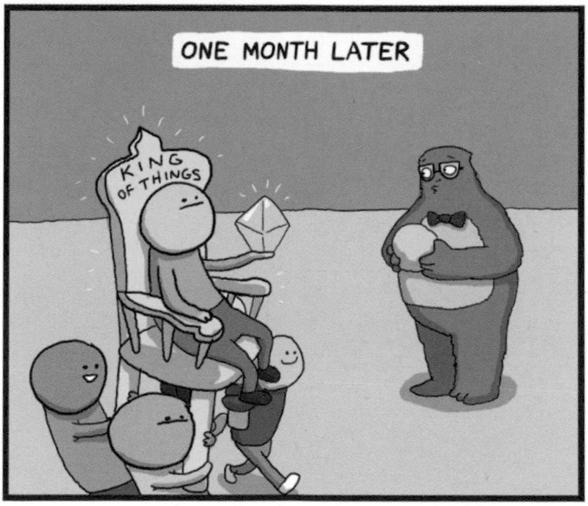

ONE MONTH LATER
KING OF THINGS

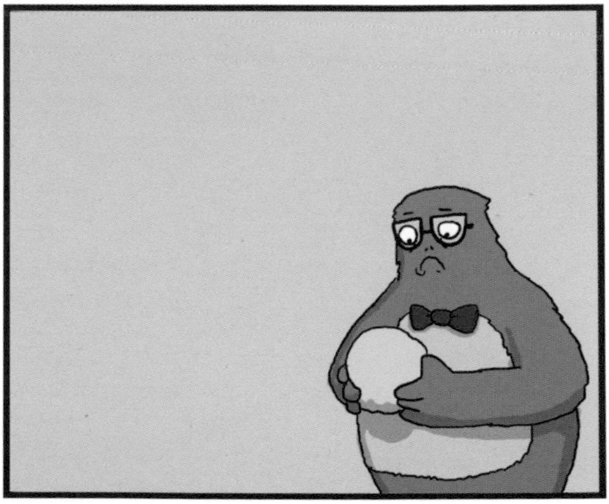

Anxiety Reform

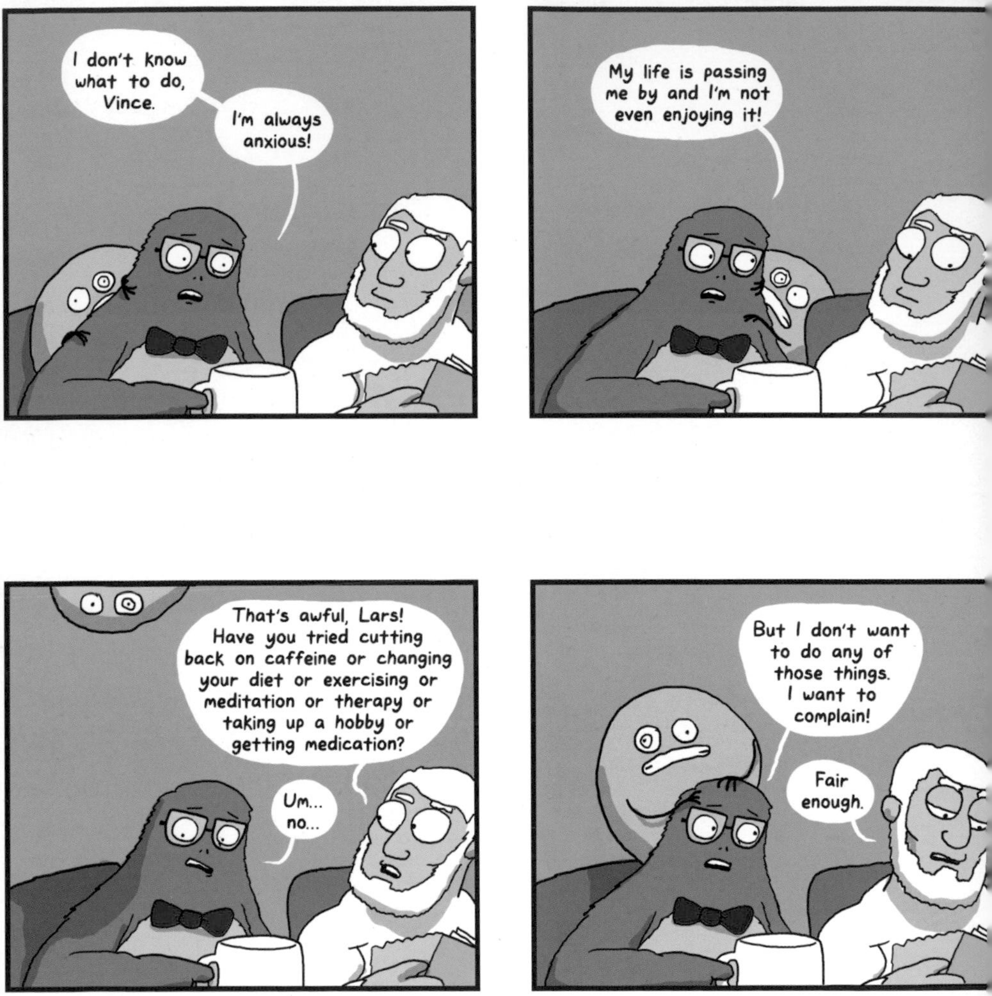
I don't know what to do, Vince.
I'm always anxious!
My life is passing me by and I'm not even enjoying it!
That's awful, Lars! Have you tried cutting back on caffeine or changing your diet or exercising or meditation or therapy or taking up a hobby or getting medication?
Um... no...
But I don't want to do any of those things. I want to complain!
Fair enough.

What Lies Beneath

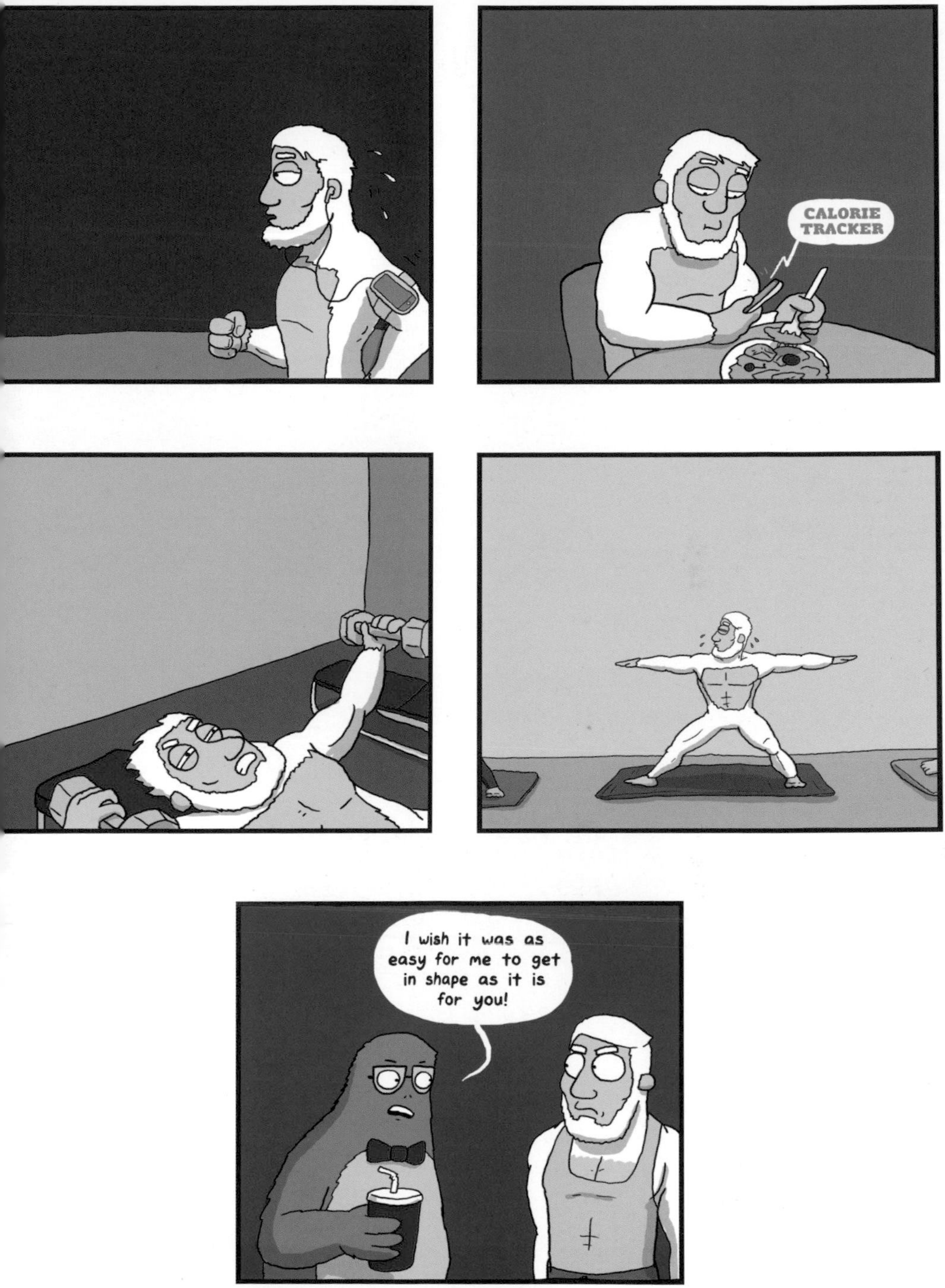
CALORIE TRACKER
I wish it was as easy for me to get in shape as it is for you!

A Quick Meditation

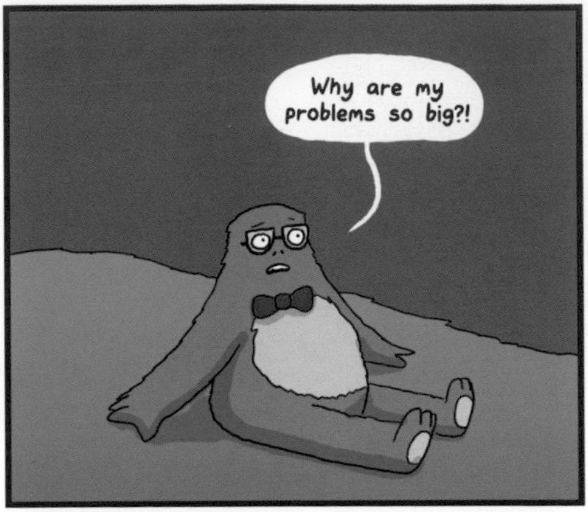
Why are my problems so big?!

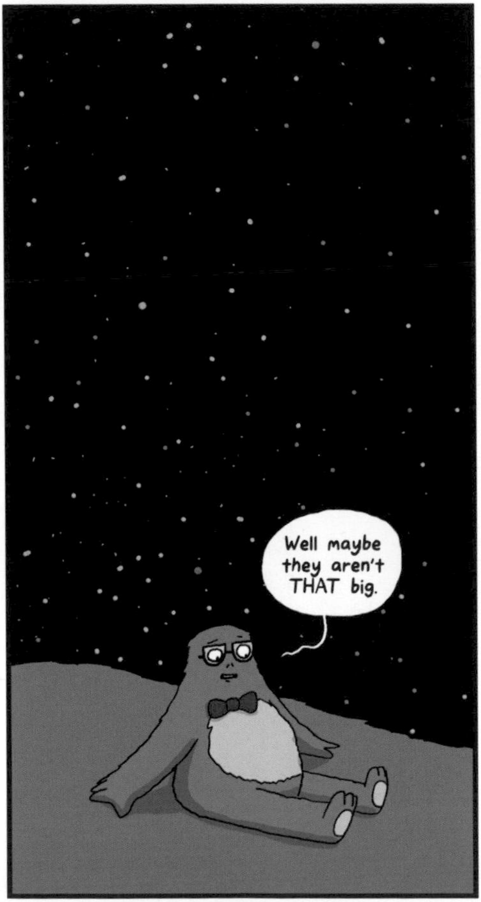
Well maybe they aren't THAT big.

Train of Thought

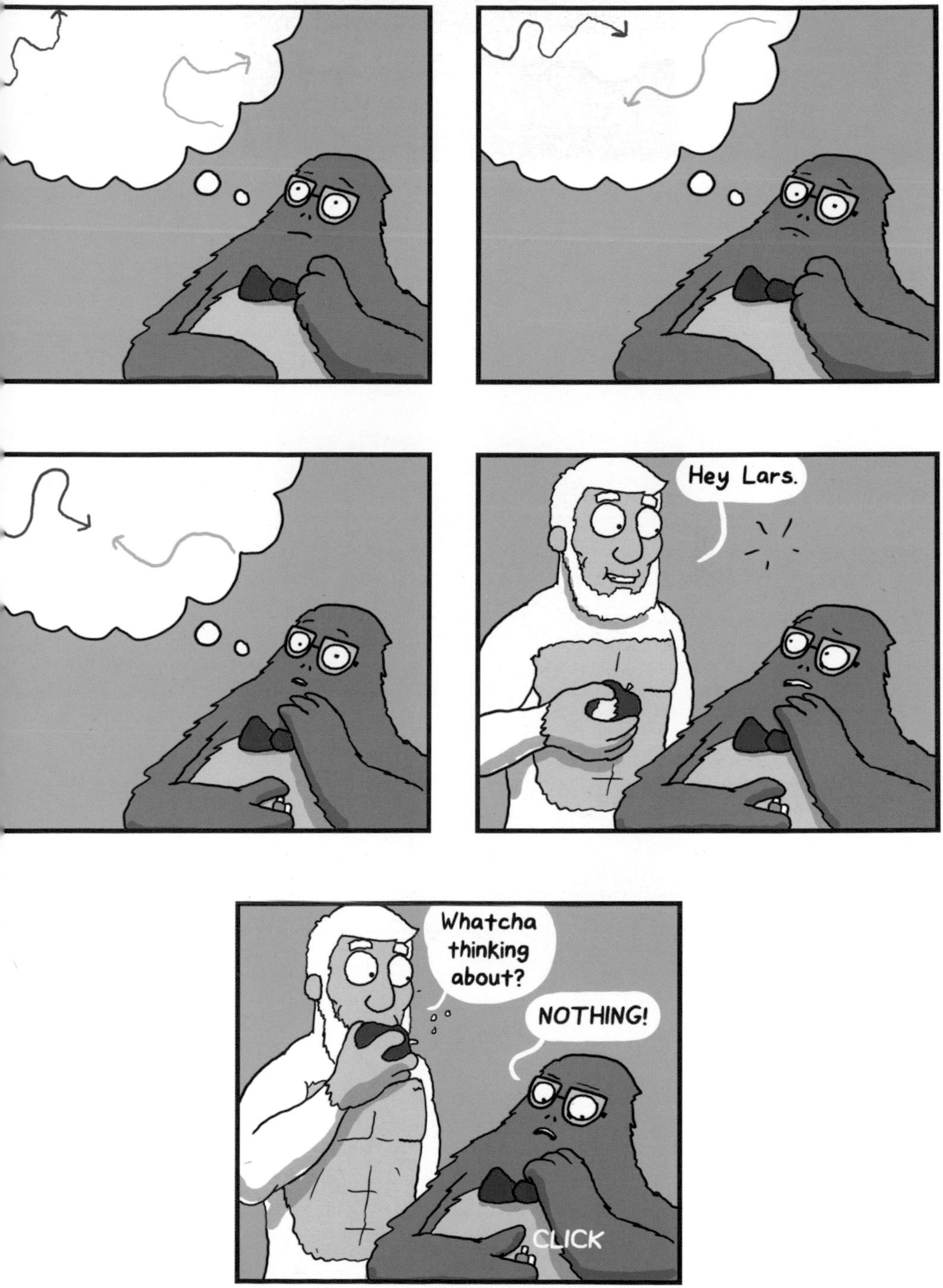
Hey Lars.
Whatcha thinking about?
NOTHING!
CLICK

The Cameo

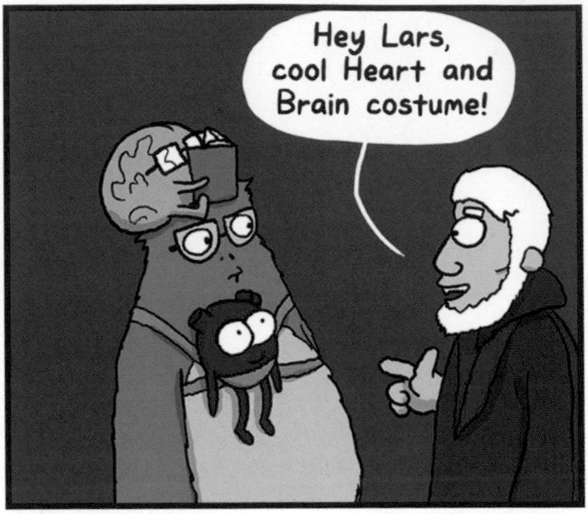
Hey Lars, cool Heart and Brain costume!

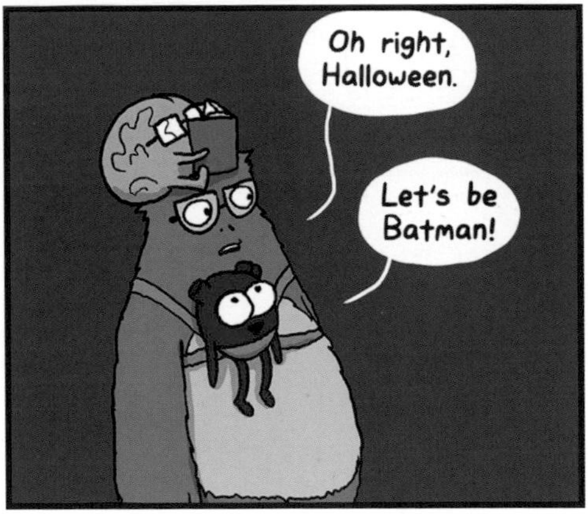
Oh right, Halloween.
Let's be Batman!

Awkward

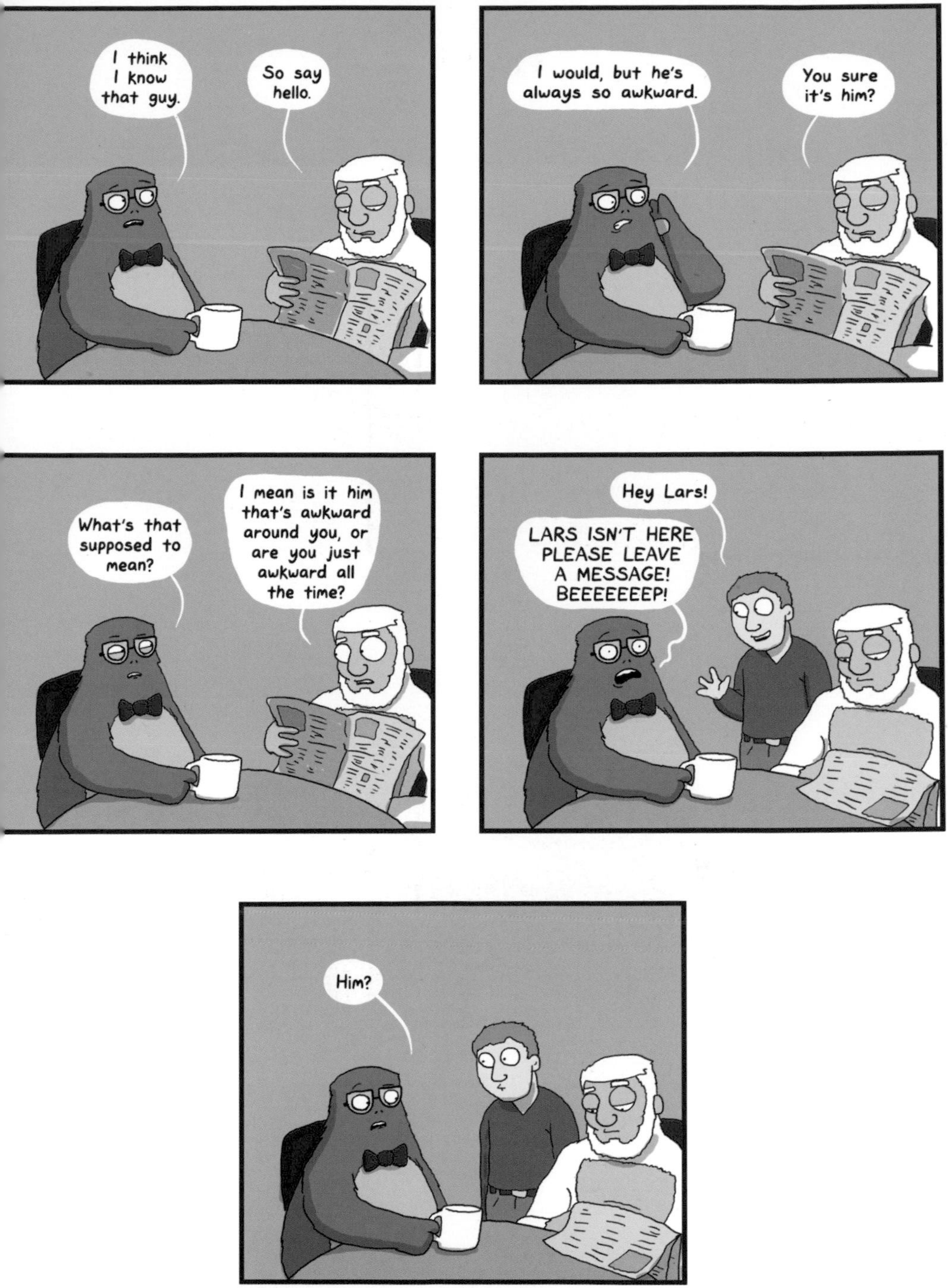
I think I know that guy.
So say hello.
I would, but he's always so awkward.
You sure it's him?
What's that supposed to mean?
I mean is it him that's awkward around you, or are you just awkward all the time?
Hey Lars!
LARS ISN'T HERE PLEASE LEAVE A MESSAGE! BEEEEEEEP!
Him?

Bonus Classics

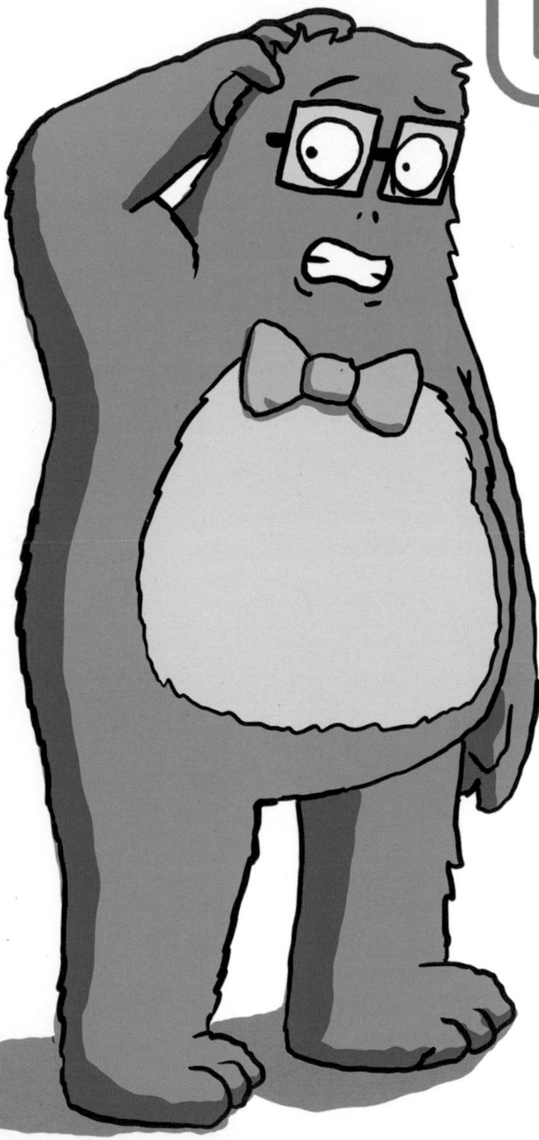

Pen Pal

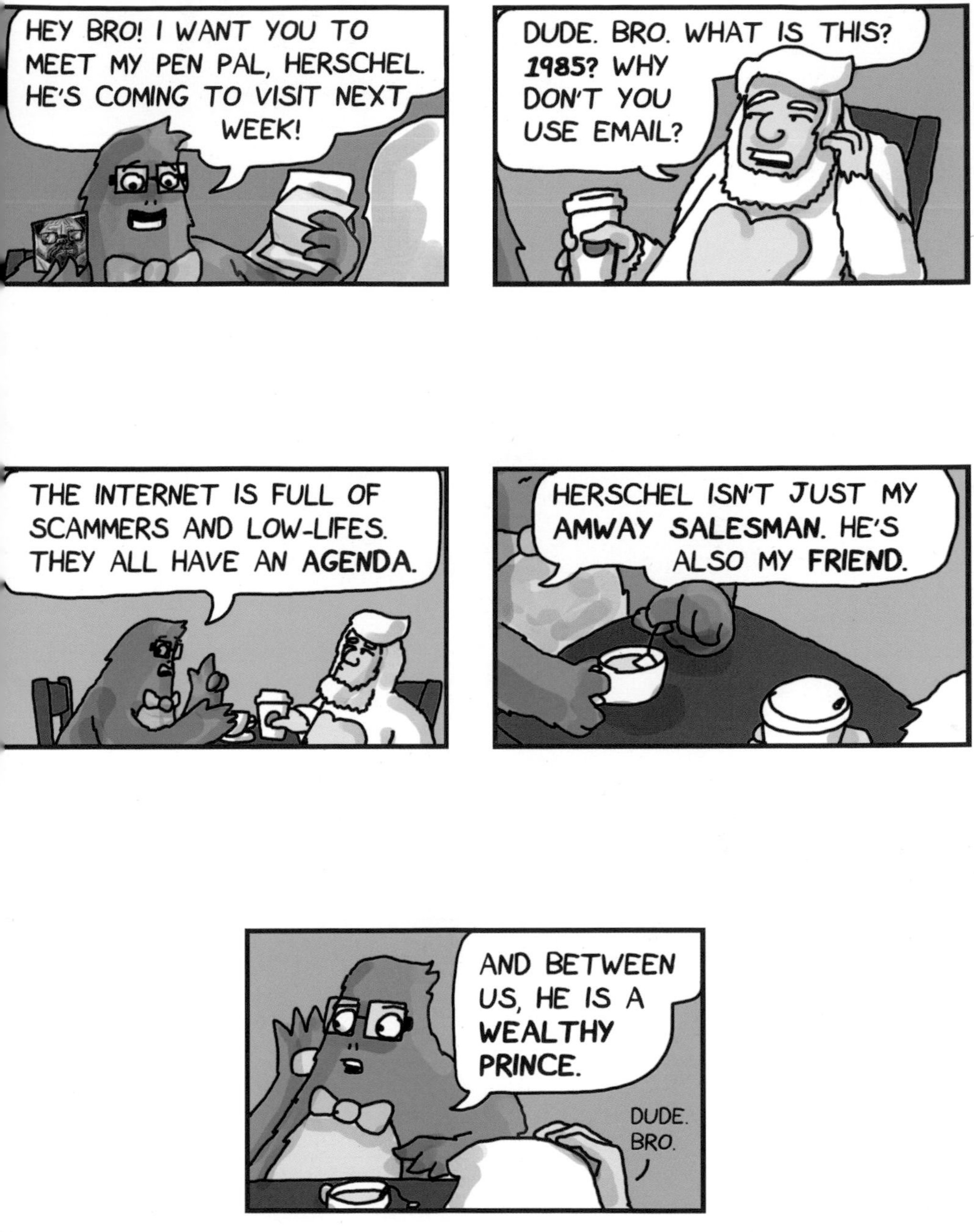
HEY BRO! I WANT YOU TO MEET MY PEN PAL, HERSCHEL. HE'S COMING TO VISIT NEXT WEEK!
DUDE. BRO. WHAT IS THIS? 1985? WHY DON'T YOU USE EMAIL?
THE INTERNET IS FULL OF SCAMMERS AND LOW-LIFES. THEY ALL HAVE AN AGENDA.
HERSCHEL ISN'T JUST MY AMWAY SALESMAN. HE'S ALSO MY FRIEND.
AND BETWEEN US, HE IS A WEALTHY PRINCE.
DUDE. BRO.

Herschel The Pug

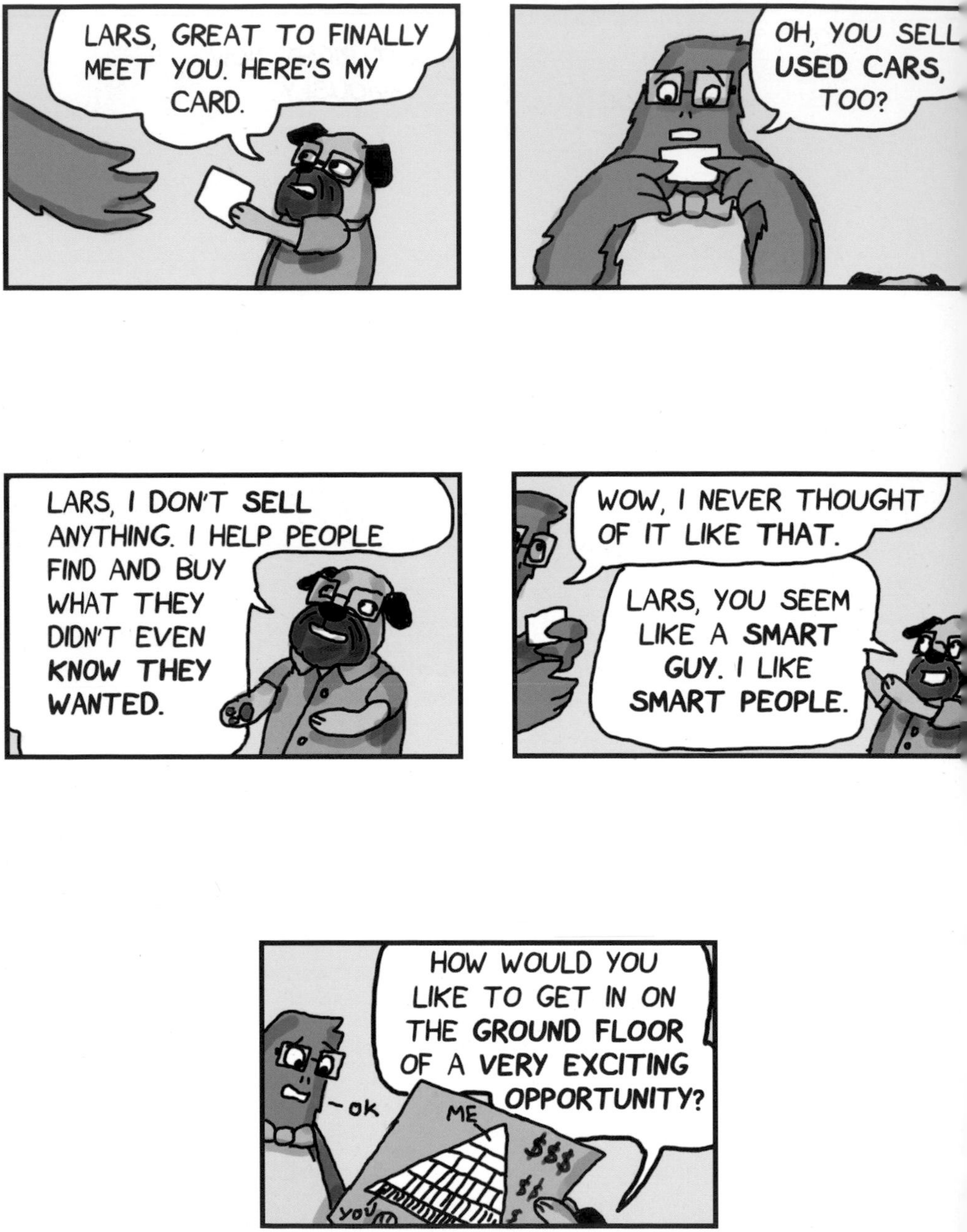

LARS, GREAT TO FINALLY MEET YOU. HERE'S MY CARD.
OH, YOU SELL USED CARS, TOO?
LARS, I DON'T SELL ANYTHING. I HELP PEOPLE FIND AND BUY WHAT THEY DIDN'T EVEN KNOW THEY WANTED.
WOW, I NEVER THOUGHT OF IT LIKE THAT.
LARS, YOU SEEM LIKE A SMART GUY. I LIKE SMART PEOPLE.
HOW WOULD YOU LIKE TO GET IN ON THE GROUND FLOOR OF A VERY EXCITING OPPORTUNITY?
—ok
ME
$$$
YOU

The Smooth Recovery

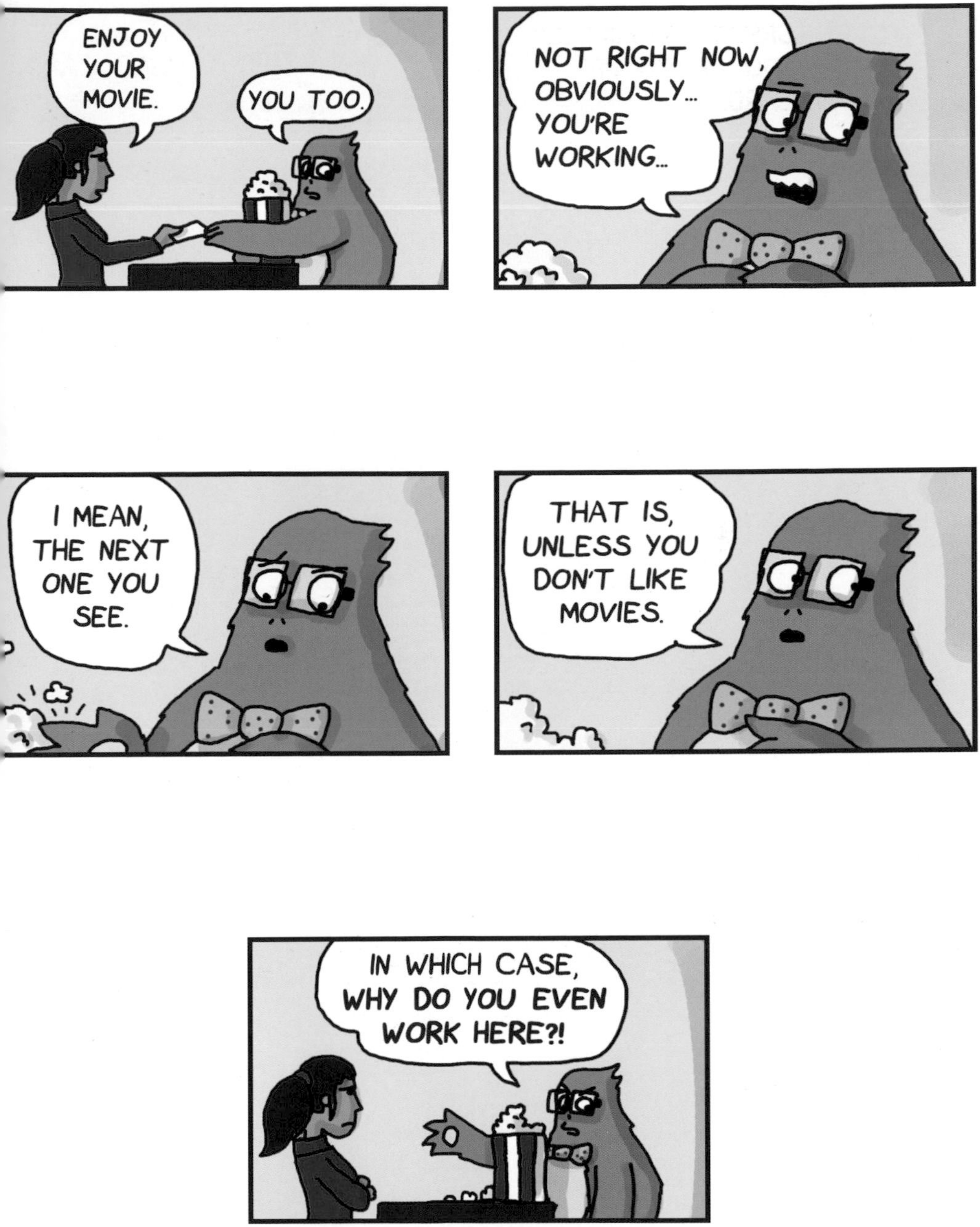
ENJOY YOUR MOVIE.
YOU TOO.
NOT RIGHT NOW, OBVIOUSLY... YOU'RE WORKING...
I MEAN, THE NEXT ONE YOU SEE.
THAT IS, UNLESS YOU DON'T LIKE MOVIES.
IN WHICH CASE, WHY DO YOU EVEN WORK HERE?!

The Ball

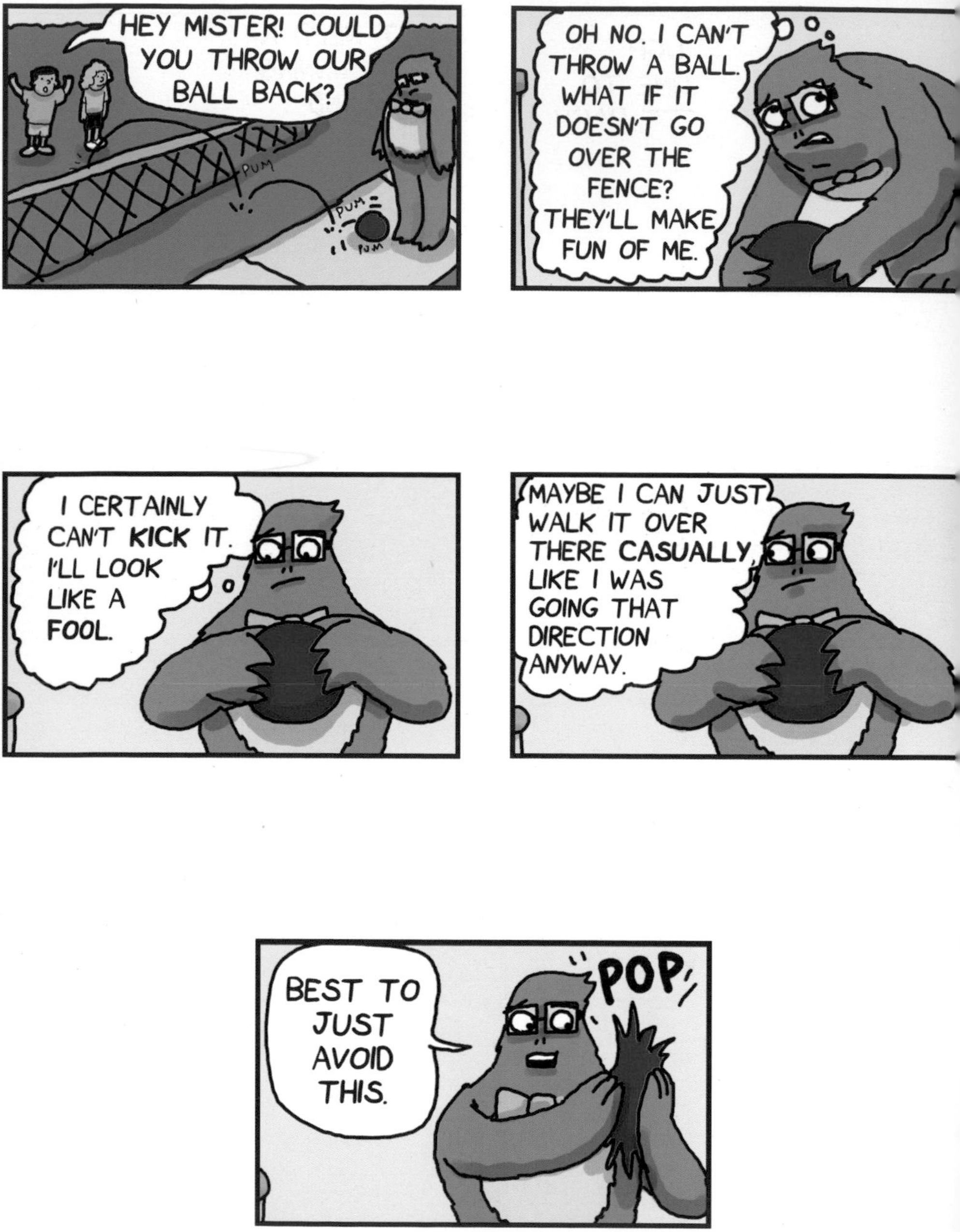

HEY MISTER! COULD YOU THROW OUR BALL BACK?
PUM
PUM
PUM
OH NO. I CAN'T THROW A BALL. WHAT IF IT DOESN'T GO OVER THE FENCE? THEY'LL MAKE FUN OF ME.
I CERTAINLY CAN'T **KICK** IT. I'LL LOOK LIKE A **FOOL**.
MAYBE I CAN JUST WALK IT OVER THERE **CASUALLY**, LIKE I WAS GOING THAT DIRECTION ANYWAY.
BEST TO JUST AVOID THIS.
POP

Running Season

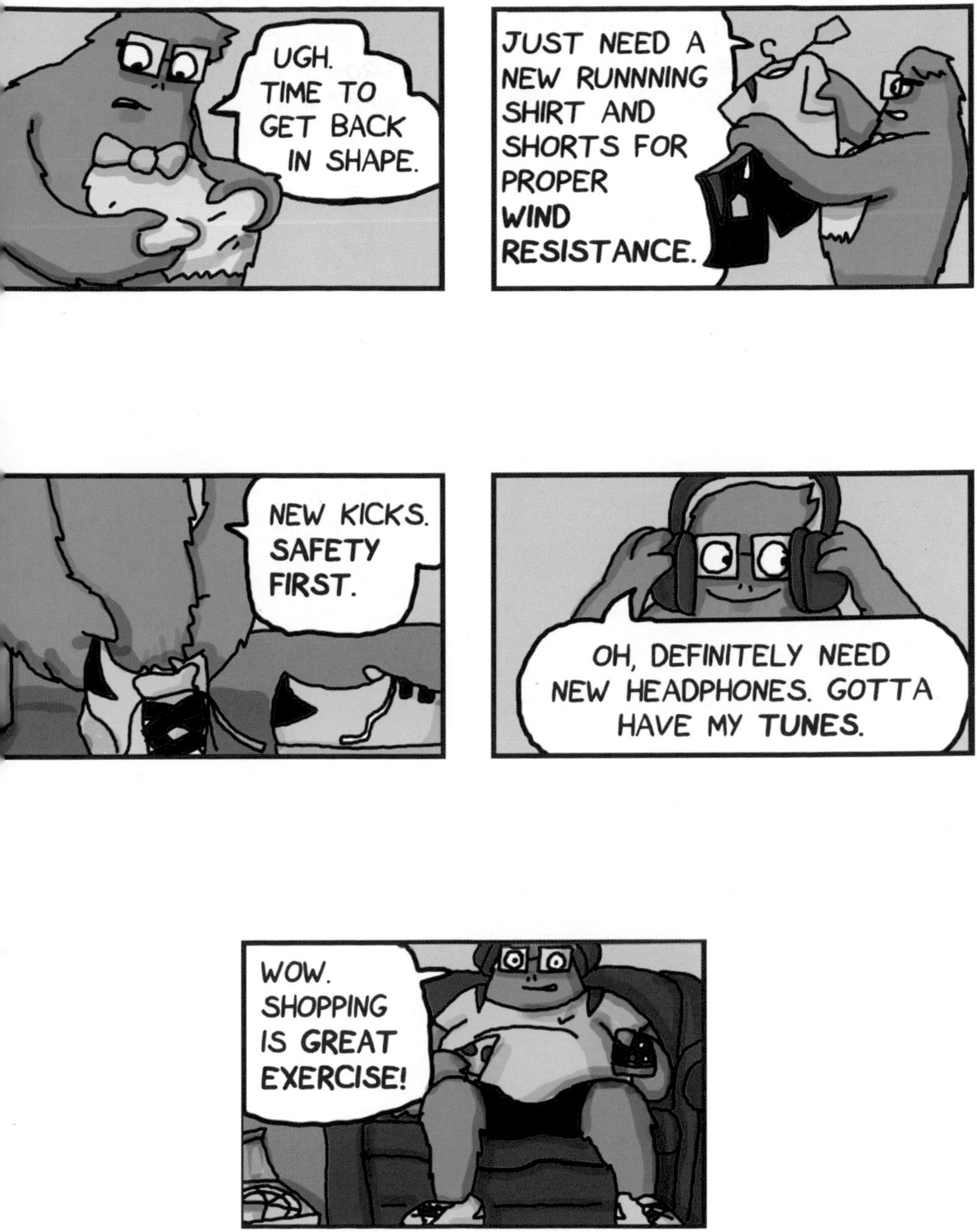
UGH. TIME TO GET BACK IN SHAPE.
JUST NEED A NEW RUNNNING SHIRT AND SHORTS FOR PROPER WIND RESISTANCE.
NEW KICKS. SAFETY FIRST.
OH, DEFINITELY NEED NEW HEADPHONES. GOTTA HAVE MY TUNES.
WOW. SHOPPING IS GREAT EXERCISE!

Guide to Plant Care

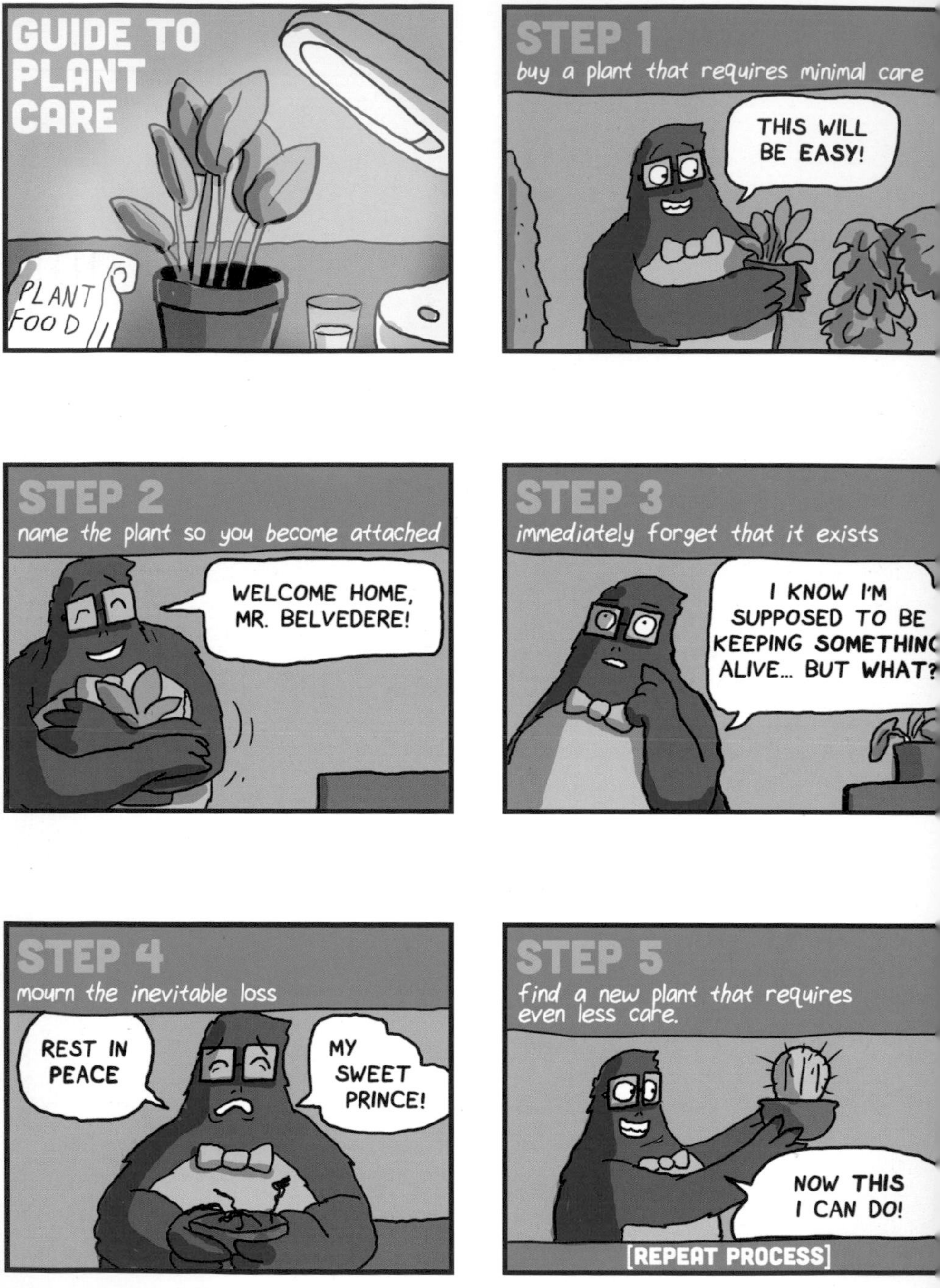
GUIDE TO PLANT CARE
PLANT FOOD
STEP 1
buy a plant that requires minimal care
THIS WILL BE EASY!
STEP 2
name the plant so you become attached
WELCOME HOME, MR. BELVEDERE!
STEP 3
immediately forget that it exists
I KNOW I'M SUPPOSED TO BE KEEPING SOMETHIN
ALIVE... BUT WHAT?
STEP 4
mourn the inevitable loss
REST IN PEACE
MY SWEET PRINCE!
STEP 5
find a new plant that requires even less care.
NOW THIS I CAN DO!
[REPEAT PROCESS]

The Patron

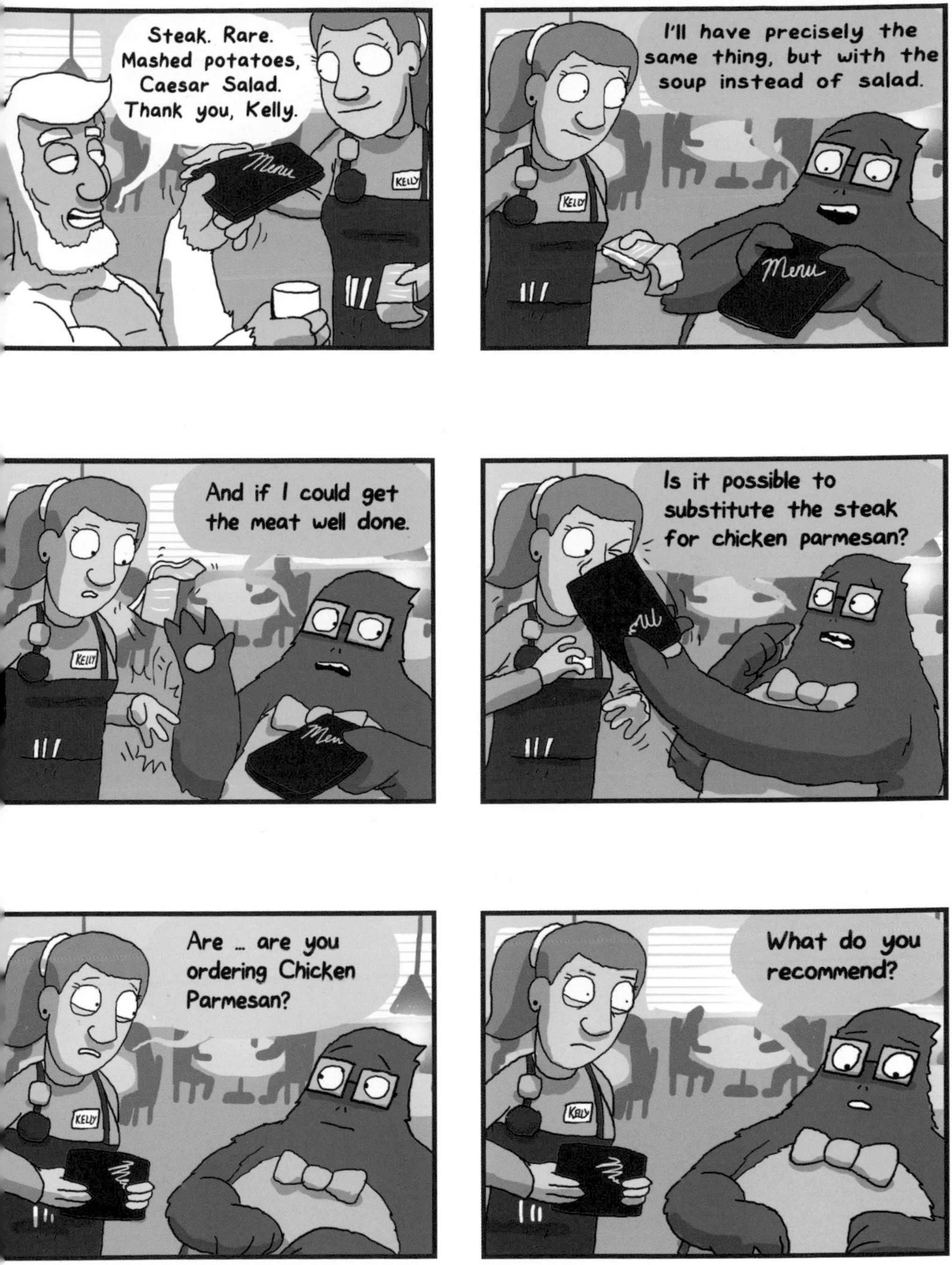
Steak. Rare. Mashed potatoes, Caesar Salad. Thank you, Kelly.
Menu
KELLY
I'll have precisely the same thing, but with the soup instead of salad.
KELLY
Menu
And if I could get the meat well done.
KELLY
Is it possible to substitute the steak for chicken parmesan?
Are ... are you ordering Chicken Parmesan?
KELLY
What do you recommend?
KELLY

Lisa's Hair

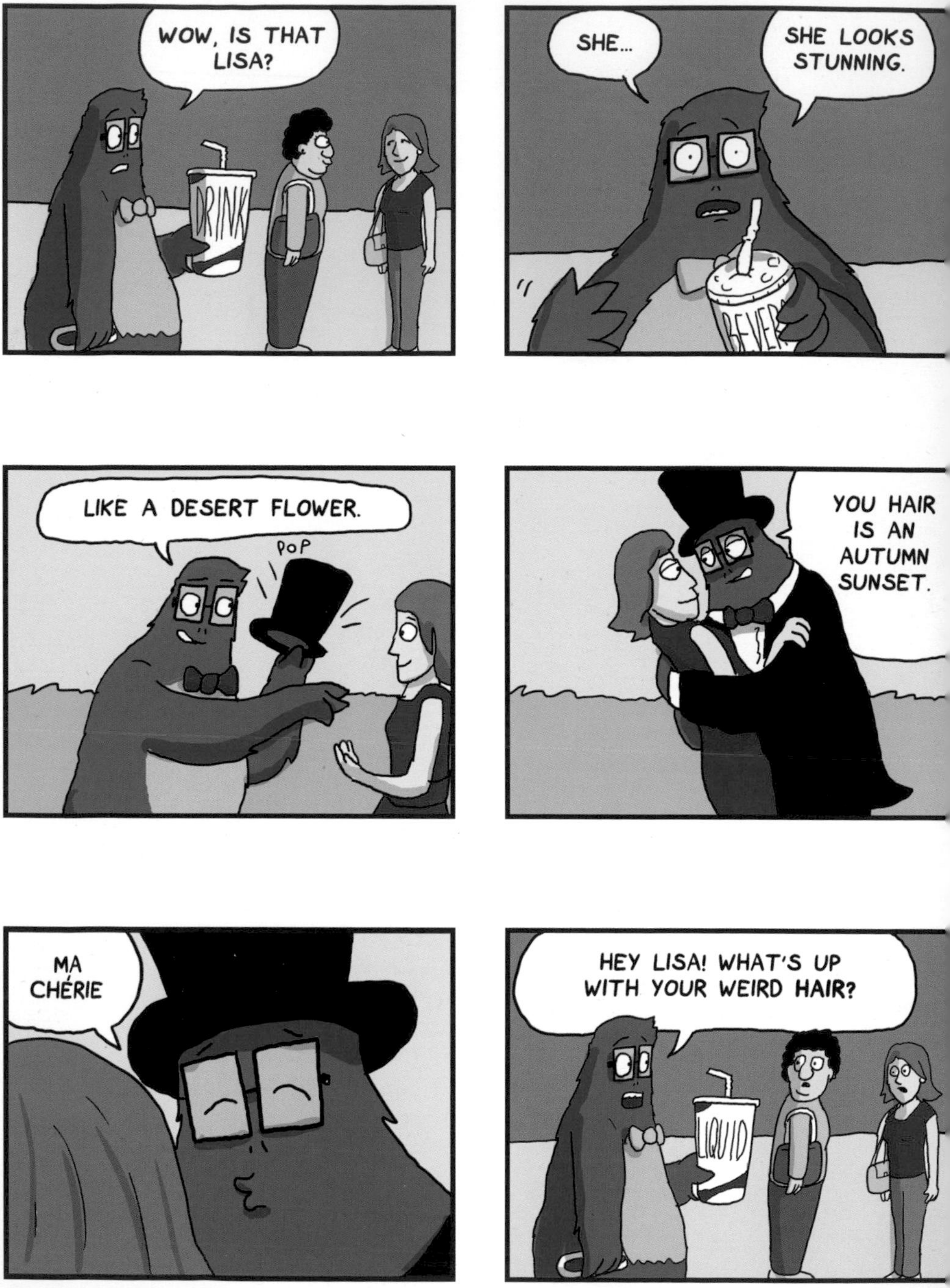

WOW, IS THAT LISA?
DRINK
SHE...
SHE LOOKS STUNNING.
LIKE A DESERT FLOWER.
POP
YOU HAIR IS AN AUTUMN SUNSET.
MA CHÉRIE
HEY LISA! WHAT'S UP WITH YOUR WEIRD HAIR?
LIQUID

Sigh

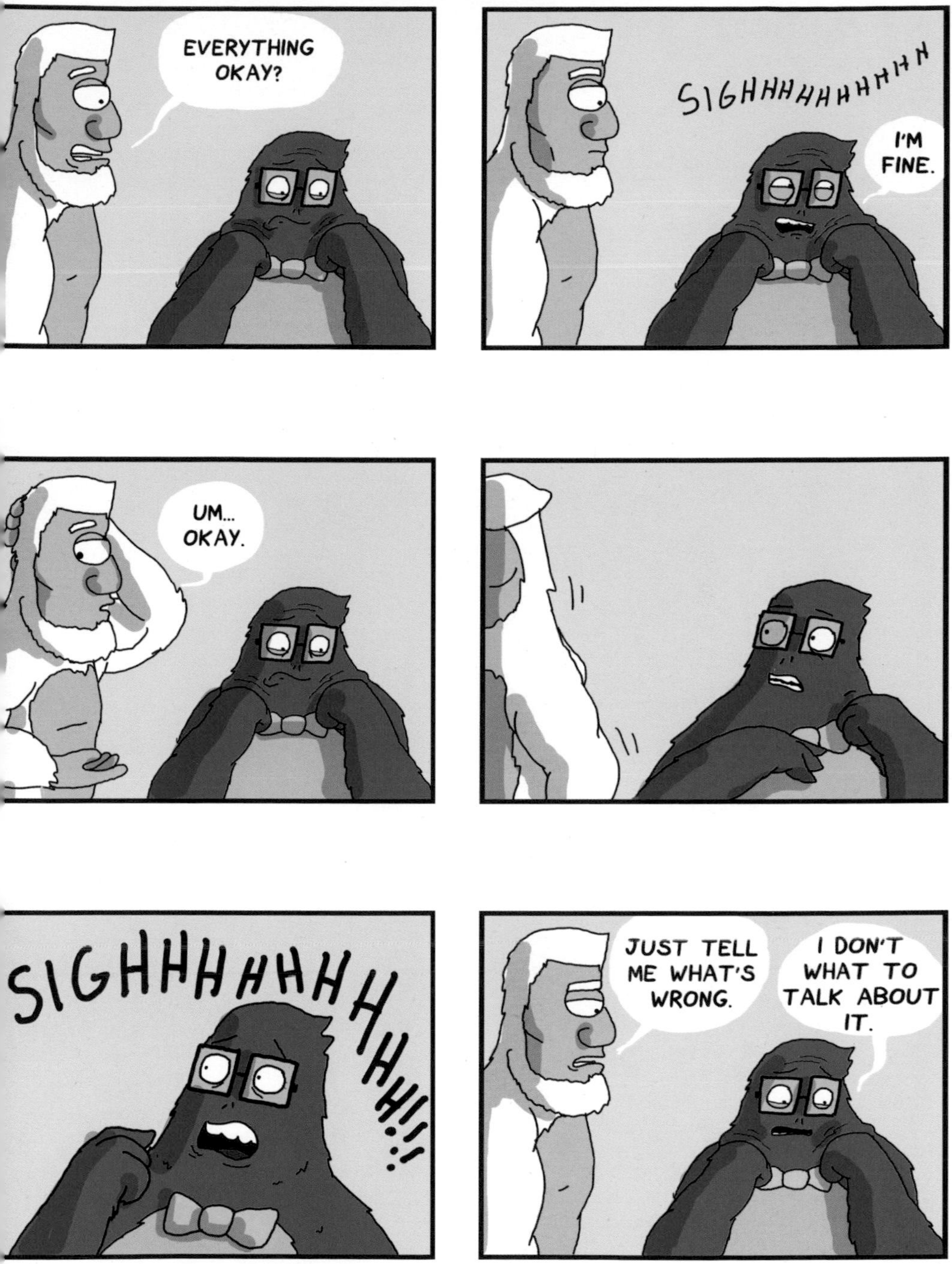
EVERYTHING OKAY?
SIGHHHHHHHHHHN
I'M FINE.
UM... OKAY.
SIGHHHHHHHHHHH!!!
JUST TELL ME WHAT'S WRONG.
I DON'T WHAT TO TALK ABOUT IT.

The Monologue

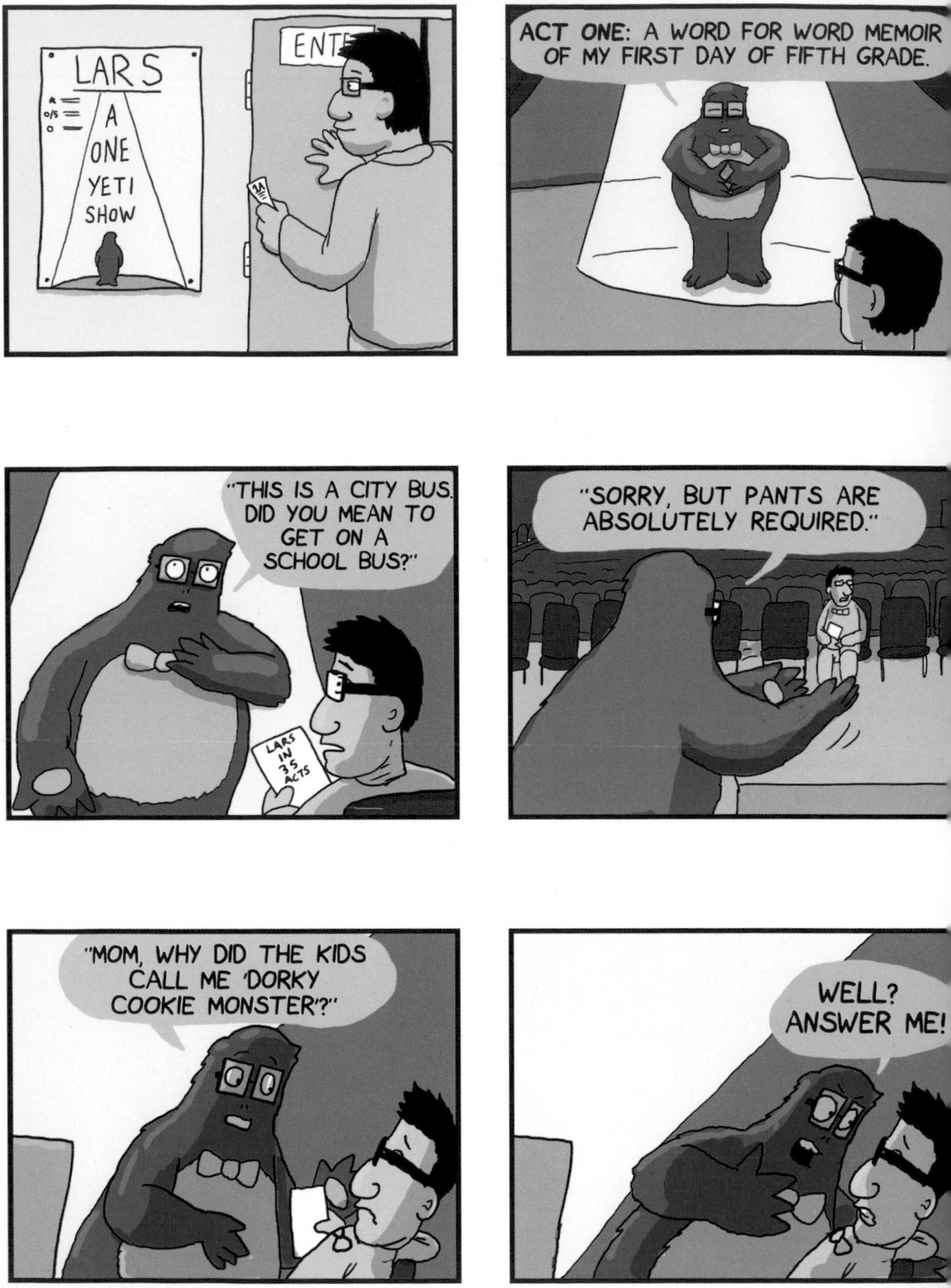
LARS
A ONE YETI SHOW
ACT ONE: A WORD FOR WORD MEMOIR OF MY FIRST DAY OF FIFTH GRADE.
"THIS IS A CITY BUS. DID YOU MEAN TO GET ON A SCHOOL BUS?"
LARS IN 35 ACTS
"SORRY, BUT PANTS ARE ABSOLUTELY REQUIRED."
"MOM, WHY DID THE KIDS CALL ME 'DORKY COOKIE MONSTER'?"
WELL? ANSWER ME!

Heart and Brain®

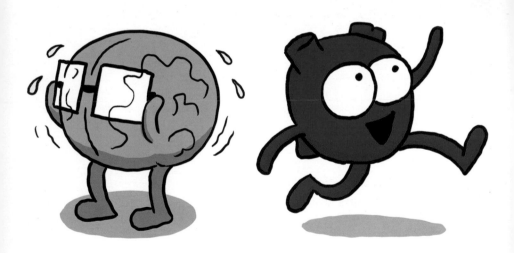

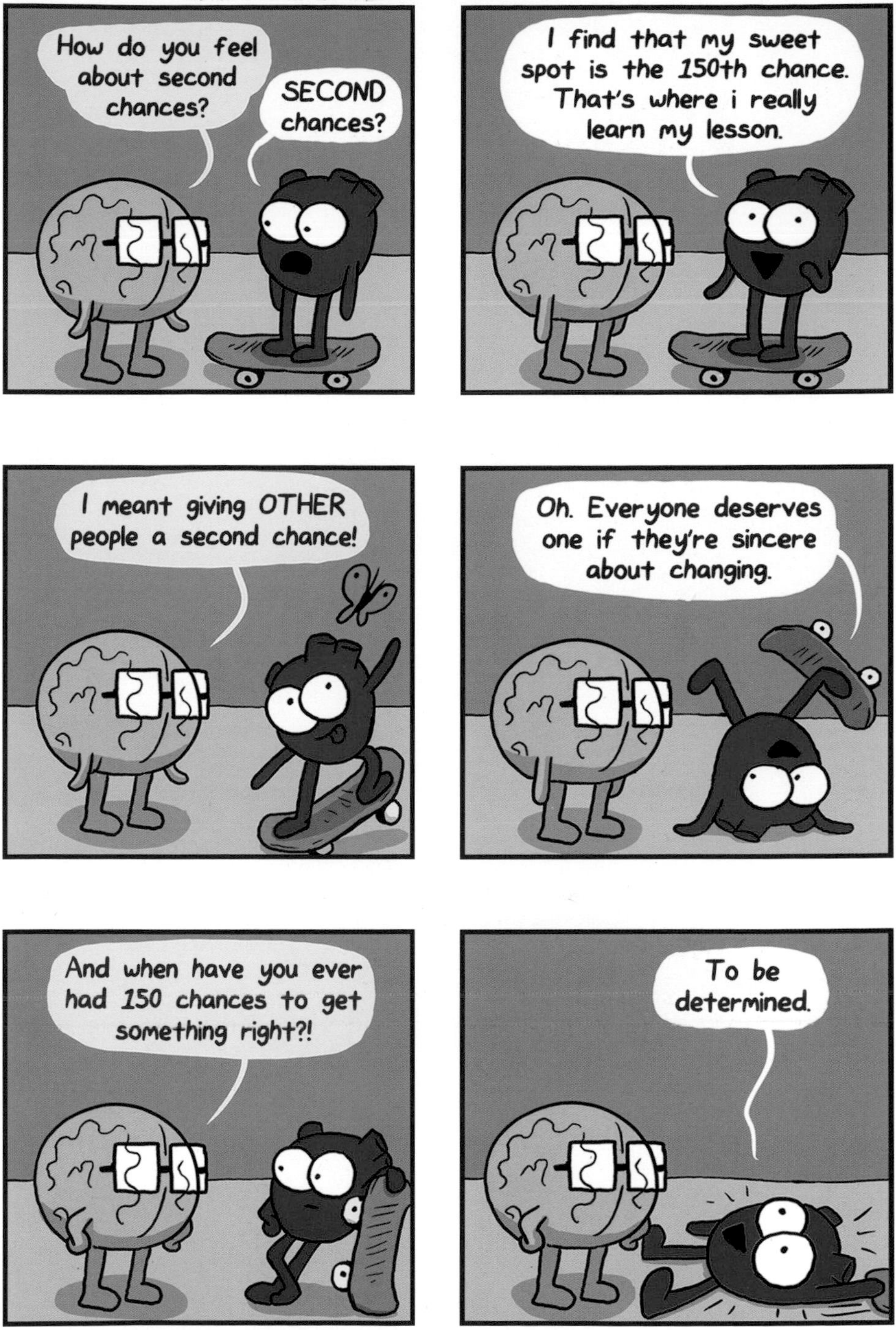
How do you feel about second chances?
SECOND chances?
I find that my sweet spot is the 150th chance. That's where i really learn my lesson.
I meant giving OTHER people a second chance!
Oh. Everyone deserves one if they're sincere about changing.
And when have you ever had 150 chances to get something right?!
To be determined.

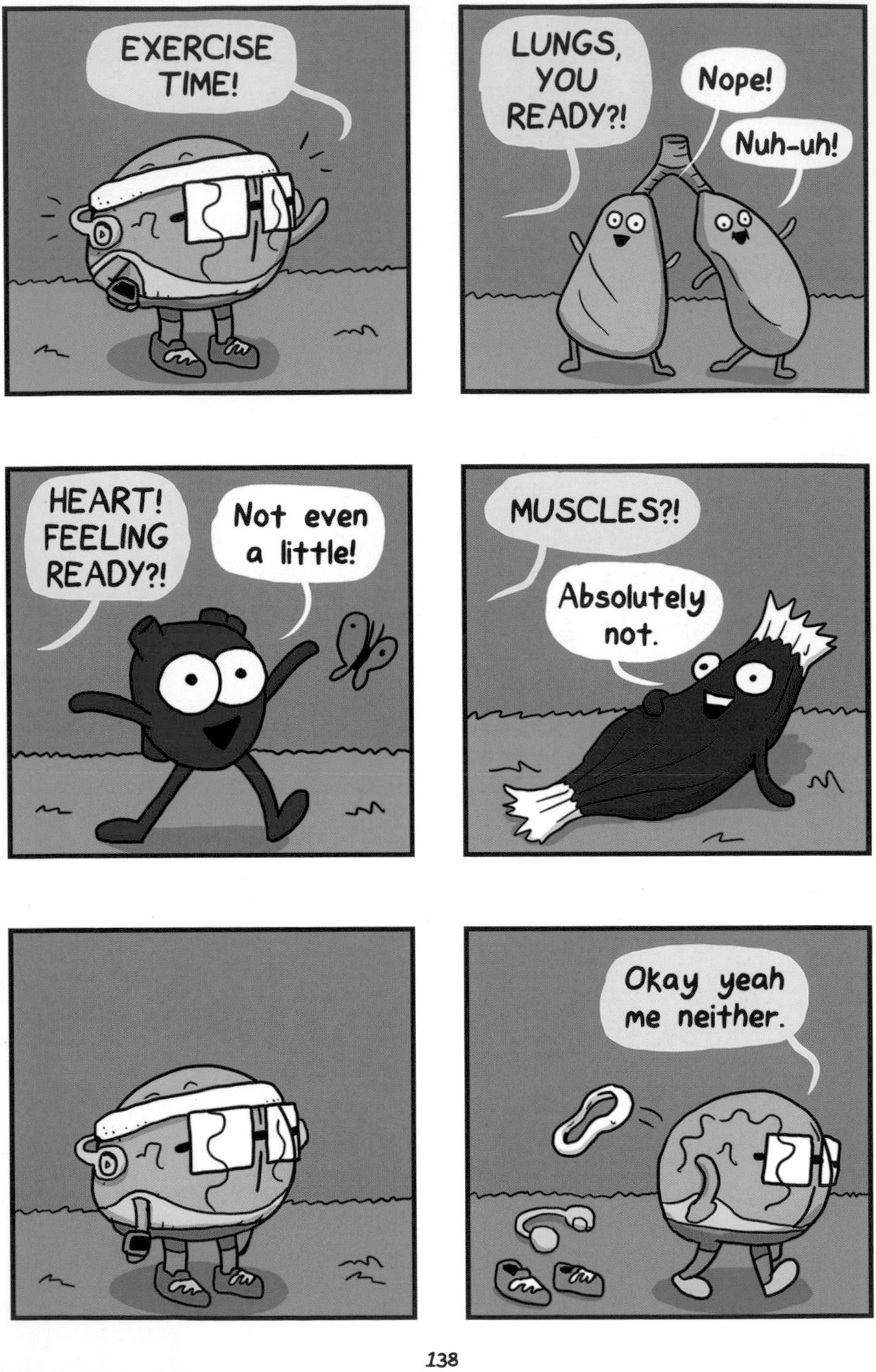
EXERCISE TIME!
LUNGS, YOU READY?!
Nope!
Nuh-uh!
HEART! FEELING READY?!
Not even a little!
MUSCLES?!
Absolutely not.
Okay yeah me neither.

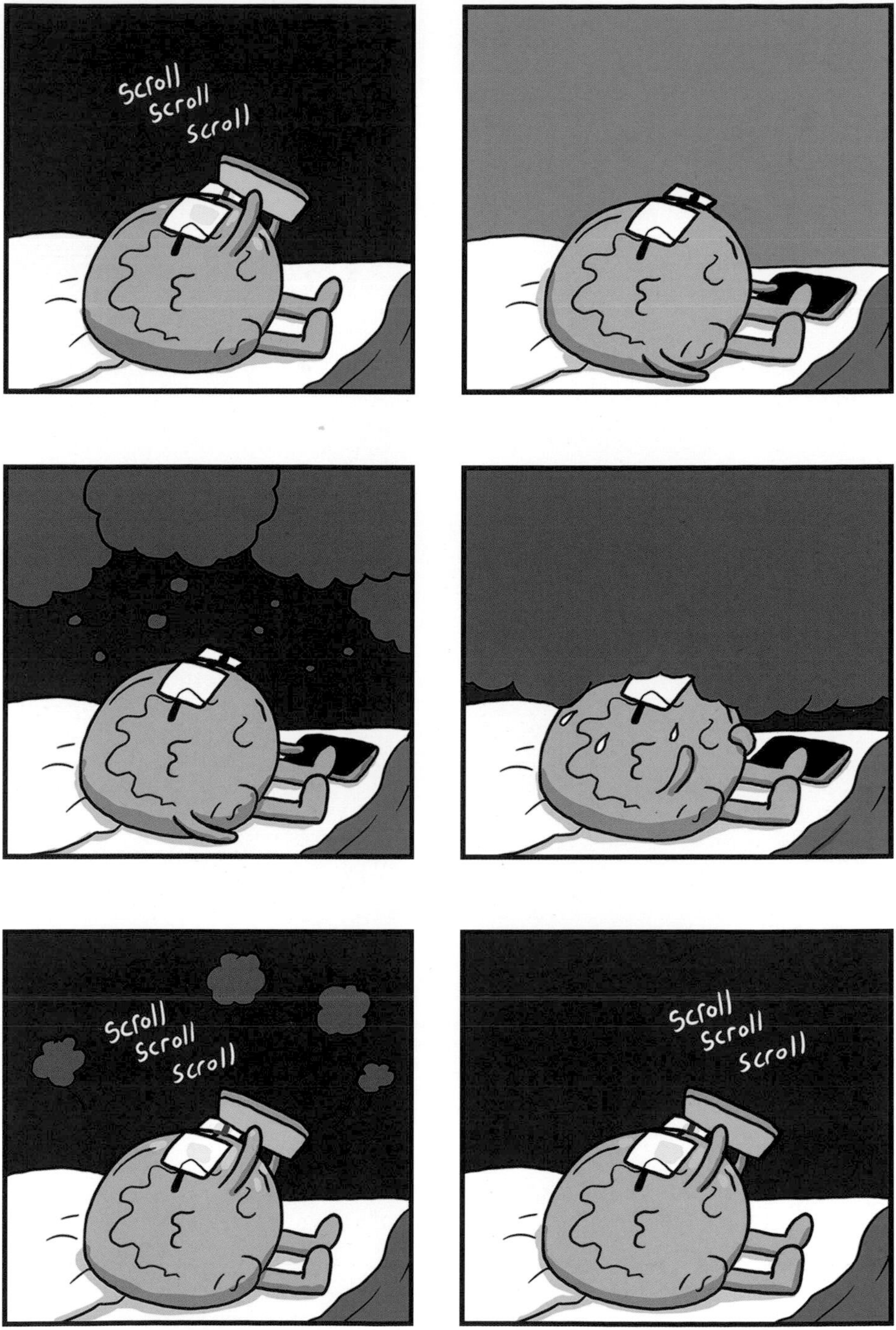
scroll
scroll
scroll
scroll
scroll
scroll
scroll
scroll
scroll

Why HIC can't HIC I HIC stop HIC-HICCUPPING!
Diaphragm is glitching. Hug your knees!
HIC!
HIC!
Try holding your breath!
TOOT
HIC!
Drink water upside-down!
GrrgGGLLL
HIC! Does any of that work?!
No idea.
CLICK

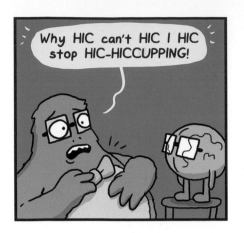

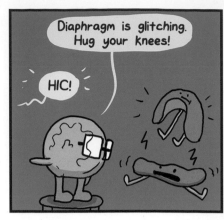

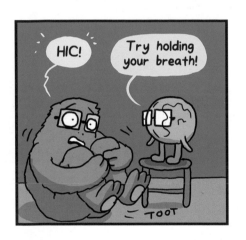

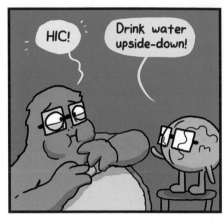

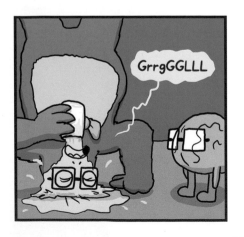

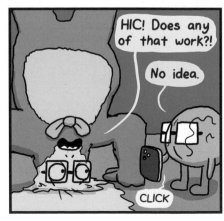

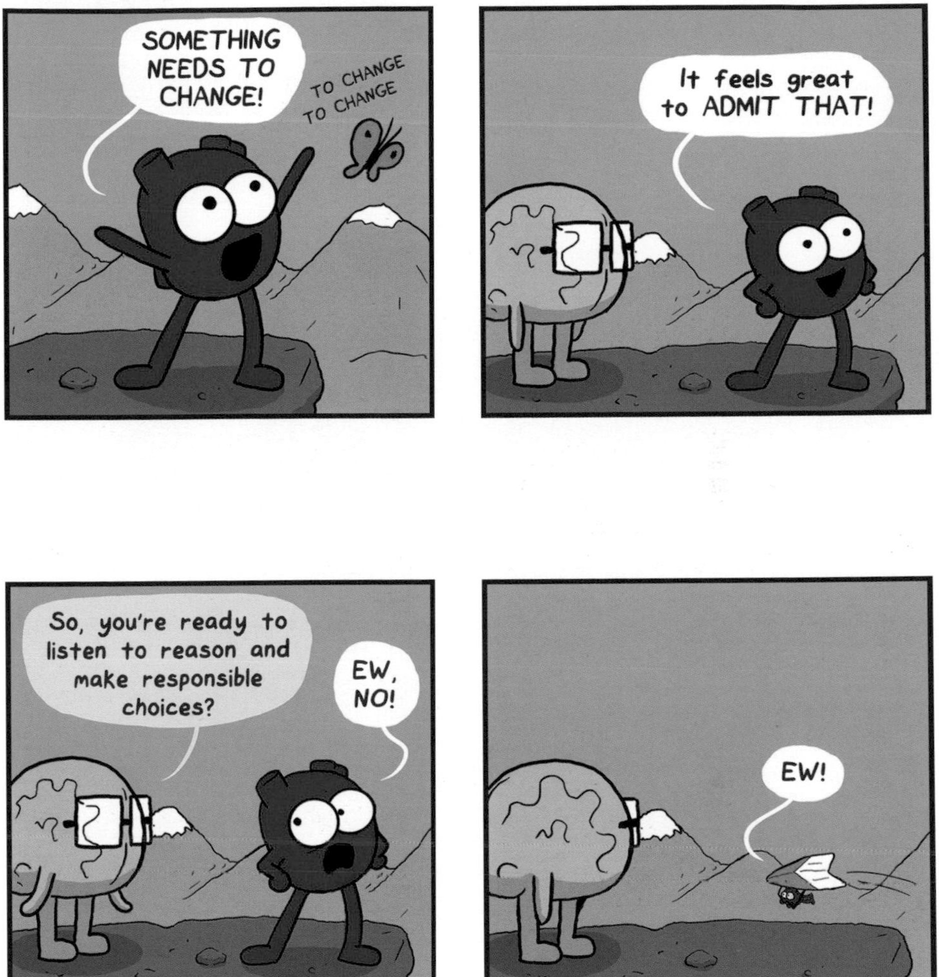
SOMETHING NEEDS TO CHANGE!
TO CHANGE
TO CHANGE
It feels great to ADMIT THAT!
So, you're ready to listen to reason and make responsible choices?
EW, NO!
EW!

VACATION
what the-
FLING!
PLAF
REALITY

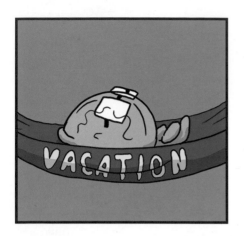

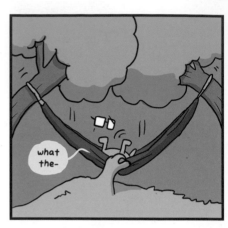

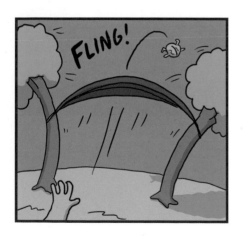

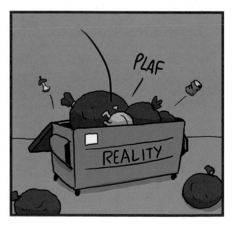

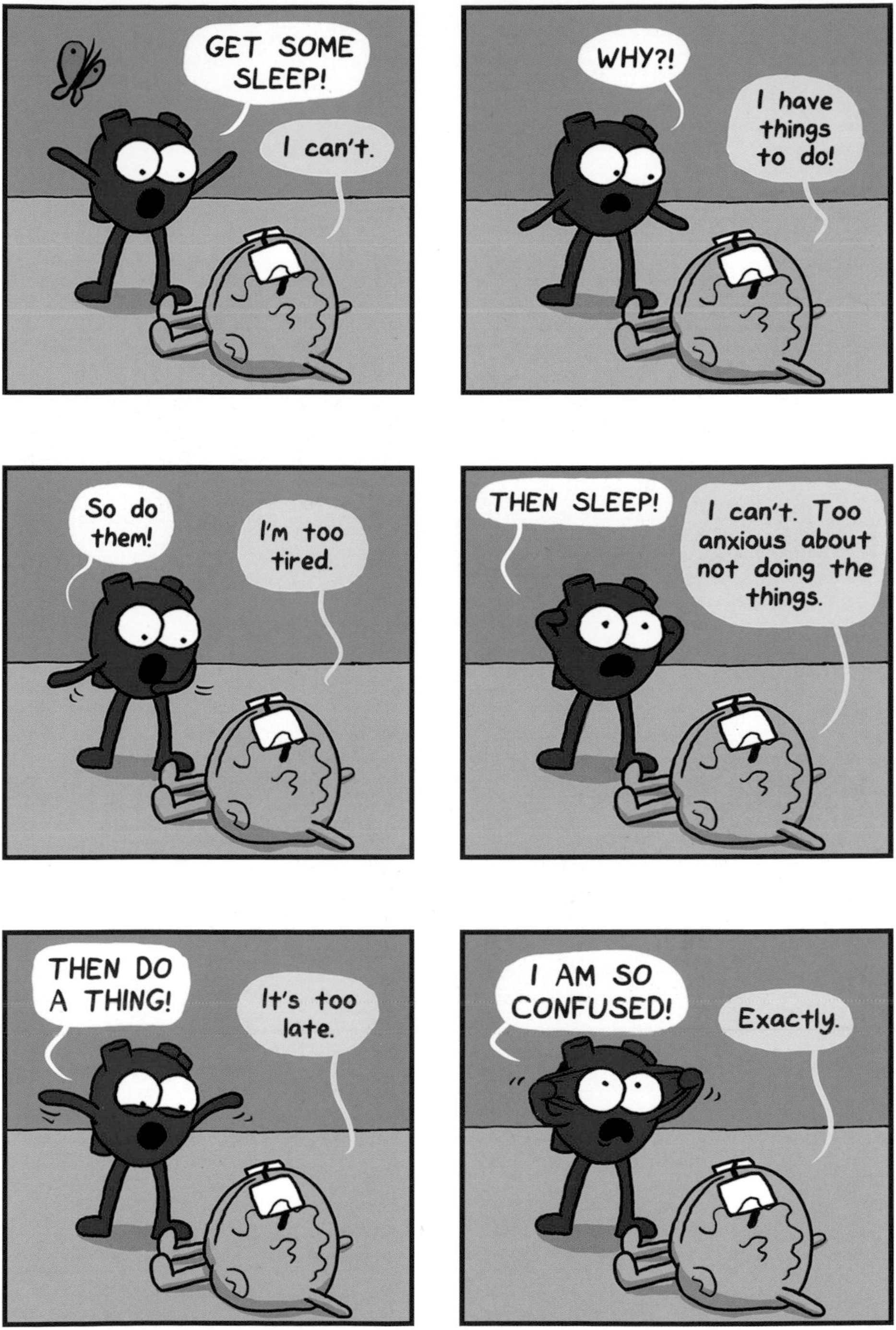
GET SOME SLEEP!
I can't.
WHY?!
I have things to do!
So do them!
I'm too tired.
THEN SLEEP!
I can't. Too anxious about not doing the things.
THEN DO A THING!
It's too late.
I AM SO CONFUSED!
Exactly.

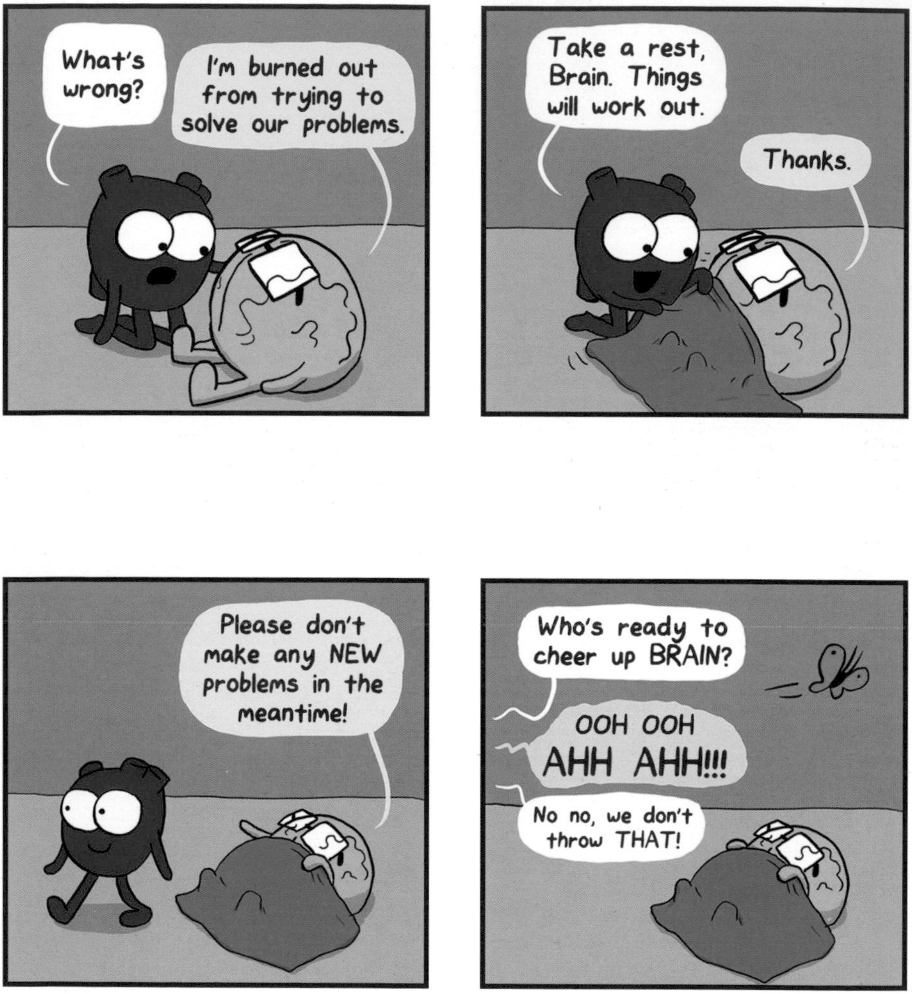
What's wrong?
I'm burned out from trying to solve our problems.
Take a rest, Brain. Things will work out.
Thanks.
Please don't make any NEW problems in the meantime!
Who's ready to cheer up BRAIN?
OOH OOH AHH AHH!!!
No no, we don't throw THAT!

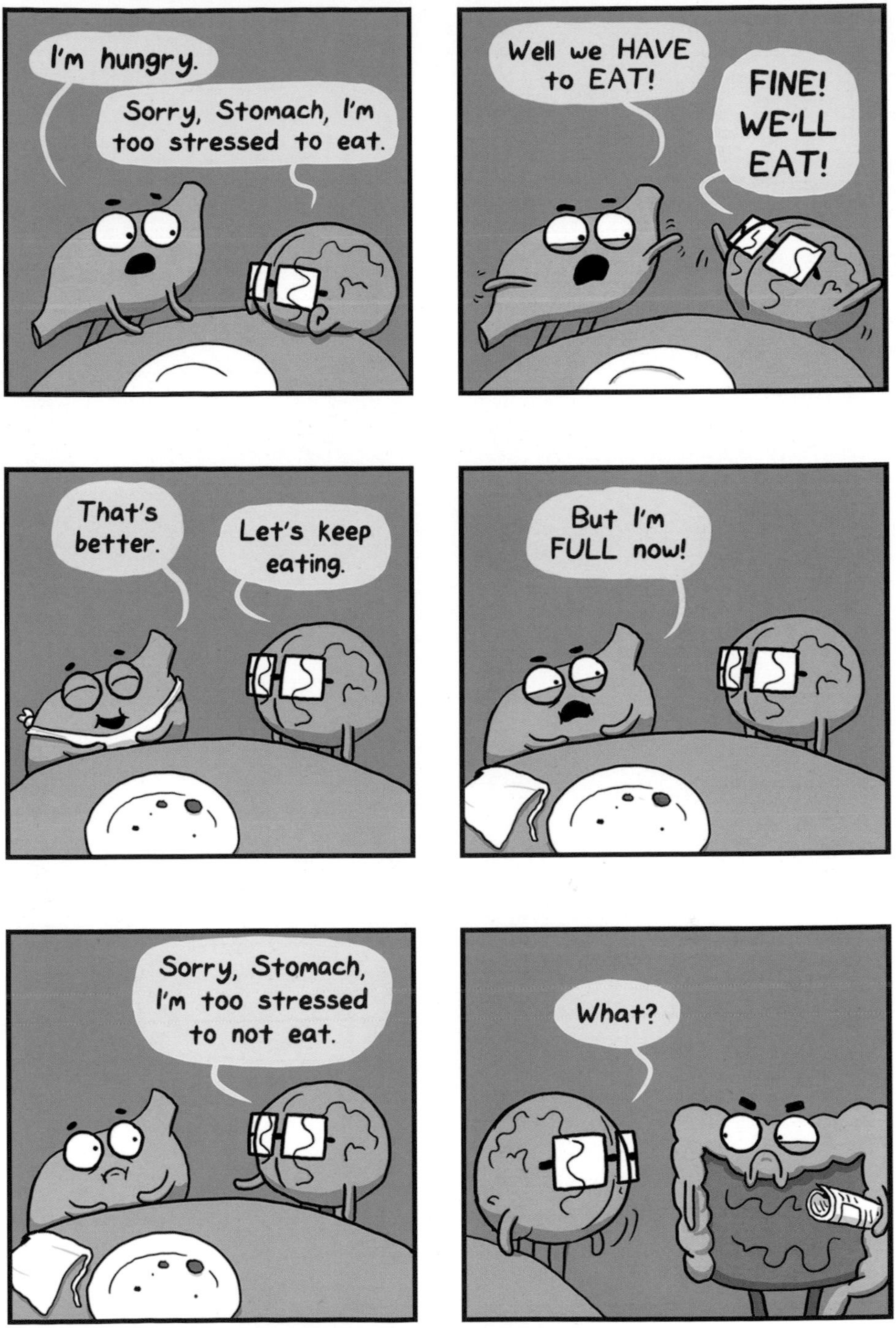
I'm hungry.
Sorry, Stomach, I'm too stressed to eat.
Well we HAVE to EAT!
FINE! WE'LL EAT!
That's better.
Let's keep eating.
But I'm FULL now!
Sorry, Stomach, I'm too stressed to not eat.
What?

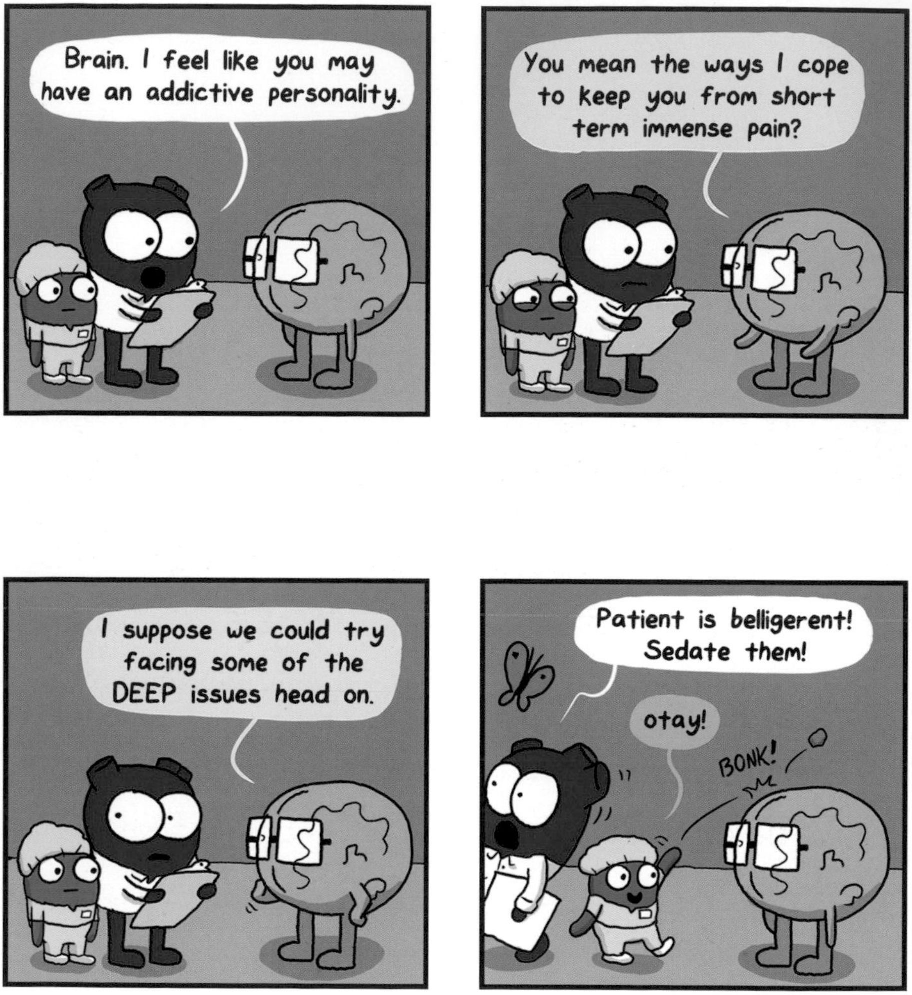
Brain. I feel like you may have an addictive personality.
You mean the ways I cope to keep you from short term immense pain?
I suppose we could try facing some of the DEEP issues head on.
Patient is belligerent! Sedate them!
otay!
BONK!

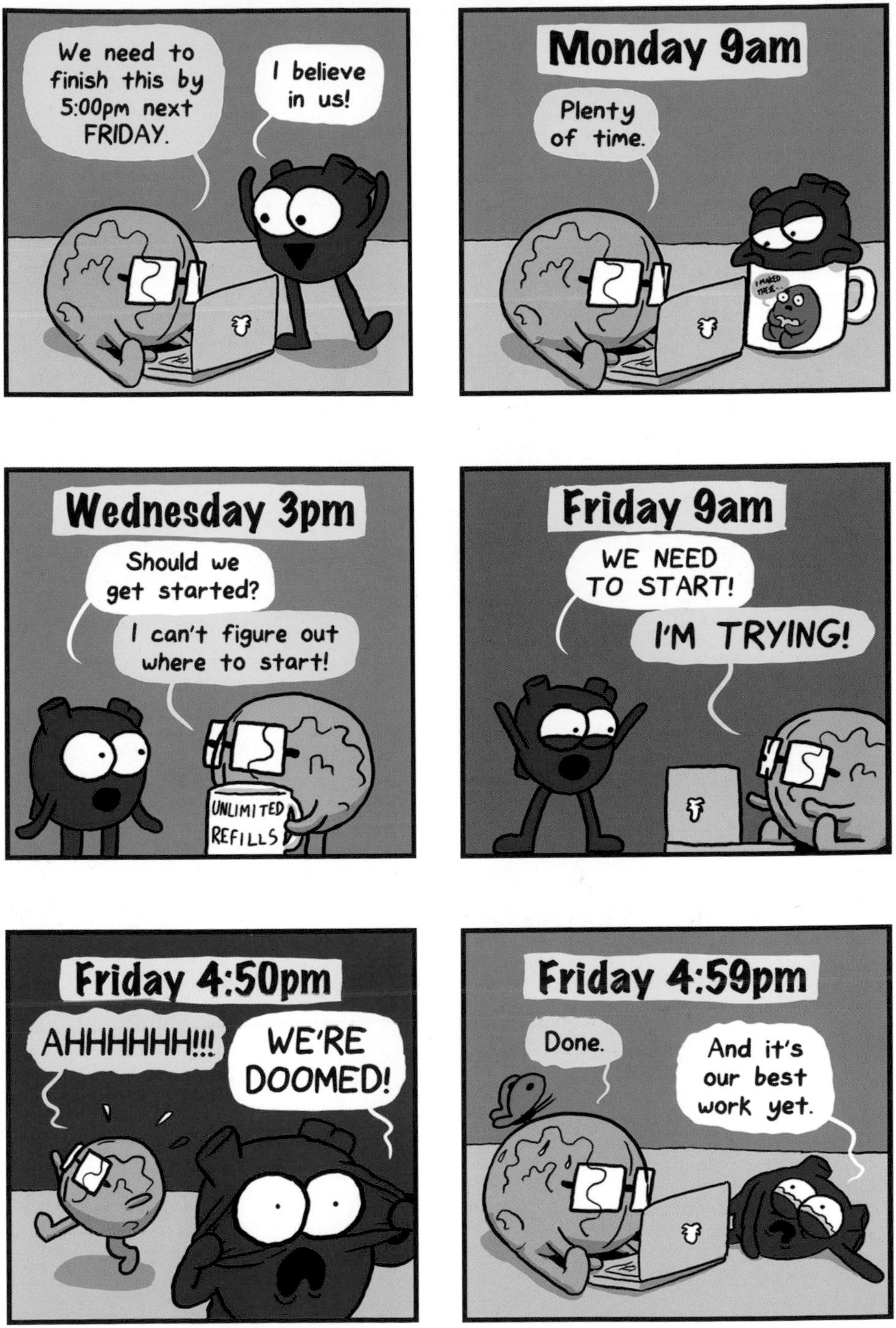
We need to finish this by 5:00pm next FRIDAY.
I believe in us!
Monday 9am
Plenty of time.
Wednesday 3pm
Should we get started?
I can't figure out where to start!
UNLIMITED REFILLS
Friday 9am
WE NEED TO START!
I'M TRYING!
Friday 4:50pm
AHHHHHH!!!
WE'RE DOOMED!
Friday 4:59pm
Done.
And it's our best work yet.